CHEROKEE NATION CITIZENSHIP

The manufacturer's authorized representative in the EU for
product safety is Mare Nostrum Group B.V., Mauritskade 21D,
1091 GC Amsterdam, The Netherlands
email: gpsr@mare-nostrum.co.uk

CHEROKEE NATION CITIZENSHIP

A Political History

Aaron Kushner

UNIVERSITY OF OKLAHOMA PRESS : NORMAN

Library of Congress Cataloging-in-Publication Data

Names: Kushner, Aaron, 1991– author.
Title: Cherokee Nation citizenship : a political history / Aaron Kushner.
Description: Norman : University of Oklahoma Press, [2025] |
   Includes bibliographical references and index. | Summary: "An exploration
   of how the Cherokee Nation of Oklahoma has defined citizenship over time"—
   Provided by publisher.
Identifiers: LCCN 2024022111 | ISBN 978-0-8061-9475-2 (hardcover)
Subjects: LCSH: Cherokee Nation, Oklahoma—Membership. | Cherokee Indians—
   Tribal citizenship.
Classification: LCC E99.C5 K87 2025 | DDC 305.897/557—dc23/eng/20240923
LC record available at https://lccn.loc.gov/2024022111

To Liara, my starlight.

Contents

Acknowledgments

WRITING A BOOK is a long campaign peppered with victories and defeats, won only by the generosity, unselfishness, and charity of those with whom you journey. To those who taught and trained me, especially Jason Jividen, Michael Krom, Jason King, Jerome Foss, Michelle Gil-Montaro, Rev. Paul-Alexander Shutt, Rev. Killian Loch, Scot Schraufnagel, Andrea Radasanu, Larry Arnhart, Matt Streb, Laron Williams, Marvin Overby, Jay Dow, and Sarah Beth Kitch, thank you for your patience, time, and dedication to helping others grow. To Justin Dyer, for taking me on as your advisee and for your continued support and counsel over the years, I am forever indebted. And to Adam Seagrave: thanks for moving me west to a new university every few years.

To my graduate cohort at the University of Missouri, Dongjin "Bro" Kwak, Katherine Becerra Valdivia, Will Holden, Yuko Sato, Nikolaos Frantzeskakis, and Angela Gjekanovikj—the finest assembly of scholars and human beings you could ever hope to encounter—for your friendship and generosity during our time together, I am eternally grateful.

To all those who inspired, read portions of, gave feedback on, critiqued heavily, and otherwise helped shape this book through their conversation, I offer my sincerest thanks, especially to (in addition to those already named above) Alessandra Jacobi Tamulevich, David Wilkins, Steve Pittz, Joseph Postell, Paul Frymer, Karen Taliaferro, Luke Perez, Brian Brayboy, Rick Avramenko, Zack German, Samuel Piccolo, Catherine Craig, Jacob Boros, Paul Carrese, and, finally, Kimberly Teehee—whose generous visit and encouragement to students at Mizzou launched this entire venture.

To the anonymous Reviewer 3, who gave me the most thorough, expansive feedback—the most extensive critique I've ever received on anything. I took it all to heart; your generous gift of time and effort was, I hope, not in vain. Additional thanks to David Chesanow, for your copyediting expertise, and to Cami Garland, for being on hand to answer all manner of citation questions. All errors—grammatical, conceptual, or otherwise—are mine and mine alone.

To my friends, colleagues, and sometimes coauthors, Sean Beienburg, Stephen Clouse, and Trevor Shelley: thank you for making this job fun.

To Lea, Dale, Chris, Nhi, and Claire: thank you for your unwavering support, advice, and love.

To my brothers, Ryan, Fr. Dan, and Thomas: I love you guys.

To Bob and Mary Ann, my parents, who taught and teach me how to live and from whom I have been given so much; I hope that in some small way what I manage to do in my life honors you.

To Clara: life with you is like watching air turn to gold, a miracle. *Ditat Deus.*

Introduction

THE DEVELOPMENT OF CITIZENSHIP IN THE
CHEROKEE NATION

I HAVE FOUND a shorthand for capturing some of the tension between the American articulation of legal citizenship and the various manifestations of legal tribal membership in the United States in a story from a dinner—a Thanksgiving dinner no less—I once enjoyed some years ago. During the meal, a fellow guest asked me what I was researching. I began to say that I was writing a book chapter on legal citizenship in the Cherokee Nation of Oklahoma. Before I could continue, my questioner cut me off, decrying Americans past and present for their racist, bigoted oppression of Cherokees and for failing to permit the latter to participate in our American polity, arguing that the United States should leave the Cherokee Nation alone. When they subsided, I continued by adding that the chapter in question dealt primarily with how the Cherokee Nation historically defined citizenship laws, which included repeatedly resisting the incorporation of many Cherokee freedmen, formerly enslaved people and their descendants, into full tribal membership. The same person then decried the Cherokee Nation for their racist, bigoted actions, arguing that the United States should punish them for this by restructuring their tribal citizenship laws. . . .

I mention this story because it highlights an important feature of the way that many Americans discuss Indigenous politics. Americans praise or defend Indigenous peoples insofar as the latter seem to adhere to American values. The moment many Americans perceive that a tribal nation, like the Cherokee Nation of Oklahoma, has done something outside the bounds of the current vogue, they pounce, demanding conformity. The concept of *citizenship* is often one of those cases.

The goal of this book is to understand the development of legal citizenship in the Cherokee Nation and thereby challenge Americans to think seriously about citizenship, both that of tribal nations and their own. In November 2017, I was fortunate enough to meet Kimberly Teehee, who went on to become the Cherokee Nation's first appointed delegate to the US House of Representatives.[1] In a small meeting with students, she spoke to us about the state of Cherokee–United States relations, especially the lack of attention that the American public has for tribal sovereignty. As scholars like Vine Deloria Jr., Daniel Heath Justice, and Ned Blackhawk have articulated, Americans, when faced with troubling colonial realities that they are neither equipped nor willing to engage with, often seek refuge in comfortable stereotypes or ignore the matter altogether.[2] This meeting changed the trajectory of my academic career; I wanted to know why so many Americans ignore Indigenous politics.

Not long after this meeting, the war of words between President Donald Trump and Senator Elizabeth Warren (D-MA) drew blood. In 2018, the senator released DNA test results that allegedly proved her Indigenous ancestry.[3] Critical reactions to the DNA test results—which concluded that Senator Warren likely had a Native American ancestor six to ten generations prior—were negative. Some Democratic Warren supporters were perplexed by the move, while Republican opponents were quick to cast Warren as insensitive to Indigenous peoples.[4] Shortly thereafter, however, Cherokee Nation secretary of state Chuck Hoskin Jr. issued a statement condemning the use of DNA tests to establish citizenship in tribal governments: "Sovereign tribal nations set their own legal requirements for citizenship, and while DNA tests can be used to determine lineage, such as paternity to an individual, it is not evidence for tribal affiliation. Using a DNA test to lay claim to any connection to the Cherokee Nation or any tribal nation, even vaguely, is inappropriate and wrong. It makes a mockery out of DNA tests and its legitimate uses while also dishonoring legitimate tribal governments and their citizens, whose ancestors are well documented and whose heritage is proven. Senator Warren is undermining tribal interests with her continued claims of tribal heritage."[5] This reaction is striking because Senator Warren did not publicly, to my knowledge, claim Cherokee Nation *citizenship*, yet Secretary Hoskin was concerned in his response with protecting the exclusivity of tribal citizenship. There seemed to be some disconnect between these events—a lack of common definitions for key terms.

The key term here is, of course, citizenship. Hoskin further explained his understanding of this term in an article in the *Cherokee Phoenix*:

As I discuss citizenship with non-Native friends, I talk about my family table. During holidays, our family table is shared by my immediate family, and friends we do not get to see that often. They are all welcome and loved as we share food, stories and laughter.

However, if something tragic were to happen to me or my wife, not everyone at that table would be entitled to inherit my house or become legally responsible for my kids. Those friends at my table will no doubt be critical in healing and providing love for those left behind, but it is my immediate family that will have their own rights and responsibilities in the eyes of the law.

This concept of family is key to understanding why citizenship matters. Everyone who cares about us as Natives are welcome, but at critical moments those that have legal and cultural standing have a unique place with specific rights and responsibilities.

That is why it offends us when some of our national leaders seek to inappropriately ascribe membership or citizenship to themselves. They would be welcome to our table as friends, but claiming to be family to gain a spot at the table is unwelcome.

Like all families we have successes and challenges that need to be addressed. We want our friends to join us in these fights, but we need them to understand they are fighting for our citizens' benefits, not their own.

We know that many people across the nation have treasured family stories about having Native lineage. There is nothing wrong with being proud of that.

However, every day, people make claims of Native heritage and Cherokee ancestry across the country to take advantage of laws intended to level the playing field for Indian Country. These claims, made for personal advancements by profiteers, are like a guest at my table saying they've had a seat there all along.[6]

A tribal citizen, according to Hoskin, is someone whose "ancestors are well documented and whose heritage is proven," a member of the "immediate family" with certain "rights and responsibilities in the eyes of the law." Cherokee Nation *citizenship* is, therefore, a legal articulation of and an attempt to preserve authentic tribal belonging, which also confers certain rights and responsibilities.[7]

How is this understanding different from citizenship in the United States? The term "citizen," as used in the Americas, is a product of European colonialism, one that forces an arbitrary distinction between the individual and the community. Early Americans concluded that allegiance to their community should be the result of a "contract resting on consent."[8] "Consent" here is an artificial construct whereby individuals agree to common constraints, or laws. The citizen is, therefore, one who agrees to certain common limitations on their behavior. This tie between the individual and the community, however, is "contractual and volitional, not natural and perpetual."[9] The family would thus not be an apt metaphor for describing citizenship in the United States. Although citizenship laws in the United States have been flavored with their own particular blend of exclusion and rejection, in America citizenship "has in principle always been democratic," based on the premise (if not always the reality) that anyone can consent to become an American.[10]

It is important to note here the difference between the terms "citizen" and "member" as Indigenous nations (within the United States) use them in the twenty-first century. "Member" is used in several senses concerning human belonging, of which two are most relevant: (1) "relating to part of a living body organism," and (2) "relating to an individual or constituent element within a social or other organizational structure."[11] "If one understands Native peoples as genealogically or organically related communities who share a common language, values, and territory," legal scholars David E. Wilkins and Shelly Hulse Wilkins suggest, "then the term *member* is certainly apropos."[12] The meanings of the word "citizen" convey more strongly rights, duties, and privileges: "(1) an inhabitant of a city or a town, especially one possessing civic rights and privileges; and (2) a member of a state, an enfranchised inhabitant of the country, as opposed to an alien."[13] Tribal nations today use the term "member" far more frequently than "citizen"; the Cherokee Nation, however, uses "citizen" in their constitution and laws. The public debate

4

between Warren and Hoskin thus involved a discussion of Cherokee Nation *citizenship*.

Senator Warren and Secretary Hoskin each emphasized ancestry, but the latter connected ancestry with citizenship. Hoskin did not say, however, that simple ancestry is equivalent to citizenship either: "We are citizens through historical documentation, adopted laws and a shared language and culture that make us unique," Hoskin wrote, emphasizing that a particular set of shared experiences lies at the core of Cherokee Nation citizenship.[14] The Cherokee Nation today grants legal citizenship only to those who can prove lineal descent from someone listed on the Dawes Rolls. The Dawes Commission compiled citizenship rolls for the Cherokee and other tribal nations from 1898 to 1907, which federal officials used to allot land to approved tribal citizens ahead of Oklahoma statehood.[15] Instead of tracking the amount of "Cherokee blood" in an individual's veins, the Cherokee Nation instead relies on legal document trails linking specific persons to the Dawes Rolls.[16] Since the Cherokee Nation has become three contemporary federally recognized tribal governments—linked by family, history, and culture, if not always law and politics—the reliance on the Dawes Rolls is not a statement of mere Cherokee ancestry but rather the ancestry of a specific community of people living in Indian Territory during allotment.[17] While Senator Warren officially apologized to the Cherokee Nation in February 2019, the incident again made salient a centuries-old tension between the United States and Indigenous peoples: Who is a tribal citizen and who gets to decide?[18]

In response to Warren's apology, Cherokee Nation spokesperson Julie Hubbard commented that she was glad that they had now reached the understanding that "being a Cherokee Nation tribal citizen is rooted in centuries of culture and laws not through DNA tests."[19] This practice of defining tribal citizenship by reference to the Dawes Rolls, however, has not always been the case. Yet, as Kimberly Teehee pointed out to me, the American public is largely unaware of this history. Political science as a discipline fares similarly.

THE LAY OF THE LAND

The evolution of academic knowledge is like a child developing sight. We first encounter something—some historical political event, perhaps—as a dark formless blur. Gradually, nearsighted, we distinguish contours, edges, and begin to see in black and white. As time passes and we sit with the light, we adapt to color and depth, which reveal things for what they are: complex objects in space and time. Consider the ratification of the United States Constitution. To understand what happened, where do we begin? A useful duality, in black and white, is that *Federalists* supported ratification and *Anti-Federalists* opposed the same.[20] Sit with these debates for a while, however, and we see that while James Madison and Alexander Hamilton both supported ratification, each had some starkly different ideas about how that Constitution should be interpreted. Likewise, Melancton Smith, Patrick Henry, and Robert Yates had varying (and far less coordinated) reasons for opposing the Constitution. The duality was a necessary starting point, but incomplete.

Consider in the same light how political science has engaged with settler colonialism and the United States. The discipline has distinguished contours, edges, but remains largely committed to the duality George Washington identified in his public addresses: there's the United States on one side, Indigenous nations on the other. Political scientists have, of course, revealed a great deal of nuance in all sides of the ratification debates. When it comes to understanding Indigenous politics, however, tribal nations are often treated as a monolith, as victims of American cruelty and/or a group America needs to include but has not.[21] As political theorist David Myer Temin puts it, political science has focused on *inclusion* instead of *decolonization* or understanding nuances in Indigenous regimes themselves.[22]

Scholars of literature and history over the past twenty years have drawn depth and color from the relationship between the United States and Indigenous Peoples, especially in their work on the Cherokee Nation.[23] Kirby Brown, Joshua B. Nelson, Daniel Heath Justice, and Jace Weaver, among others, have challenged common black-and-white stereotypes, both of Native Americans generally and Cherokee people specifically, in their studies of literature and literary figures past and present.[24] Christopher B. Teuton's work on Cherokee storytelling adds layers of critical nuance to academic conversations about the Cherokee Nation, especially about what it means to be a *traditionalist*.[25] Historians like Tiya Miles, Julie L. Reed, Andrew Denson, and Rose Stremlau have lent their talents to uncovering the complexities of race, spirituality, and political life in the Cherokee Nation.[26] Yet political science has not followed suit.

Political science, according to political theorist Kennan Ferguson, hates American Indians. "The formations of political science as a discipline have erased Native identity, Native philosophy, and Native history from its areas of concern" because of the former's normative commitment to American politics.[27] Since Indigenous thought "overtly oppose[s] many of the values that [the] United States presumes"— among these, the correctness of majoritarian democracy, American exceptionalism, political individualism, and abstract understandings of citizenship that divorce individuals from their communities and glue them back together with law—political science has found it expedient to marginalize Indigenous politics in favor of reinforcing American political thought as a flawed but ultimately correct understanding of the best regime in practice.[28] Ferguson calls for changes to "indigenize the study of political science," which should include a "recognition of the extensive history of Native treatments of power and politics in land now claimed by the United States," an "acceptance of the importance of work by contemporary Native scholars," and a commitment to the presumption of equality between Native and European narratives.[29] By including, consulting, and valuing Indigenous political scholars and thought, Ferguson argues, political scientists might build upon the important work currently being done in other disciplines.

Ferguson's critics have argued that he did not go far enough in stating the radicalness of indigenizing political science, a process that, according to political scientist Lauren M. MacLean, would challenge "our normative understandings of the American political system as a whole" as well as the "dominant epistemological assumptions" of the discipline.[30] David Wilkins was similarly pessimistic about the prospect of indigenizing the discipline, stating that "disciplinary intellectual imperialism, swaddled in the flag of American exceptionalism, means that those who have power and influence in our field have no incentive to question, let alone change, the existing paradigm."[31] Institutes of higher education are not incentivized to support research that criticizes the foundations of the American Regime.

Political scientist Franke Wilmer praised Ferguson's diagnosis of the problem in political science and highlighted two of Ferguson's suggestions. The first is a question of definition: "The categories and concepts of the discipline transpose poorly onto indigenous experiences and practices because they are the product of an academic enterprise that springs from the perspectives of European colonial settlers."[32] Wilmer referred to the Haudenosaunee, to the 1978 "*Basic Call to Consciousness, Address to the Western World*," which stated that "spiritual consciousness is the highest form of politics," a concept outright rejected in American political thought.[33] The second suggestion, reinforced by preeminent scholar Linda Tuhiwai Smith's work, is a question of decolonizing ourselves, meaning that scholars must challenge contemporary norms in political science that exclude Indigenous political actors and thought.[34]

In response to these arguments, political scientist Paul Frymer, while agreeing with Ferguson's presentation of the situation in political science as a whole, pointed out that the discipline is far from barren in terms of Indigenous political research.[35] There has been, according to Frymer, a "recent revival of interest in Native American politics, particularly in . . . American political development where concerns with temporality and ideological construction are central to the field."[36] American Political Development (APD) is a field where Indigenous political thought and practice may find a sustainable home within the broader discipline due to its ability to address and take seriously both history and political ideas.

Cherokee Nation Citizenship: A Political History is situated within the growing political development tradition of prioritizing Indigenous political ideas, history, and practices.[37] By focusing on a single Indigenous regime, the Cherokee Nation, this book challenges the dominant duality within political science by sitting with it for a while and exploring its depth. The politics of the Cherokee Nation as a sovereign nation are worth studying in their own right, not simply as part of the larger conglomeration of Indigenous Nations in the United States. We can work to decolonize the field by using its strengths to reveal truths in the political developments of Indigenous regimes.[38] This study is, therefore, a Cherokee political development project that builds upon the methodologies of APD research to answer questions that the field has not yet asked.

8

SEARCHING FOR CHEROKEE POLITICAL DEVELOPMENT

One of the primary interests in political development studies lies in conceptualizing processes of change and contemplating their implications for the regime.[39] A political development is "a durable shift in governing authority," where "authority" means the exercise of control over persons by institutions and "shift" means a change in the "locus of direction of that control."[40] This requires a detailed articulation of political history. Adaptive decision-making, which leads to durable shifts in policy, takes place within an environment shaped by certain political ideas. We begin by searching for foundational ideas.

A *foundational* idea is "an idea offered in political discourse as a first cause or ultimate justification for a general political position or orientation."[41] For example, the "ultimate justification" for seat belt laws is that human life is valuable and should be protected while driving. *Policy* ideas, conversely, "are encountered as tangible political phenomena in the practical political world."[42] Presuming that human life is valuable and should be protected, that idea, when translated into the "practical political world," could suggest seat belt laws. This strategy of categorizing ideas as either *foundational* or *policy* in this book helps us organize ideas into clearly defined packages that may then change over time.

Policy ideas are fairly straightforward: laws and institutional rules are types of policy ideas. Foundational ideas, however, are more difficult to discern and require interpretation. There are a few different ways that we can identify foundational ideas. One way is by reading and analyzing how Indigenous scholars have interpreted cultural traditions and other stories to ascertain both implicit and explicit values therein meant to influence behavior. Another way is by looking at laws and other rules and working backward to find the underlying principles. Taken in tandem, these two approaches can help us find a starting point for beginning to understand foundational ideas in Cherokee Political Thought that relate to tribal citizenship.

That starting point is a pyramid of ideas, a tool that serves as a shorthand for Cherokee Political Thought. Attempting to define any political thought is like trying to tackle a moving car. Idea pyramids are useful, not because they provide definitive definitions of complex

9

ideas, but because they allow us to view snapshots of the relationship between certain foundational ideas and corresponding policy ideas in a given time frame.[43] In an idea pyramid, foundational ideas sit at the bottom, supporting policy ideas at the top. Foundational ideas, "as core ideational commitments, are in some sense immutable and thus do not often change."[44] Policy ideas change more frequently to retain and realize foundational ideas. "Foundational ideas answer *why* policy ideas are implemented, and [policy] ideas answer *how* foundational ideas are practiced in the real world."[45] Figure 1 shows the outline of an idea pyramid.

Throughout this book, I will refer to this tool to help trace the development of citizenship in the Cherokee Nation of Oklahoma to see how foundational ideas have been interpreted differently by different actors in different eras. Legal citizenship—or how nations understand themselves—is developed through a negotiated process over time. Political ideas matter, history matters, and institutions—the "rules and procedures that structure behavior and provide incentives, norms, and resources that shape it"—matter.[46] In the course of Cherokee Nation history, the United States has exerted great force against them, influencing

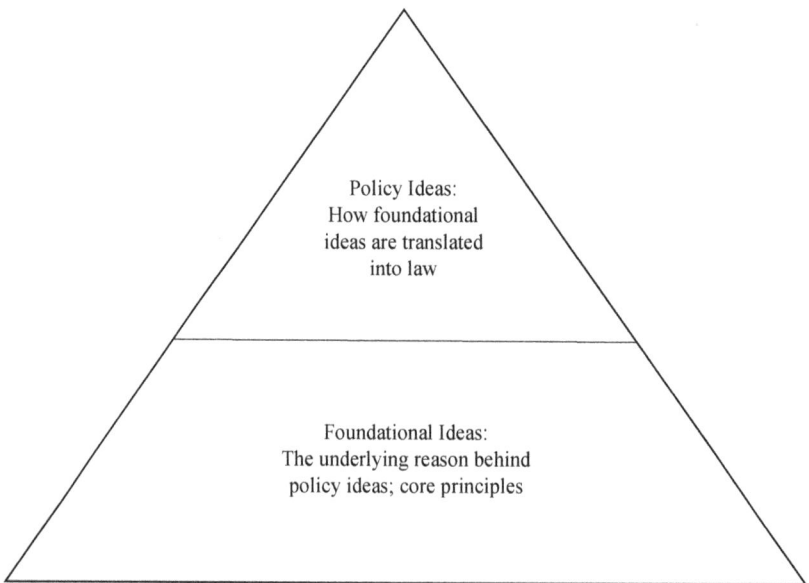

Figure 1. Sample Idea Pyramid

their politics in various ways which will be examined presently. This book, however, is *not* a study of United States Indian policy, although specific policies and attitudes are explained where necessary. This book is a study of the Cherokee Nation regime as a sovereign regime, not as a by-product of the United States' colonialism. As such, I focus on Cherokee Nation innovations and citizenship policies as they have occurred throughout history.

Before the imposition of European settlers, tribal nations like the Cherokee Nation identified themselves "by genealogy (culturally derived, not fractions of blood), by land, by language, and by spiritual traditions and values."[47] Before the 1820s, Cherokees' preferred mode of identification came via membership in one of the seven matrilineal clans.[48] Cherokee kinship structure was dynamic and fluid: custom permitted adoption into the tribe if a clan was willing. This mode has changed over time, first centralizing under a nationalistic impulse by a regime that used blood (Cherokee parentage) in lieu of clan as its means of legal identification before being co-opted by treaty agreements and acts of Congress that forced the adoption of those without Cherokee blood or clan.[49] Today, tribes "generally have the power to determine their own membership," although "Congress has the power to define membership differently from the tribe when necessary for *administrative purposes.*"[50]

Administrative purposes include census-taking for land allotment and tribal termination and requiring the Cherokee Nation to adopt freedmen as citizens at the end of the Civil War. Felix S. Cohen, lawyer and architect of the "Indian New Deal" during the FDR Administration, also noted that when property was involved, the federal government could step in at any time.[51] The United States Supreme Court decided in the case of *Santa Clara Pueblo v. Martinez* (1978) that tribal governments "retained as one of their inherent powers the right to decide who could or could not be citizens of their nations."[52] Since then, the federal government has generally been loath to involve themselves directly in tribal citizenship cases but has ruled—in 2017, for instance—against the Cherokee Nation in favor of full tribal citizenship for Cherokee freedmen.

While the mode for determining citizenship has changed, the goal of the Cherokee Nation has remained consistent over time: to articulate a means to keep citizenship exclusive. Put another way, citizenship laws have changed to ensure the continuity of the tribe as a cohesive whole. An initial duality suggests itself. Since 1800, citizenship laws have appeared to take on two forms: *blood as ancestry* and *blood as culture*. Proponents of the former have argued that keeping citizenship exclusive requires recognizing first and foremost Cherokees by blood. Chief Wilma Mankiller, for example, stated in 1984 that freedmen "should not be given membership in the Cherokee tribe. That is for people with Cherokee blood."[53] More recently, in 2021, one council member posed a rhetorical question to their fellow legislators at a tribal council meeting: "What does it mean to be Cherokee anymore?" They answered themselves: being a "blooded Indian."[54] Proponents of the latter argue instead that, rather than restricting citizenship by blood, citizenship ought to be reserved for those who have shared in common experiences. In 2017, Marilyn Vann, president of the Descendants of Freedmen of the Five Civilized Tribes Association, argued that, since her ancestors walked the Trail of Tears, labored to build Cherokee cities, and helped "make the tribe," freedmen are an intrinsic part of Cherokee culture that do not merely reside alongside Cherokees but belong as Cherokees due to their ancestors' shared experiences.[55]

Sit with this duality for enough time, however, and we see that, while it is a good starting point, it is incomplete. "Blood as ancestry" could mean different things, like having a Cherokee mother, father, or both. It could also encompass those adopted by Cherokee clans and their descendants. Similarly, "blood as culture" could convey shared experiences in a particular place, like Indian Territory, or, more broadly, shared experiences of those who strive to adhere to traditional lifeways across the continent. The development of citizenship in the Cherokee Nation reveals rich nuance in how citizenship has been articulated and interpreted over time. The reality is that negotiated processes that create policy are complicated in any nation.[56] This book aims to articulate how and why.

The Cherokee Nation, under current principal chief Chuck Hoskin Jr. (elected in 2019 and again in 2023), has worked to expunge all references to blood restrictions articulated in Cherokee law. These actions have proved controversial, especially in 2021, when, at the urging of the Cherokee Nation attorney general Sara Hill, the Cherokee

Nation Supreme Court struck the words "by blood" from the Cherokee Constitution without a constitutional amendment.[57] A year later, in May 2022, the Council revised Title 26 of the Cherokee Nation Code relative to elections.[58] The old stipulation stated that, to be eligible to run for elective office, each candidate must submit, among other things: "*Proof of citizenship and membership by Indian blood consisting of his or her certificate of degree of Indian blood card and a Cherokee Nation citizenship card*" (emphasis added). This provision now reads: "*Proof of Citizenship and a Cherokee Nation Citizenship card.*" The internal debate over Cherokee identity, as it has been a perennial part of Cherokee Nation politics for centuries, is likely to continue.

THE WAY FORWARD

The chapters in this book are designed to highlight and understand shifts in Cherokee Nation citizenship laws. Chapter 1 covers the time period between 1710 and the ratification of the first Cherokee Nation Constitution in 1827. In the eighteenth century, Cherokees generally determined tribal belonging by membership, via birth or adoption, in one of the matrilineal Cherokee clans. Colonization, changing demographics, and acculturation (which included the practice of chattel slavery) introduced patriarchal norms that over time demanded a transition toward a more male-dominated society. Their constitution and the laws of the 1820s increasingly favored the heirs of Cherokee men, especially those who had married non-Native women, who had no clan (also called bilateral citizenship). Those who had Black ancestors were an exception to the rule, as racial prejudice inspired laws designed to exclude these people from citizenship.[59]

Chapter 2 features the era between the 1827 constitution and 1866 treaty between the Cherokee Nation and the United States after the Civil War. The Cherokee Nation had crafted a governing document that appeared, on the surface, like a state constitution in America in an attempt to appease neighboring whites and the federal government while at the same time articulating their nationhood. Americans hungry for land and resources opted instead to ethnically cleanse the Southeast by sending Indians west.[60] Cherokees reasserted their sovereignty with an act of union and a new constitution in 1839; internal strife and external pressures, however, led to siding with the Confederacy in the

Civil War. The Treaty of 1866 treated the Cherokees as a conquered people and became the legal basis for certain peoples' claims to Cherokee Nation citizenship. Freedmen, Delawares, and Shawnees thereafter derived their citizenship status from both the treaty and Cherokee Nation law, the former's authority superseding the latter.

Chapter 3 covers the era following the Treaty of 1866 up until the dissolution of the Cherokee Nation in 1907. Dismissal and aggression by United States officials toward both Cherokees and freedmen contributed to a crisis of governance in the Cherokee Nation. Beset on all sides by individuals hungry for land, Cherokee attempts to assert sovereignty against the United States coincided with American attempts to destroy the tribe and all remnants of tribal land holdings. Allotment was the destruction of communally held lands, Cherokee Nation authority, and Cherokee Nation citizenship.[61] Indian Territory officially became Oklahoma in 1907, and Cherokees were given United States citizenship to assimilate them into American culture.

Chapter 4 focuses on the era between 1907 and 1975, the period of tribal termination, when United States officials exerted direct control over tribal affairs and attempted to destroy tribal entities and cultures through forced assimilation. This chapter covers how the people of the Cherokee Nation carried on and how foundational ideas retained their enduring appeal and power. This era witnessed a concerted American effort to impose a definition of citizenship as a statement (how the administrative state understands citizenship) instead of citizenship as an active way of life (citizenship not simply defined by eligibility for government services but by individual and communal sacrifice) upon Cherokees. "Allotment utterly transformed the Cherokee body politic" and "remains the great rupture in this history."[62]

Chapter 5 features the Cherokee Nation from the creation of the 1975 constitution to the present (2023). It covers attempts to disenfranchise freedmen, the constitutional crisis of 1999–2006, when the government underwent massive restructuring, and the most recent culmination of the freedmen citizenship debate in a 2017 US district court ruling. Contemporary Cherokee Nation citizenship policies retain the desire to keep citizenship exclusive but now use the Dawes Rolls as a baseline by which to restrict citizenship.[63] The chapter concludes by addressing the Cherokee Nation citizenship debate in 2020–2021 that included a decision by the Cherokee Nation Supreme Court to strike the words "by blood" from the Cherokee Nation Constitution and the fallout.

Chapter 6 reflects back upon the history of citizenship laws in the Cherokee Nation and the lessons that Americans can learn from that development. Cherokee Nation citizenship policies, designed to keep citizenship exclusive, when they changed, did so in ways intended to preserve certain foundational ideas. Policy ideas changed so that foundational ideas could stay the same. Certain key threads, core foundational ideas running throughout Cherokee history, include valuing interdependence, respect for the past, working in the present, and passing down a stable identity and purpose to the future.[64] Hospitality—or "generosity," as Native American studies professor Tom Holm puts it—is another overarching value tied to the foundational idea of ᏍᏏ (gadugi).[65] Gadugi, which Julie L. Reed interprets as coordinated work for the common good, and which Christopher Teuton calls "a Cherokee value in which people come together to help one another," has pervaded Cherokee political life for centuries.[66] The word gadugi itself translates to "cooperative labor (involving a community)" and was popularized in the modern Cherokee Nation by Chief Chad Smith, who used it as an organizing principle for Cherokee governance.[67] This foundational idea endures today in the Cherokee Nation despite hundreds of years of removal, allotment, termination, and assimilation policies designed to stop it.

CITIZENSHIP AND THE GOOD LIFE

"American Indian identity," wrote Chief Chad Smith in 2013, "and the seizing of that identity by non-Indians . . . provides insight into the national character of America and American's own search for identity."[68] Claims to Indian heritage—or tribal citizenship—by non–Indigenous Americans are dangerous because such claims erode the sovereignty of Indigenous regimes. Americans have historically claimed Indigenous heritage to partake in land allotments, monetary payouts, and lower college tuition rates, among other things.[69] The ease with which Americans assume Indigenous identities speaks to something broken in United States citizenship and in the American idea of what it means to live a good life.

Alexis de Tocqueville appreciated this deficiency in America's democratic mores. Obsessed with equality in public life, Americans create for themselves private inequalities while at the same time publicly proclaiming that their private associations are equal in value to one another.[70] This obsession with equality consequently conditions Americans toward *small ambitions*: "All want constantly to acquire goods, reputation, power; few envision these things on a grand scale."[71] As Americans become habituated to fulfilling small, base desires, they become more likely to "love success much more than glory."[72] We might read "glory" in this case as "virtue," something noble and difficult to obtain. It is not difficult to envision how such a people might in turn come to view *citizenship* as a statement rather than as a way of life requiring sacrifice of them. Citizenship thus risks transforming into a box to check so that individuals can continue working and acquiring material possessions in private.

The United States is experiencing an identity crisis. Alexander Hamilton and James Madison's vaunted system, predicated on the idea that striving and competition will ultimately hold Americans together, has failed to generate a stable, unifying cultural foundation from which citizens may draw meaning. Americans today instead find more meaning in individual identity and in other private associations than in whatever "American culture" might be. Part of the problem is that our founders' vision of the "good life," if one can rightly point to such a vision, is itself predicated on the idea that there is no one good life, that human beings can find meaning in admitting that there is no true meaning in their public lives—that their own individual vision of a good life is equal to anyone else's. This notion is, however, unsatisfying.

We see here the long trend of non–Indigenous Americans claiming Indigenous heritage and citizenship step into the light.[73] Many of these cases are and always have been about base material gain. But there is also something comfortable for Americans when they can reach back into some forgotten past (or, more accurately, forgotten to themselves) and boldly exclaim, "I *really* belong to this group!" or "These are my *real* people!" Of course, living in America, many Americans also lack the patience to acknowledge, let alone act upon, what belonging to a culture actually requires.[74] We instead consume cultures, picking our preferred meat off of their bones, discarding the rest at our leisure. Vine

Deloria Jr. said as much when he wrote that *"white culture* destroys other culture because of its abstractness. As a destroyer of culture it is not a culture but a cancer. . . . Indian people . . . are becoming distrustful of people who talk equality because they do not see how equality can be achieved without cultural separateness."[75]

Part of the problem lies in certain strands of American liberalism. This liberalism, political theorist Patrick J. Deneen argues, "is understood to be the greatest possible freedom from external constraints, including customary norms" that consequently "disassembles a world of custom and replaces it with promulgated law."[76] The law, replacing culture, must continually expand to regulate an ever-greater number of behaviors, creating a distant, abstract "Empire of Liberty" that suffers only the sovereignty of the individual—and, far too often, the white individual over others.[77] The American retreat into unmoored individualism has created a restless population, eager for truth and belonging, yet either unwilling or unable to sublimate themselves in order to belong anywhere. Belonging, after all, requires a certain type of humility, an act of the will that preferences the good of others over personal desires.

Cherokee scholars have seen the danger, the potential for disconnection, in American political thought and culture for a very long time. In a world dominated by Western liberalism, Daniel Heath Justice writes, we become "disconnected from one another, from the plants and animals and elements upon which our survival depends, from ourselves and our histories and legacies. When we don't recognize or respect our interdependencies, we don't have the full context that's necessary for healthy or effective action."[78] "The Keetoowah way," according to Tom Holm, "is exactly the opposite of a western tradition that emphasizes disharmony, greed, and deception. . . . [T]he idea of having a respectful relationship with the natural world is inherent in Cherokee language, the sacred history, the blessed elements of earth, wind, fire, and water, and the ceremonies performed to ensure the continuity of the Keetoowah ethos."[79] Crosslin Fields Smith, Hastings Shade, and other Cherokee traditionalists have also noted that much of the disconnection in the United States comes from American individualism.[80]

The consequences of such individualism are startling.[81] It leads to a loss of friendships, history, nature, and, ultimately, a stable sense of self.

Without a firm sense of identity, Americans seek to shield themselves with some discovered identity in place of authentic self-actualization. From the beginning, political scientist Michael Rogin notes, "liberalism insisted on the independence of men, each from each other, and from cultural, traditional, and communal attachments."[82] It is therefore not surprising that many Americans would find Indigenous identities— which have such a solid foundation in antiquity and which have survived the last five hundred years of contact with colonizing civilizations— attractive targets to make up for their own lack of meaningful attachments. In short, many Americans want an identity like that forged by the Trail of Tears and Allotment, but without the trauma.

Consider Chief Chad Smith's description of *gadugi*, which stands in stark contrast to how many Americans understand religious belief or cultural traditions—personally meaningful, but publicly meaningless. Smith declared: "ᏍᏕ (*gadugi*). We must live by it. Not because it is the right thing to do—even though it is. Not because it is the strategic process to save the Cherokee Nation—even though it is. But because it is the principle, the perspective, and the opportunity for us to pause and enjoy ourselves, our lives, and our kin by doing something worthwhile."[83] Cherokee leaders have consistently argued that Cherokee culture contains something good, true, and beautiful, and that adhering to that tradition is *something worthwhile* that elevates human life. Maintaining that practice requires sacrifice and humility. As Smith's ancestor Redbird Smith once proclaimed, "A kindly man cannot help his neighbor in need unless he have a surplus and he cannot have a surplus unles [*sic*] he works. . . . Our pride in our ancestral heritage," Redbird Smith said, "is our great incentive for handing something worth while to our posterity."[84]

Vine Deloria Jr. argued that sovereignty consists more of "continued cultural integrity than of political powers and to the degree that a nation loses its sense of cultural identity, to that degree it suffers a loss of sovereignty."[85] The development of citizenship in the Cherokee Nation may be seen as a quest to protect its sovereignty, a quest that is ongoing. Citizenship in the Cherokee Nation is rooted in a distinct cultural tradition—not stagnant but dynamic and adaptable. The goal of this study is *not* to presume to know what it means or how it feels to *belong* to the Cherokee Nation, but to highlight the complexity of tribal citizenship laws—not as an identity to be assumed at leisure by Americans seeking a vague sense of distant meaning that asks nothing of them, but as part of a negotiated process that developed over time, defining the contours of a sovereign nation. Understanding how citizenship has developed in regimes like the Cherokee Nation can help teach Americans what it means to be a citizen—the type of citizen Benjamin Franklin alluded to when he informed Elizabeth Powel that the convention had created a republic (if they could keep it)—with all of the sacrifice that entails.

CHAPTER 1
CLAN MEMBERSHIP AND
THE OLD LAWS
1710–1827

BEFORE THE AMERICAN Revolution, an Indian trader named Sam Dent, who had married a Cherokee woman, beat and murdered her while she was pregnant.[1] Dent's wife belonged to the ᏗᏠᎠ (Aniawi), or Deer Clan, whose members decided to kill Dent in keeping with the law of blood, or Blood Law, which demanded retribution for the murdered woman.[2] Since the survival of the Cherokee matrilineal clans "depended on the clan's women," this particularly devastating loss demanded swift action.[3] Fearing for his life, Dent fled to Augusta, Georgia, and there "to appease them and satisfy . . . [the Deer Clan] did then purchase a female slave name of Molly" to offer her as "remunerations for the wrongs he had done."[4]

This transaction proved agreeable to the Deer Clan, under the "then existing usages & customs of said Nation"; Molly, formerly enslaved in Georgia because of her race, was officially adopted into the Deer Clan as a result.[5] Now a member in a Cherokee clan, Molly, taking the name Chickawa, became Cherokee herself and "enjoyed the liberty of freedom."[6] She would later, as a full member of Cherokee society, marry and have two sons. Her race, in this respect, did not matter. A key element of Blood Law was about "replacing an individual who was lost with someone who could take on the deceased person's role in the community."[7] Since Chickawa herself was a member of the Deer Clan, so also were her children from that point on; the family thereby also assumed the communal obligations of clan life. Thus did clan membership confer belonging in the Cherokee Nation at the end of the eighteenth century.

THE CLAN SYSTEM AND EARLY MORES

Charles Renatus Hicks, who rose to prominence in the ᏣᎳᎩᎯ ᎠᏰᎵ (Tsalagihi Ayeli), or Cherokee Nation, as a gifted interpreter and leader during the early nineteenth century, wrote in 1826 that while the Cherokees' "original institutions" and "emigration" had escaped living memory, there could be "no doubt that their institutions began to decline when their intercourse commended [sic] with the whites."[8] Those original institutions and their perpetuation, which relied upon an oral tradition, quickly became enmeshed with well-articulated, written European and Protestant Christian ideas. Cherokee people took what they perceived as most valuable from those ideas and used them to transform their society so that, by as early as 1810, tectonic shifts occurred in their legal thinking.[9] These shifts, however, were not a complete departure from traditional mores but rather part of a larger process of adaptation.[10] While leaders like Charles Hicks were part of a growing movement to refashion Cherokee governance into a constitutional republic, these efforts were not nearly the end of traditional mores that they are often depicted as.[11]

Before Cherokee leaders adopted the term "citizen" and applied it to themselves, the clan system governed Cherokee life.[12] Cherokee people primarily defined themselves against other tribes, and eventually against European colonists, not by skin color, language, or race but by membership in a Cherokee clan, acquired via birth or adoption, calling themselves ᎠᏂᏴᏫᏯ (aniyvwiya), which means the "Real People."[13] Clan membership was matrilineal. If a woman was a member of the Deer Clan, so were her children. Her partner, the father of her children, did not belong to her clan—and could not, due to Cherokees' understanding of incest.[14] A father's children, therefore, were not his clan relatives. The fundamental male influence in a child's life came from their uncles, with their mother's eldest brother taking precedence. To understand Cherokee clan-kin relationships, we must "think in terms of the blood family, not of the connubial family."[15] Cherokee clan members believed that they literally shared a common blood, not a symbolic blood; transformation, as in the case of Chickawa, occurred during adoption.[16] These relationships structured Cherokee life, conferring rights and duties.

The basic right that stemmed from having a Cherokee mother was clan membership. Mothers and members of a mother's blood family, especially her brothers, had a subsequent duty to raise, instruct, and support her children.[17] This is not to say that fathers were totally absent but rather that the matrilineal and matrilocal nature of Cherokee society did not incentivize fathers, who belonged to a different clan, to take primary responsibility for their biological children. The concept of marriage, therefore, did not exist among the Cherokees in the European sense. Partnerships were fluid; monogamous marriages were short-lived (generally but not exclusively: there are a number of documented cases of long-lasting marriages), since either party could end the relationship at will.[18] While monogamy was the norm, polygamy was also permissible and practiced well into the nineteenth century.[19]

Cherokee Nation elder and spiritual advisor Crosslin Smith writes that "the clans are for human growth and spiritual duty. For those who take their clan seriously, they are used for structuring one's life and for answering questions such as: Who am I? What is my purpose? In the truest sense, the clans play a major role in shaping one's nature."[20] Cherokee clans cultivated a "web of social welfare fail-safes," reinforced by kinship bonds and a communal obligation to coordinate work for the common good, or ᏍᏏ (*gadugi*).[21] Cherokees "did not view individual want as a failure of the individual in need; it was a failure of the entire community" to abide by *gadugi* and their kinship duties.[22] The tribal policy of holding land in common reinforced *gadugi* as well, as individuals in need could have access to whatever natural resources were available.

Irish trader James Adair, who had gone to live among them in 1735, described their system of sharing and reciprocity: "[Cherokees] are so hospitable, kind-hearted, and free, that they would share with those of their own tribe, the last part of their provisions, even to a single ear of corn; and to others, if they called when they were eating . . . An open and generous temper is a standing virtue among them . . . When the Indians are travelling in their own country, they enquire for a house of their own tribe; and if there be any, they go to it, and are kindly received, though they never saw the persons before—they eat, drink, and regale themselves, with as much freedom, as at their own tables . . ."[23] This ethos was not derived from pity or sympathy but rather from Cherokee communal understandings of unity: "At its best, the clan system served as an adhesive for unity and allegiance that kept the total nation connected."[24] Clan members, as Adair witnessed, had a duty toward other clan members and took care of them. The communal consensus on ᎣᏍᏓᏗ ᎢᏳᏅᏁᎯ (*osda iyunvnehi*), understood as right living, or "the continual act of perpetuating positive well-being for the community," helped the decentralized Cherokees thrive.[25] This consensus included their hospitality ethic, which was in turn rooted in one's clan-kin. Cherokee extended families "included all other clan members" whose duties required that that same hospitality ethic be shown toward local neighbors.[26] Hospitality obligations included offering protection from attack, feeding the hungry, clothing the naked, caring for orphans, and sheltering those without a home. Colonial officer Henry Timberlake described a communal ceremony in the 1760s, during which Cherokees collected funds to help the poor:

> When any of their people are hungry, as they term it, or in distress, orders are issued out by the headmen for a war-dance, at which all the fighting men and warriors assemble; but here, contrary to all their other dances, one only dances at a time, who, after hopping and capering for near a minute, with a tommahawke in his hand, gives a small [w]hoop, at which signal the music stops till he relates the manner of taking his first scalp, and concludes his narration, by throwing on a large skin spread for that purpose, a string of wampum, piece of plate, wire, paint, lead, or any thing he can most conveniently spare; after which the music strikes up, and he proceeds in the same manner through all his warlike actions: then another takes his place, and the ceremony lasts till all the warriors and fighting men have related their exploits. The stock thus raised, after paying the musicians, is divided among the poor.[27]

For Cherokee communities, "right living" meant ensuring that actions conformed to their understanding of harmony and balance; they crafted a cosmovision that could be remembered, reinforced by a rich oral tradition and communal ceremonies.

A VISION OF THE GOOD LIFE

Scholars Heidi Altman and Thomas Belt write that humans are anomalous in the Cherokee cosmovision, "stuck in the midst of supernatural plants, animals, and other beings; guests in a complex spirit world."[28] Humans thus find themselves peculiar beings seeking to fit into the already functioning world. To do this, people must "observe a system of natural laws instilled through oral tradition, balance themselves among their antagonists and protagonists, and preserve a neutral position."[29] Traditionalist Hastings Shade referred to this neutral position as "a reflective practice, or way of being, focused on living in accord with Cherokee values to establish *tohi* (peace or flow) in body, mind, and spirit."[30] To live with *tohi* is to "stand in the middle": "*ayetli tsidoga*, or 'I stand in the middle.'"[31] Christopher Teuton calls this a vision of the "good life."[32]

The human position in the cosmos may only be understood in context. Not only must humans understand themselves in relationship to plants, animals, and other beings but, Crosslin Smith writes, they must also be "in complete communion" with themselves, "mind, body, and soul."[33] As human beings have "free will," Altman and Belt write, they are afforded the choice between right and wrong actions—and face the consequences of each.[34] The world exists in a precarious balance, kept in order (or thrown into disharmony) by human action.[35] Children would traditionally learn their role as human beings (and consequently what constitutes right or wrong actions) "by being taught the names, stories, and customs of the other creatures with whom we share life."[36] The goal of this and other traditional practices is not simply to impart knowledge of the world but to *know* it in a dynamic, living way.

Tradition, writes sociologist Eva Marie Garroutte, "tells you the way you are *supposed* to be. It has to give us *good*. It has to give us *growth*. It is the lessons that were taught us by the ancient ones and the elders to help us be a better person, and closer to the Creator."[37] Yet, Cherokee tradition "is not simply what was known and practiced in the past."[38] Tradition is instead, argues scholar Clint Carroll, "a shorthand and accessible (if imperfect) way to communicate concepts, behaviors, practices, ethics, and values that are grounded in cultural forms and identities of a people."[39] Tradition is living knowledge shared across generations, growing and changing and adapting as the Cherokee community makes it its own. At the heart of this tradition, according to Christopher Teuton, is storytelling.[40]

There are no definitive versions of traditional Cherokee stories; stories are about sharing, teaching, and learning, so the focus belongs there.[41] One of the most often cited stories is the Origin of Corn and Game—the story of 4M (Selu), Corn Mother, and ᎣᎾᏗ (Kanati), Lucky Hunter.[42] One version of the story tells the life of Selu and her husband, Kanati, the original woman and man, who lived in harmony on the banks of a river with their son.[43] In private, Selu would produce corn and beans for her family by rubbing her stomach and underarms respectively; in this manner, the family never ran out of food. Kanati also provided a continual source of food by bringing meat from the forest.

While playing by the river, their son met another boy, who called himself his older brother. The older child claimed that his mother had thrown him in the river; Selu and Kanati, upon hearing this, knew that the child had been born of blood that Selu had washed off in the river. The family took him in, calling him "he who grew up wild." Soon after, the "Wild Boy" persuaded his brother to follow Kanati on his hunt, to together find out the secret of his continual success in procuring meat.[44] They discovered that Kanati would go to a cave, remove the large stone at the entrance, and shoot the first animal that emerged. Replacing the stone, he would return home with meat. When Kanati had left, the boys attempted to replicate the feat, but instead freed all the animals from the cave, shooting at them for sport as the creatures fled. Kanati, realizing what the boys had done, punished them by freeing the remaining animals: insects which stung the boys for their impudence. Kanati told the boys, "Whenever you were hungry, all I had to do was to come up here and get a deer or a turkey [for you. Now] you have let out all the animals, and after this . . . you will have to hunt all over the woods [and you may not find any]."[45] The boys returned home while Kanati went back into the woods to hunt.

At home, they complained to Selu that they had no food. Selu told the boys to wait while she went into the provision hut, where the boys had never been. The Wild Boy convinced his brother to spy on Selu to see what she did to produce food.[46] The two witnessed Selu rubbing her stomach and underarms, producing corn and beans. Convinced that Selu was a witch, the boys resolved to kill her. Selu, however, "knew their thoughts" and directed the boys, after they had killed her, to drag her body around in a circle seven times and then seven times within the circle. She told them to "stay up all night and watch, and in the morning you will have plenty of corn."[47] The boys, however, did not do as she asked, instead dragging her body only in small patches, which caused corn to grow only in select spots instead of covering the entire earth. Wherever Selu's blood fell, corn sprang up.

Kanati, after seeing that his boys had killed Selu, traveled to the Wolf clan to ask the chief to kill the boys for their crime. The boys, however, were aware of the plot and able to plan for it and survive, killing many of the wolves in the process. Kanati, who did not expect his boys to survive, kept traveling farther away from home. The boys followed him east, toward the Sun Land, eventually catching up with him. Kanati next led them to a dangerous swamp, again leaving them behind. The boys discovered a panther living there but could not kill it, as their arrows had no effect. They fled to again rejoin their father. Losing Kanati once more, the boys came upon a group of cannibals, who captured and attempted to eat them, throwing the Wild Boy into a cooking pot. The cannibals, however, were unable to harm them. Summoning lightning using splinters from a tree that had been struck, the boys vanquished their cannibal captors. They yet again caught up to Kanati, who continued without them once more, reaching the end of the world. When the brothers finally reached him, they found him, to their surprise, seated with Selu. Their parents instructed them to go back to live where the sun goes down; after staying there seven days, the boys traveled back to the darkening land, becoming known as the Thunder Boys, who can to this day be heard talking to each other in the rumbling of thunder.

Different versions of the story have different elements. Christopher Teuton and Hastings Shade write "Kanati" as "Kanadi"—"Lucky One" or "Smart Hunter."[48] In Crosslin Smith's telling, the boys were twins, mortal children of two immortal parents.[49] A version recounted by scholars Jack and Anna Kilpatrick, depicts Selu living in a house with two grandsons who, while they could procure meat, were sustained by Selu's gift of corn.[50] The boys do not kill Selu when they discover how she produces food but break her heart by refusing to eat. Before she dies, Selu instructs them in the ways they ought to cultivate and harvest corn. They do so, but their home remains incomplete: "Their home needed a woman."[51] One of the boys marries and creates a family, sharing the teachings of Selu (and life-sustaining food) with the next generation and, eventually, with all Cherokee people. Yet, across different narratives, core elements remain the same: the boys seek knowledge of that which they do not know; they are afraid of or do not at first take seriously what they discover; and Selu dies, but not before sharing the secret of how to grow corn to sustain life. "Stories of the first woman, Selu," Joshua B. Nelson writes, "reinforce the traditional centrality of women's power. Selu is the Corn Mother, without whose gift of corn, the Cherokee would not be."[52]

Selu and Kanati's story, according to scholar Carolyn Ross Johnston, "emphasizes Selu's sacrifice of her life and her gift of corn."[53] The tale teaches hearers that if they showed respect and gratitude while not breaking taboos, "the blessings of the Corn Mother might return."[54] A Cherokee woman's power "derived from their ability to give and sustain life . . . [B]lood was believed to be the ultimate symbol of women's power. Selu's blood was shed as she sacrificed her life and gave the gift of corn."[55] It is therefore unsurprising that clan membership was determined through the mother's bloodline. For a community to flourish, men and women must live in harmony with one another, taking care to balance out each other's powers.[56] "Selu, and Corn-Mother and First Woman of the Cherokees," Daniel Heath Justice writes, "is balanced in her deep agricultural wisdom by her husband Kanati, Great Thunder and First Man, an unerring hunter and woodsman."[57]

Selu and Kanati personified the ideal divisions of labor in Cherokee society, modeled proper behaviors, and explained both the importance and origination of corn, beans, and game. Their story "expresses the way in which Southeastern Indians regarded hunting and agriculture."[58] Men hunted and women gathered. Selu physically gave birth to corn and beans and, through her death, these things were made available to all, much like a dying seed bears fruit. The story explains why corn does not grow everywhere and why hunts sometimes end in failure. Selu and Kanati explained to Cherokees why men and women in their society lived the way that they did, "occupying separate categories that opposed and balanced each other."[59] Men and women performed different tasks, followed different rules of behavior, and engaged in different rituals. As a result, they knew little of each other's lives, since crossing boundaries involved a certain amount of danger. Cherokees essentially understood their society in absolute terms and worked hard to conform to those expectations.

Like Selu and Kanati, Cherokees divided labor by gender. Men hunted because Kanati hunted and procured meat. Women followed

Selu's example and farmed and were primarily responsible for agriculture, which made up the bulk of the Cherokee diet. A Cherokee person's
job, anthropologist Theda Perdue writes, "was an aspect of his or her
sexuality, a source of economic and political power, and an affirmation
of cosmic order and balance."[60] Due to the connection between women
and corn, women held considerable status; moreover, Cherokees relied
heavily on the crop for subsistence.[61] Corn was more reliable than the
hunt; Cherokees even considered meat more debilitating than corn
and "its consumption problematic for those who faced various kinds
of trials."[62]

As for their children, the boys, especially the Wild Boy, do not respect
boundaries. His understanding of how to survive is "simple and irrever-
ent."[63] He is not interested in the long, arduous, and careful process by
which wisdom is acquired and implemented, nor does he initially care
to know the deeper significance of how humans ought to live rightly in
the world. "Of their two sons—the Thunder Boys—one (Tame Boy) is
born of their loving union within the structure of their ordered home,
but the other, wilder son (Wild Boy) emerges undomesticated from
the blood of Kanati's prey that Selu washes in a stream."[64] The Wild Boy
causes the dispersion of resources, technology, and knowledge essential
for Cherokee survival and therefore shapes the natural world into the
one that Cherokees know. Yet despite the fact that the Wild Boy and his
brother were initially both braggarts and "reckless rule-breakers" who
sowed chaos on earth, their story is one of redemption.[65] The Thunder
Boys, by some traditions, eventually learn to work for the communal
well-being of the Cherokees, "making recompense through the assumption of individual responsibility and generously sharing food and labor
with the earliest Cherokees."[66] There is a major emphasis on restoration
in the Cherokee cosmovision. Even the Wild Boy's mistakes have positive outcomes, thanks to his choice to make amends.

Traditionally, any who heard the "Origin of Corn and Game" and
its explanation had to "bathe in the running stream at daybreak" after
the recital "while [a] medicine-man went through his mystic ceremonies
on the bank."[67] This story reinforces the need for a closed system, one
that is not only skeptical of outside influences but actively seeks to purge
destabilizing knowledge from its people because such knowledge could
have a corrupting influence. While there are many different versions

of the Origin of Corn and Game, each version, historian Rose Strem-lau suggests, emphasizes adaptation and restoration, not despair.[68] Although things are not the way that they were in ancient times, there is still a correct way to live, a pattern of behaviors that may be considered *most human*, a vision of a good life that permits human beings to live in harmony with the world and one another.[69] This *good life*, writes Daniel Heath Justice, is the result of intentional, "balanced participation in the responsibilities of peoplehood. It isn't something that exists in the ideal abstract, as a timeless and fixed state of being . . . ; it requires atten-tive, ongoing engagement and continual contextualization in order to endure and thrive."[70]

The Origin of Corn and Game is but one story among many. The lessons in each of these are even more numerous—including some inap-propriate for sharing with outsiders.[71] Certain core themes and values emerge, however, when considering what it means to live a good life in a Cherokee *sgadug* (community). These values, according to traditional-ist Benny Smith, "include *gadugi*, 'People coming together as one and working to support one another,' and *ulisgedi detsadayelvsesdi*, 'Treat each other's existence as being sacred or important.'"[72] Joshua B. Nelson writes that "balance, boundary crossing, harmony, righteousness, and purity are among the more salient concepts of Cherokee religion, along with community responsibility."[73] We see these values practiced in how Cherokees organized themselves communally.

CHEROKEE POLITICAL LIFE

In the European sense of the term, the Cherokee people did not pre-side over a *domain*, as there were no demarcated legal boundaries; they simply knew what was theirs and what was not.[74] By 1700 "the Chero-kee Nation consisted of sixty-four towns," loosely categorized as upper, middle, and lower towns, depending on their geographical locations.[75] These towns, or villages, were politically autonomous. Edmond Atkin, member of the South Carolina Governor's Council and Indian trader, reported on the status of Cherokee towns in 1755, noting particularly the differences between the upper and lower towns.[76] "The upper and lower Cherokees," Atkin wrote, "differ from each other, as much almost as two different Nations." The upper Cherokees were "much more war-like," yet were better protected by the mountains than their southern neighbors; the lower Cherokees, "whose Towns being the most and Nearest [are much exposed], are glad to accept the Mediation of the So. Carolina Government," due to their more precarious position.[77] The middle towns were, according to Atkin, much more like the upper than the lower in character and disposition toward war. Cherokee towns had two different governmental structures that depended on the status of the tribe vis-à-vis conflict: a white (peace chief) government and a red (war chief) government.[78] The former reigned in all matters excepting war, "essentially a stable theocracy composed of the older and wiser men of the tribe."[79] The latter, run by younger Cherokees, exercised its authority during wartime and was "flexible, responsive to changing conditions."[80] Leadership was thus given up and transferred to those recognized as the most capable in a given situation.

To encourage consensus, the Cherokee councils were democratic bodies where anyone, man or woman, who wished to speak could speak, no matter how unpopular their words. Councils did not meet to legislate the way that Europeans did; they met to reach consensus.[81] Cherokees did not reach popular consensus by voting but rather by slowly dissolving the opposition.[82] Those who did not agree with the majority either compromised or withdrew. The goal of a council was not to coerce dissenters but to conciliate differences. Cherokees believed that harmony and unanimity "should prevail."[83]

The belief in harmony and consensus extended to the Cherokee justice system. No town or national council had the authority to create police forces, so clan "custom and public opinion" maintained order.[84] Leaders selected other tribal members to mete out punishments against individuals guilty of harming the community; these depended on the severity of the crime. Charges of treason, arson, incest, or witchcraft typically merited death.[85] Cherokee Blood Law was exercised to restore harmony after an individual killed a member of (typically) another clan.[86] Blood Law involved the clan members of a homicide victim, usually brothers, exacting retribution on the murderer, whether by capturing someone to fulfill clan responsibilities or killing someone. The clan was the only body with coercive authority, and "only in cases of homicide or incest."[87] Public disdain followed in the wake of most nonviolent crimes. Cherokee society was so close-knit, however, that such public shaming—including "ear cropping, insult, public disgrace, and stoning"—was often enough to keep the peace.[88]

Cherokees believed, legal scholar Rennard Strickland argued, that the natural law, or rules of conduct, were not created by men but instead existed as "a sovereign command from the Spirit World."[89] The law, as such, did not mandate or restrict behavior, but rather revealed a natural order.[90] John Haywood, in his *Natural and Aboriginal History of Tennessee*, published in 1823, described a public recitation of the law:

> The great beloved man or high priest addresses his warriors and women giving all the particular and positive injunctions, and negative precepts they yet retain of the ancient law. He uses very sharp language to the women. He then addresses the whole multitude. He enumerates the crimes they have committed, great and small, and bids them look at the holy fire, which has forgiven them. He presses on his audience by the great motives of temporal good, and the fear of temporal evil, the necessity of a careful observance of the ancient laws.[91]

When the lawgiver, dressed in the orator's costume and wearing in his hair the wings of a raven, "spoke the law, he was reading the meaning of history and tradition contained in the tribal wampum."[92] Wampum beads of different colors symbolized significant events.[93] This law, recited annually, was simple. Cherokees would have known it by heart.

Community ceremonies emphasized the value of restoration for wrongdoing and reminded participants that the spirits, not human beings, governed them through the natural laws. The Green Corn Ceremony, for example, required purification and restitution; individuals could not participate if hostility with another remained.[94] Since Cherokee tradition highlighted the individual value of each member to the community, cultivating harmony required pardoning offenses by this annual ceremony, where the Sacred Fire, polluted by wrongdoings, was reignited, burning away transgressions. Celebrated in July or August, Green Corn became the occasion for the "forgiveness of debts, grudges, adultery, and all crimes except murder." This ceremony forced a restoration of the internal order regardless of the parties' desire for reconciliation.

The forgiveness of trespasses was more important for the community than the individual's will to forgive.[95] The bond between individuals, clans, and nature was intensely spiritual, bolstered by story and symbol.

BELONGING IN THE CHEROKEE NATION

Clan members had responsibilities to live in certain ways that protected the natural world.[96] Their desire for exclusive membership flowed directly from their understanding of themselves as uniquely situated to sustain life on earth. At the same time, this desire of Cherokees to continually perform traditional dances lest the world "come to an end," as Chief Wilma Mankiller put it, was coupled with an understanding of interconnectedness and a hospitality ethic that sustained Cherokee life.[97] While Cherokees did not appear to have proselytized their religious beliefs in the manner of Christianity or Islam, they considered many of those who lived among them, when adopted, fully Cherokee themselves upon experiencing and cultivating the same lifestyle despite not being solely of Cherokee blood. Culture, not blood, determined who was Cherokee. The mode of determining who participated in Cherokee culture was belonging to a clan. Those who experienced clan membership and participated in Cherokee culture *belonged.*

Based on descriptions of their laws, taken in conjunction with their sacred stories, we begin to understand a community of people, bound by *blood as culture*, who believed in an intimate attachment between the spiritual and physical worlds, an interconnectedness between all beings.[98] Their oral tradition was reinforced and upheld by each member's lifestyle and behaviors. Among the foundational ideas in Cherokee thought stand *aniyvwiya, tohi*, and *gadugi*—which together emphasize oneness, a living history, natural interconnectedness, and the obligations human beings have to those beings with whom they are interconnected.[99] Cherokee people belonged to a clan, abided by *gadugi*, and preserved the harmony, the interconnectivity, between human beings and nature.

Early visions of the good life were inherently exclusive, restricted to those who lived in the ways that their spiritual traditions and cultural mores encouraged. Figure 2 displays the status of Cherokee belonging

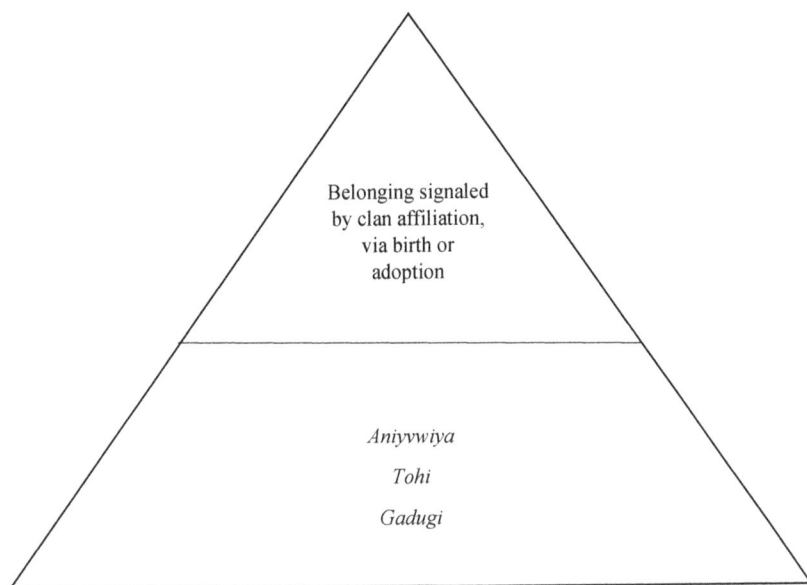

Figure 2. Foundational and Policy Ideas about Cherokee Nation Membership, Pre-1827

in the eighteenth century, leading up to the eventual centralization of Cherokee society by the 1820s. Membership depended on whether one belonged to a Cherokee clan and on whether one lived in a way that conformed to the Cherokee belief system, which entailed *right living* and acting for the social good.

The southeastern Indians, noted James Adair, each "distinguish[ed] himself by his respective family" and regarded their "own particular lineal descent" above any other.[100] These communities predicated on kinship and clan membership perplexed European colonizers, whose own ideas of citizenship or belonging were emerging from the Enlightenment.[101] While the British Empire treated as *subjects* anyone living in its colonies, including Indians, "after 1776, Americans distinguished between citizens, 'who collectively possess sovereignty,' and noncitizens such as Indians" who were not consenting members of the republic.[102] From this classification came centuries of assimilation, removal, and termination policies designed to abrogate Indigenous ideas of belonging in favor of United States liberal citizenship.

CONTACT AND ADAPTATION

A Spanish army under the command of Hernando de Soto was the first European expedition to record an encounter with the Cherokees. By the time of de Soto's expedition, Cherokees extended their influence from Virginia to Alabama and from Kentucky to the Carolinas—roughly 70 million acres of hunting grounds.[103] In 1540 about five hundred Spaniards riding horses, dragging captives, and looking for gold stumbled upon a Cherokee town, called Guasili.[104] De Soto and his officers stayed in the chief's house and accepted gifts from the Cherokees, whom the Spanish described as peaceful and hospitable despite having few possessions.[105] Although he and his men had caused so much destruction elsewhere, de Soto seems to have left the Cherokees unharmed when he departed after a few days. Cherokee culture and habits remained largely unaltered by European mores until around 1710, when trade between Cherokees and the British of Charles Town (in the Province of Carolina) significantly expanded.[106]

The British encountered the Cherokee people enjoying a sprawling territory—territory that, to British eyes, looked empty. Once established as trade partners, British goods, habits, mores, and religious beliefs steadily seeped into Cherokee society, producing an upheaval in their tribal communities. Rennard Strickland identified five factors that drove the Cherokees' transition "from clan to court" in the century between 1710 and 1808, which saw the first Cherokee written law promulgated in emulation of white governments.[107] These factors are: the change in the Cherokee economic system, missionary pressures, and the loss of traditional religious practices; the withdrawal of traditional factions from Cherokee politics; the increase in the number of "mixed-breed Cherokees"; and the United States' obsession with obtaining land.[108] In that century, Cherokees underwent a period of critical self-reflection to redefine themselves in a world that suddenly included written language, dogmatic abstract religions, new races, and a lust for land hitherto unknown.

Among these changes, the clash of religious beliefs became one of the most significant as missionaries flocked into the Cherokee Nation to convert those peoples into the various sects of Protestant Christianity. Early missionaries, who had officially begun to enter Cherokee territory after 1799, were shocked when Cherokees that they encountered recited back to them stories from the Old Testament, leading some, as James Adair had earlier, to believe that the Cherokees were somehow descendants of the Israelites.[109] If not exactly descendants of the Israelites, missionaries thought the Cherokees' religious beliefs at least similar in critical ways to those of the Christians.[110] This misunderstanding is attributed to the life and adventures of a man named Christian Gottlieb Priber, who lived among the Cherokees in the 1730s and 1740s.[111]

Often mistaken for a French Jesuit—and so derogatorily painted by the British when Priber attempted to turn the Cherokees against them—Priber was a German political idealist who attempted to create what he called a "Kingdom of Paradise" among the Cherokees.[112] This "kingdom" was intended to be an "asylum for debtors, Transport Felons, Servants & Negroe [sic] Slaves in the two Carolinas & Virginia."[113] Priber arrived among the Cherokees and immediately ingratiated himself there by adopting their habits and dress, by learning their language, and by marrying a Cherokee woman.[114] Priber earned the ire of the British, Adair complained, by convincing the Cherokees that the British had swindled them out of their lands and by giving them a "prodigious high opinion of their own importance in the American scale of power."[115]

Before being exiled from Germany for his political ideas, Priber had planned for decades to create a utopian society, one predicated on an idea of true equality and freedom. Antoinne Bonnefoy, a French trader, encountered Priber in 1741 and recorded Priber's designs for his Kingdom of Paradise: "The form of the government should be that of a general society of those composing it, in which, beyond the fact that legality should be perfectly observed, as well as liberty, each would find what he needed, whether for subsistence, or the other needs of life; that each should contribute to the good of society, as he could."[116] This republic would be independent, not affiliated with any colonial power in Europe. Priber saw in the Cherokees, a communal society with a strong hospitality ethic that instructed them to care for one another, the opportunity to mold them into his political ideal.

In this republic, Priber told another trader named Ludovick Grant, "there would be no superiority; that all should be equal there; that he would take superintendence of it only for the honor of establishing it."[117] All material goods, including clothing, shelter, and furniture, would be held in common and each member would work according to his abilities for the common good. Even more radically to the ears of the traders, in the Kingdom of Paradise, men, women, and children would be held in common: the adults would be free in terms of marriage and sexuality and the children would be raised by the community away from their birth parents and educated to cultivate their "genius."[118] Priber found among Cherokees a social and political system that seemed ripe for refinement into his vision. Priber soon crowned a man named Moytoy "emperor" of this republic and whom Priber himself served in a support role as the "imperial majesty's principal secretary of state."[119] Priber, himself highly educated and skilled, taught the people how to measure and weigh materials, which gained him much prestige.[120] He also spread among them stories from the Old Testament, which some Cherokees incorporated into their own knowledge systems when they proved useful for their explanatory power or for dealing with other whites whom they encountered.

Priber's actions, however, especially his efforts to drive a wedge between the Cherokees and the British at Charles Town, who were their major trade partners, incited a British plot against him. The capital of Priber's empire was to be at a place called Coosawattee, located nearer the French than the British, further leading to discord between the two. The British made a few attempts to capture Priber but were repulsed each time when they discovered just how much the Cherokee people were attached to him. Despite British efforts, his comrades refused to let Priber go. Priber's downfall came in 1743 when he was captured by Creek Indians, allies of British general Oglethorpe.[121] A celebrity in captivity, Priber fascinated his captors and visitors with his magnetic personality and ambitions, but more so for the way in which he appeared to have completely committed to the Cherokee way of life. Priber would die in captivity, but not before rejecting a chance to escape. Adair relates that on one occasion, a stockpile of munitions caught fire near the prison in which Priber was held. Although the guards told Priber to run for safety, giving him the chance to escape, the captive simply lay prone on the floor of his cell before emerging from the fire unscathed, explaining to his stunned guards that he was in no danger from smoke on the ground or from the explosion, which shot straight up into the air. Adair related his story and Priber's eventual starvation with a mixture of awe and irritation, stating that "happily for us, he died in confinement, though he deserved a much better fate."[122]

Incidents like the encounter with Priber show the tendency of Cherokees to deal in good faith with whites who seemed to understand and who lived culturally as Cherokees did—and that of whites' attempts to exploit the adaptable Cherokee society for their own ends. While the Cherokees did not adhere to Priber's vision for a utopian society, they did retain memory of the stories he told and the lessons he taught in their oral traditions. As historian Emmet Starr suggested, Cherokees appeared to have forgotten Priber entirely, although certainly not the biblical stories he shared with them, as Cherokees later related these stories to missionaries with ease.[123] Knowing some of the stories in the Christian tradition, the Cherokees were in that sense, according to Starr, primed to accept Christianity when it was more fully articulated in the nineteenth century.

SPIRITUALITY AND RELIGION

The Cherokee religion was administered by medicine persons, who constructed answers to spiritual questions each on their own, drawing from their rich oral traditions.[124] The mass introduction of Christianity brought these spiritual leaders and healers into contact with questions for which they had no answers, such as the origin of good and evil, whether humans had eternal souls, and how white men not only existed but also had books that seemed to answer their questions.[125] Medicine men employed Old Testament narratives as support for their mythology to fill in gaps where their own stories did not explain certain things. Cherokees adopted elements of these biblical stories as their own, especially the Garden of Eden, the Mosaic Law, and the Great Flood.[126]

Apart from providing answers to cosmic philosophical questions that many Cherokees had, Christian missionaries, with some notable exceptions, instructed Cherokees to completely give up their traditional mores, including ceremonial dances, ball play, and the division of labor between men and women.[127] Indeed, Protestant theology taught the Cherokees to completely cleave vulgar business and politics (the purview of men) from home and virtue (the purview of women).[128] Since Protestant sects disregarded the Blessed Virgin, the only female role model these missionaries had to offer the matrilineal Cherokees was Eve, who, by disobeying God, had brought sin into the world.[129] Many Cherokees resisted Protestant Christianity and its prescriptions for women as a result, preferring Selu, who had given them gifts and taught them how to live properly. But this does not represent the entire experience. Some Cherokee women, like Catharine Brown, converted to Christianity, finding in that faith strength and hope in a manner that did not diminish her Cherokee identity.[130] Women took on "conspicuous and influential roles as teachers and community leaders," contributing to the Christianization of the Cherokee Nation; historian William McLoughlin claimed that the majority of converts were, in fact, women, who, because of their prominent position in Cherokee culture, sustained the spreading evangelization.[131]

The missionaries at the Brainerd Mission—located along the South Chickamauga Creek from 1817 to 1838—were perplexed that Cherokees did not seem to contemplate God, sin, or the afterlife.[132] One missionary asked a Cherokee woman whether "she had many thoughts about God, the Great Spirit. She replied 'I do not think much about him.'" When asked if she thought herself a sinner, she answered, "No." Neither did she know where her spirit would be when her body died: "She did not know that it would be anywhere."[133] The missionaries found that their beliefs differed from Cherokee beliefs on many fundamental issues:

The Cherokee concept of the after-life projected a life similar to this life where souls of dead slipped back and forth at will, often through the portals of dreams, visions, and spiritual omens. The Cherokees had no one 'Great Spirit,' who created all, but rather had many spirits with which the Great Spirit blended. The missionaries also found their beliefs in contrast to the Cherokees' beliefs in reference to 'sin.' The Cherokees believed that all life existed in balance, a harmony of man, nature, and spirits. For example, a man was balanced by a woman, hunting was balanced by farming, Cherokee was balanced by non-Cherokee . . . The concept of 'sin' as disobeying God was foreign to the Cherokees for the evil came, many times, from a man violating the balance of nature. If a man killed a deer without the proper ceremony, imbalance occurred, and evil came upon him and his family.[134]

Missionaries thus focused not only on convincing Cherokees that they were individually sinners through the words of St. Paul—"since all have sinned and fall short of the glory of God"—but also of the concept of sin itself.[135]

Many Cherokees were amenable to Christian teachings, part of which appeared to have come from their own tradition, since in some places they had been telling stories with elements borrowed from the Old Testament for decades.[136] This resulted not in a simple abandonment of old mores but rather in a complex melding of faiths and practices.[137] "The two religions," Joshua B. Nelson writes, after all "share several important dispositions . . . like prayer, fasting, and worship."[138] Faith spread at the intersection of traditional old ways and Christianity—both beliefs sustaining and dynamic for those involved.[139] The civilization that Christians brought with them was also attractive in many ways, especially technologies like mirrors, guns, clothing, and agricultural tools. The increase in possessions, however, brought with it a great gulf between the haves and the have-nots, which many missionaries encouraged by associating Christian discipline and self-restraint with prosperity and Cherokee "savagery" with poverty.[140] Those who increased in wealth among the Cherokees therefore found such distinctions appealing— and indeed Christianity flourished especially among those who had intermarried with whites and who had raised plantations in the manner of whites, partaking also in the practice of slaveholding.[141]

SLAVERY IN THE CHEROKEE NATION

Slavery existed in parts of North America long before European settlers arrived. Though slaves were traditionally taken as prisoners of war, according to historian Rudi Halliburton Jr., there appeared to have been a commercial traffic in some places as well.[142] From the time of their earliest contact with Europeans, Cherokees had engaged in a practice of quasi-slavery and forced adoption among their Indian captives—a practice later used in the treatment of Caucasian and African prisoners as well.[143] The term "quasi-slavery" here reflects the old Cherokee practice of claiming slaves from rival tribes as spoils of war; "most of the slaves [were] probably prisoners, [but] not all of the prisoners were slaves."[144] Although this quasi-slavery was widespread among Cherokees at first contact, chattel slavery as an institution did not exist prior to European settlement.[145] Once introduced by English traders, Cherokees were quick to accept the European brand of slaveholding as one of the benefits of white civilization.[146] English traders in the seventeenth century began to establish themselves among the Cherokees through marriage and the spread of material wealth.[147] The legacy of slavery among them was passed down through a combination of cultural pressure, assimilation, and family heritage.

Many Cherokees also took to institutionalized slavery because of the benefits they received from stealing or returning runaway slaves.[148] English and French colonists frequently urged Cherokees to sell them slaves stolen from the plantations or villages of their European adversaries. In return, colonial powers typically promised access to powerful weapons and ammunition. The return or barter of runaway slaves became so common that Cherokees were often known colloquially as "slave catchers."[149] Whether through trade, theft, or personal benefit, chattel slavery gradually became a part of Cherokee society in a way that normalized the practice and invested many Cherokees in the colonial status quo. In everyday life, the addition of slaves was a boon for Cherokee women, who lacked the same level of farming skill as enslaved peoples they could acquire from their neighbors, and for Cherokee men, who could spend more time hunting, bartering, or at war.

In the beginning, the Cherokee relationship to slaveholding was characterized more by *otherness* than by racism. The tension between Anglo-dominated slaveholding society and Native Americans has been well-documented, but many tribes, including the Cherokees, grew to feel a particular antipathy toward Black persons as well.[150] For whites, who harbored a racial animosity toward Blacks and Indians alike, Indian slaveholding represented a potential alliance of natural enemies and threatened white civilization.[151] However, for the Cherokees, who did not possess a concept of race as such, *foreignness* initially determined their perceptions of outsiders.[152] Their eventual disdain for Black persons likely emerged out of their desire to emulate their American neighbors and the sustained practice of slaveholding itself.[153]

Since they had encountered Europeans and enslaved peoples at the same time, and typically together, Cherokees did not sharply distinguish between the two and considered both inferior.[154] However, according to historian Kenneth W. Porter, there is no evidence that the northern tribes made any distinction between Black and white persons based on color until white society told them to.[155] In fact, Cherokees only identified Black persons with servitude after they developed a need for additional laborers on plantations because of white attitudes.[156] Ultimately, clan-less outsiders were just that: outsiders who, though bringing some benefits to the tribe, threatened the power of the sacred relationships between nature, kin, and community. Those threats grew continually up through the early half of the nineteenth century, until the US government officially decided to remove tribal nations off of their lands to make room for American expansion.

REVOLUTIONARY WARS AND REVOLUTIONARY PEACE

The politics in the Americas during the late eighteenth century have been well-documented elsewhere and are largely outside the scope of this book.[157] Cherokees' roles in the major conflicts and events attending the transition from European to United States rule in North America, however, tended to shape early American Indian policies, ultimately affecting how Cherokees defined themselves as a people. During the Seven Years' War, also known as the French and Indian War, many Cherokee towns initially aligned themselves with the British, their major trade partners. Relations between the two soon soured, however, leading to a conflict with the British and particularly with neighboring colonists in Virginia. The Treaty of Long-Island-on-the-Holston (1761) officially ended the conflict, although animosity and violence continued between Cherokees and colonists.

Cherokees originally went to war to rectify the imbalance caused by acts of violence. These acts of retaliation were not intended to be drawn-out entanglements but rather short campaigns that satisfied the law of blood for blood.[158] This understanding of conflict as short-lived and retaliatory frequently brought Cherokees into conflict with colonists due to the desire to right wrongs committed against them. Colonists, refusing or unable to understand the Cherokee conception of retaliation, saw such acts not as actions meant to right wrongs but as declarations of war against the entire colony. For the Cherokees, after all, "two wrongs could make a right" and "one bad turn deserved a counter bad turn and together, balanced one against the other, they made everything smooth."[159] What Cherokees viewed as violence to right the wrongs of previous violence—at which point the matter would be settled—colonists viewed as a reason to perpetuate further brutalities as in a state of war.

As the French and Indian War came to an end, "British officers concluded that settlers, rather than Indians, posed the greatest threat to imperial peace and order on the frontier."[160] To prevent further conflicts, the British attempted to protect Indigenous peoples from the colonists, who had already drawn hard racial lines between themselves and their native neighbors. James Adair lamented British colonial treatment of the Cherokees and the constant violence and murder that was sustained between them: "We forced the Cheerake [sic] to become our bitter enemies, by a long train of wrong measures, the consequences of which were severely felt by a number of high assessed, ruined, and bleeding innocents—May this relation, be a lasting caution to our colonies against the like fatal errors!"[161] The colonists, however, were more than willing to continue expanding into the worlds of the Cherokees and other nations at the latter's expense if it meant solidifying themselves as a prosperous people.[162]

As the American Revolutionary spirit boiled over, most tribal leaders adopted a policy of neutrality, willing to wait to see which side was winning before committing themselves and preferring to be paid in some way by both British and Revolutionaries.[163] Cherokee people were in a difficult position. The British desired native neutrality to coax Loyalists in the colonies to rally to the crown; yet they also wanted the tribal warriors to attack Revolutionaries, distracting them from British targets. British superintendent John Stuart issued seemingly conflicting messages to the Cherokee towns as a result.[164] Unwilling to wait while other Cherokee chiefs deliberated, war chief Tsiyu Gansini (or Dragging Canoe), son of a peace chief named Little Carpenter, fell in with British plans to assault the Revolutionaries.[165] Speaking before the people in 1775, Dragging Canoe gave an impassioned speech:

> Whole Indian Nations have melted away like snowballs in the sun before the white man's advance. They leave scarcely a name of our people except those wrongly recorded by their destroyers.

Where are the Delawares? . . . They have been reduced to a mere shadow of their former greatness. We had hoped that the white men would not be willing to travel beyond the mountains. Now that hope is gone. They have passed the mountains, and have settled upon Cherokee land. They wish to have that usurpation sanctioned by treaty. When that is gained, the same encroaching spirit will lead them upon other land of the Cherokees. New cessions will be asked. Finally the whole country, which the Cherokees and their fathers have so long occupied, will be demanded, and the remnant of the Ani Yvwiya, *The Real People*, once so great and formidable, will be compelled to seek refuge in some distant wilderness. There they will be permitted to stay only a short while, until they again behold the advancing banners of the same greedy host. Not being able to point out any further retreat for the miserable Cherokees, the extinction of the whole race will be proclaimed. Should we not therefore run all risks, and incur all consequences, rather than to submit to further loss of our country? Such treaties may be alright for men who are too old to hunt or fight. As for me, I have my young warriors about me. We will hold our land. A-WANINSKI, I have spoken.[166]

Dragging Canoe, born around 1730, widely known for his hatred of white men, was angered by a 1775 arrangement with whites in which Cherokees agreed to part with their lands in modern-day Kentucky and a portion of those lands in Tennessee.[167] This new loss of Cherokee lands and power enraged him, further fueling his resentment of the colonists and their strong-arm tactics.[168] Dragging Canoe planned to attack the Holston settlement on July 21, 1776, but was given away by his cousin, Nanye'hi (Nancy Ward), the "beloved woman of the Cherokees," who warned the settlers of the impending violence.[169] The Cherokees were eventually driven from the region when the colonists amassed a much larger militia, roughly 6,000 strong, and destroyed all of the Cherokee villages they could get their hands on, those both hostile and neutral.[170] While other Cherokees sued for peace, Dragging Canoe and his warriors established a new home near Chickamauga and continued to assault white colonists in middle and eastern Tennessee to great effect.

Nancy Ward, for her part, followed what Daniel Heath Justice cites as the "Beloved Path," a difficult road that "sought balance between concessions to a ravenous empire and defiance against being swallowed up completely."[171] As she witnessed a world coming undone, she worked, using her considerable intellect and status, to preserve a defiant peace—not a peace at any price, but a peace when it seemed necessary to preserve her people.[172] Married to a white man and willing to oppose Dragging Canoe on his warpath, Nancy Ward followed a "tradition that saw strength and survival in adaptation."[173] However, she would not and could not consent to the further breakup of tribal lands and stood against land cessions into her old age.[174]

While the British resolved their struggle against the Revolutionaries in 1783, conceding victory for the time being, Dragging Canoe and his militant Cherokees did not. Most of the Cherokee Nation had been decimated: the Revolutionaries had "destroyed their crops, appropriated their property and burned fifty of their towns and reduced the people to dire destitution."[175] A further outrage: peace treaties were signed that gave colonists millions of acres of land. Dragging Canoe and Young Tassel (also called John Watts), nephew of Old Tassel (or Corn Tassel), who became the well-respected peace chief of the non-belligerent Cherokee towns, did not partake in these treaties but rather chose to continue their campaign of violence against white encroachment.[176] In 1785, the United States and the Cherokees signed the Treaty of Hopewell, which declared peace, defined new boundary lines between the two peoples, promised friendship, and gave the Cherokees a right to a delegate in Congress.[177]

In 1785, Chief Old Tassel issued a stern rebuke to United States commissioners even as the two sides were signing a peace treaty, remarking that whites should simply accept the intractable differences between their disparate regimes and stop attempting to turn Cherokees into Americans:

> Indeed, much has been advanced on the want of what you term civilization among the Indians; and many proposals have been made to us to adopt your laws, your religion, your manners and your customs. But, we confess that we do not yet see the propriety, or practicability of such a reformation, and should be better

pleased with beholding the good effect of these doctrines in your own practices than with hearing you talk about them, or reading your papers to us upon such subjects.

You say: Why do not the Indians till the ground and live as we do? May we not, with equal propriety, ask, Why the white people do not hunt and live as we do? . . . The great God of Nature has placed us in different situations. It is true that he has endowed you with many superior advantages; but he has not created us to be your slaves. *We are a separate people!*[178]

Yet, after the treaty, white squatters refused to leave Cherokee lands and the general harassment continued. By 1788, Cherokees, still under pressure from the American government and white settlers, were "in a furor," and it was all that Chief Old Tassel could do to maintain the peace.[179]

Dragging Canoe and his Chickamauga band of the Cherokees, however, were undeterred and remained defiant against colonist brutality in Tennessee. The violence continued, despite the peace treaty. In June 1788, Old Tassel and his family were invited to the headquarters of one Mayor James Hubbert by American colonel John Sevier's men. Under the flag of peace, the chief came unarmed and, along with his son and two others, was ushered into a vacant building, where they were shot dead.[180] The beloved chief's murder rallied many of the previously peaceful Cherokees to Dragging Canoe's cause. Dragging Canoe, "with the entire nation seething with the war spirit," recognized Little Turkey as principal chief of all the Cherokees—a huge step toward unification of the Cherokee people.[181]

A group of Cherokees, including a teenage boy called The Ridge (also known as Major Ridge) who would grow up to have a permanent impact on Cherokee history, chased after the soldiers responsible for killing their old chief. The "lust for scalps," however, prevented the Cherokees from annihilating the entire force.[182] "If thoughts of avenging Old Tassel had heightened their frenzy," scholar Thurman Wilkins relates, "the irony is that among the soldiers who had escaped was the man who had [actually] killed the old chief."[183] Dragging Canoe continued his campaign until his death in 1791, after an all-night celebration of recent victories.[184] His actions in Tennessee during those years helped consolidate Cherokee cultural resistance to white encroachment in defense of their lands; he was and is, Daniel Heath Justice writes, a "reminder of the willingness of some people to kill and die in their defiance of U.S. imperialism."[185]

THE UNITED STATES AND *CIVILIZATION* POLICIES

The Cherokee Nation, during the early period of United States domination of the continental core, experienced geographical, ideological, and identity fragmentation. Many Cherokees and other Indigenous peoples chose to move west of their own accord to avoid altercations with settlers or their fellow Indians.[186] United States officials were more than happy to let them go.[187] Since they wanted land, Americans saw these migrations as beneficial and quickly rushed to scoop up what remained.[188] This tendency of some Indians to simply move west on their own formed the unspoken understanding underlying the first US federal Indian policy, often referred to as a *civilization* policy.

Early Americans wrestled with what to make of Indigenous nations (usually in the halls of government, without their input); the *Federalist Papers* themselves are permeated with an uncertain mixture of fear and envy in their treatment of Indians, alternatively describing them as hostile threats (*Federalist* Nos. 3, 7, 24, 25) or as potential trade partners (*Federalist* Nos. 24, 40, 42). In both cases, as a monolithic group. The US Constitution itself acknowledges American Indians as a separate category of persons, leading many US officials to conclude that Indians rightfully belonged outside of the American political community.[189] During the civilization policy era, initially spearheaded by President George Washington through the influence of his secretary of war, Henry Knox, the US government avoided confronting the most vexing problems of Indian-white relations, like the major political gulf that existed between their disparate regimes, and instead focused on maintaining peace agreements while giving tribal nations aid.[190] "Civilizing" Indians in this period meant instructing them on how to build towns, cities, farms, schools, churches, and seats of government to emulate American mores.[191]

Washington's Indian policy called for "a system corresponding with the mild principles of Religion and Philanthropy towards an unenlightened race of Men, whose happiness materially depends on the conduct of the United States," to help guide US officials toward peace and friendliness with their neighbors.[192] His solution to ending the Indian wars was to impart "the blessings of civilization" to the Indian tribes, as may "suit their condition."[193] If the tribes were "civilized" in the American fashion, Washington mused, they might be more amenable to trade as good-natured neighbors attached firmly to the United States. The president's plan for the relationship between Indian tribes and the United States was therefore to teach the "unenlightened" Indians how good government—and civilization—ought to work by example. Through commerce—unbiased, ethical commerce—the United States could show Indians the benefits of a peaceful market economy.[194] Through the regular, unbiased application of the law, US officials could teach Indians how a codified legal system works and benefits human beings. A bad example of these things, Washington cautioned, could turn their neighbors from the lure of "civilization."

Yet Washington's policy, in practice, was not followed in the states. It was "the misfortune of the Indians," Alexis de Tocqueville wrote, that they encountered "the most civilized and, I shall add, the greediest people on the globe"; they received from their instructors "oppression and enlightenment at the same time."[195] Americans, while teaching Cherokees the "arts of civilization," simultaneously crushed them in the same competitive economic markets that they insisted Cherokees join. This "fatal competition" would inevitably lead to new divisions within Cherokee society, Tocqueville claimed, as successful acculturated individuals thrived while traditionalists, seeing nothing satisfying to be gained from playing the American civilization game, chose to hold tight to their old ways.[196] While Tocqueville did not see nuance in how Cherokee people reacted to the United States, his articulation of American greed certainly rang true.

Subsequent presidential administrations were inclined to follow Washington's example while exploiting these societal divisions as well.[197] President Thomas Jefferson's letter to the Cherokee Nation on May 4, 1808, largely reiterates Washington's civilization plan but with added encouragement to remove beyond the Mississippi.[198] In his message, Jefferson asked whether Cherokees were ready "to be our brothers instead of our children."[199] For Jefferson, this meant giving up hunting and sharing land in common; it meant men adopting regular jobs and women remaining at home to care for children and perform house chores rather than the farming to which they were accustomed. American Protestant Christian social mores, in effect, prepared one for citizenship. Importantly, Jefferson's was not a racial prohibition but a cultural one—a hope that many acculturating Cherokees latched onto.

Later that same year, the Cherokee Nation drafted and signed its first written law. On September 11, 1808, Chief Black Fox, Pathkiller, Toochalar, and Charles R. Hicks, secretary to the Council, signed a law creating a "national police force for the protection of property" and the general protection of its citizens from theft.[200] By the 1800s, the Cherokees had become a propertied people, as many profited from trade relationships and their own businesses. While land was still held in common, individuals owned slaves, livestock, plows, guns, and spinning wheels as individuals.[201] Women had the same rights of ownership as men, but neither nonmember whites nor enslaved persons could own anything. Critically, the 1808 law also protected children "as heirs to their father's property, and to the widow's share."[202] From this, property law would develop into a refined system, one uniquely Cherokee, by the time of their removal from Georgia.[203]

Property ownership and inheritance presented a difficulty for the Cherokee clan system. The white system of inheritance and ownership was, after all, based on the concept of a family with a single head-of-household father and mother, who passed property on to their children. Cherokees cherished kin relationships where the mother's clan, not the father's, claimed children in a world without much individual property at all. "In essence," Rennard Strickland argues, "the matrilineal social structure was supplanted. The new system built upon the strong parent-child relationship."[204] This upheaval had many implications for membership in the Cherokee Nation, among them that men, their property, and lineage began to take precedence over women in political life.

The Cherokee Nation's early written laws display attempts to consolidate government authority over an increasingly centralizing—and, paradoxically, dividing—community. Many of these laws, like the Council's attempt to end clan revenge killings in 1810, reflected the growing acculturation movement within the Cherokee Nation and attempts to align Cherokee practice with United States legal standards.[205] In 1810, Chief Black Fox signed the law outlawing the practice of clan revenge, which was inherently opposed to European ideas of the uniform application of the law.[206] The gulf between Cherokee elites and the average tribal member grew ever larger during this period. Cherokee leaders were increasingly fluent in English, mission school educated, and well-off adherents to the Christian religion. The laws passed reflected these tendencies as lawmakers attempted to both "civilize" their Cherokee brethren and position the tribe to defend itself against the onslaught of American expansion.

Another impetus for these first written Cherokee laws was Chief Doublehead's arrangement in 1805 to sign away reserved Cherokee lands to the United States in exchange for a private land grant for himself. Doublehead was a Cherokee warrior of some renown, having gained fame in the wars against the United States when he took part in a number of Dragging Canoe's campaigns.[207] In 1794 he had been selected an official spokesperson for the Cherokee Nation and had conferred with Washington himself on behalf of the Cherokees.[208] Doublehead had become a staunch ally of Colonel Return J. Meigs, US Indian agent, and proponent of acculturation "as Jefferson had described it."[209] Outraged, in 1807 chiefs and warriors met to decide Doublehead's fate for his actions. A Cherokee named Bone Polisher tried to assassinate Doublehead at a ball play but was killed instead by his target, who escaped.[210] The Ridge, who had fought with Doublehead before, tracked him down and killed him. Ridge, along with Charles Hicks and James Vann, was part of a young cohort of Cherokee chiefs who supported acculturation. Yet although Ridge and other prominent leaders favored acculturation, they did not approve of wantonly handing over Cherokees lands. The creation of a police force in 1808 and the law ending clan revenge in 1810 were, Rennard Strickland argued, intended to protect the Council's executioners and their property from retaliation from Doublehead's family.[211]

The decision of most Indigenous tribes to align themselves against the United States with the British in the War of 1812 had important implications for the Cherokees, even though towns did not officially join the British in that conflict.[212] Americans, having driven off the British yet again, were simultaneously filled with a religious fervor that seemed to direct them to their divinely ordained destiny of taking over the continent and worried about the decision of so many tribes to side against them. A renewed interest in Indian missions emerged as a way to speed up the process of civilization to both save the Indians and claim more land.[213]

The Moravians had commenced their mission work in the Cherokee Nation between 1799 and 1801; after 1815, nearly every major Protestant Christian denomination went to work setting up missions. These were supported by the Indian Civilization Act passed by Congress in 1819, which subsidized mission work in exchange for missionaries supporting US civilization policies.[214] The American Board of Commissioners for Foreign Missions, sustained by Congregational and Presbyterian churches, entered the Cherokee Nation in 1817.[215] The Baptists joined around the same time, followed by the Methodists in 1824. These missionaries, although they worked to *civilize* the Cherokees, drew the ire of neighboring frontier whites, who resented any aid to the Indians and wanted them gone outright.[216]

In 1817, members of fifty-four Cherokee towns and villages convened to draw up a plan for the future of governance in the Cherokee Nation, especially with respect to the "common property of lands."[217] Signed by Pathkiller, the six articles they adopted aimed to solidify the situation in the nation while codifying the consequences of a few key activities. Article 3, for example, stated that Cherokees who removed themselves from the limits of the nation forfeited all claim and authority of all lands held in common.[218] The agreement created a thirteen-member standing committee, into whose care they entrusted the affairs of the nation, provided that their decisions obtained the unanimous support of the chiefs of the Council. This body had the responsibility of dealing with US Indian agents to obtain annual stipends for lands ceded. The goal was to create a more unitary institutional body to deal with the Americans and, ultimately, to protect Cherokee lands.

The decision was influenced by petitions from Cherokee women, including an elderly Nancy Ward, imploring the chiefs not to part with any additional lands. These women declared it their "duty as mothers" to preserve their lands for the protection and growth of their children:[219]

Your mothers, your sisters, ask and beg of you not to part with any more of our land. We say ours. You are our descendants; take pity on our request. But keep it for our growing children, for it was the good will of our creator to place us here, and you know our father, the great president [James Monroe], will not allow his white children to take our country away. Only keep your hands off of paper talks for its our own country. For [if] it was not, they would not ask you to put your hands to paper, for it would be impossible to remove us all."[220]

Nancy Ward added that she wanted her many grandchildren to thrive on the land of their ancestors and that Cherokees should not be so quick as to sign away their blessings. While many of those gathered agreed, the Cherokees had become divided and a number of chiefs, including Charles Hicks and those in Arkansas, ultimately signed the Treaty of 1817 a few months later in July, ceding additional lands to the United States.[221] A few years later, in 1824, Secretary of War John C. Calhoun set up a Bureau of Indian Affairs within his department, which Congress confirmed in 1832.[222]

Civilization policy was having an effect, but not the exact effect that US officials like Jefferson had intended. Americans had hoped that Indians would fully assimilate into American society—and relinquish their large areas of communally held lands to new white settlements in the process. When civilizing Indigenous peoples resulted in the substantial Americanization of many tribes, including and especially the Cherokees, the United States found that eastern Indians became politically entrenched, better able to legally defend their land titles.[223] "Civilizing," instead of continuing to drive Cherokees west or dispersing them among the several states, gave the acculturated Cherokees confidence in their budding sense of nationalism. Cherokee culture, argues legal historian John Phillip Reid, had always cultivated a legalistic mind, a tendency that produced many excellent lawyers once Cherokees became proficient in United States legal terminology.[224] Nothing, however, imbued Cherokees with a national pride quite like the creation of the Cherokee syllabary.

Sequoyah, belonging to the Paint Clan, was born around 1770 to a Cherokee mother and a wandering German.[225] The young Sequoyah was sickly and suffered from arthritic knees, which made him limp his whole life. He neither spoke nor read the English language. It was common in the early nineteenth century among Cherokees to believe that the written page actually spoke to white men something that Cherokees could not hear. Sequoyah, who, Emmet Starr writes, meditated upon these things, conceived of the idea that "each mark represented a sound."[226] He created his own marks, borrowing many from English characters, and gave them distinctive sounds from the Cherokee language. He finished his great effort in 1824, an entire eighty-six-letter alphabet created by one man.[227] Its use spread like wildfire as native speakers could easily pick it up and read it when they had learned the syllables. The tables could now be turned; instead of Cherokees having to learn English to deal with whites, whites could now learn Cherokee, thus perpetuating Cherokee cultural consciousness. Both Cherokee political leaders and Christian missionaries jumped at the chance to perpetuate learning in the Cherokee language. The former caused the laws to be printed in Cherokee and in English, while the latter authored a translation of the New Testament for distribution among traditionalists who had resisted English language education.[228]

Cherokee leaders, newly encouraged by Sequoyah and the missionaries, continued to centralize their governing apparatus and adopt a legal code. Legislation created eight legislative districts in 1820, dividing up the Cherokee Nation into political sectors.[229] In an effort to further end traditional practices and solidify American family ideals, laws first discouraging and then banning polygamy were passed in 1819 and 1825 respectively.[230] Cherokees also introduced racially prohibitive laws as a means to solidify their own national identity. These were typically aimed at white men who attempted to gain control of Cherokee national assets and at free Blacks. Law passed in 1824 stipulated that all Black persons "coming into the Nation on any pretense whatsoever, shall be viewed and treated, in every respect, as intruders" and prohibited marriage between Blacks and either Indians or whites living in the nation.[231]

Cherokee politics in the 1820s was especially tumultuous. In addition to the ever-increasing pressure from Georgia and United States officials to relocate west, internal divisions steadily arose between traditionalists and the growing number of acculturated progressives—"Cherokee leaders increasingly came from an elite group of wealthy men who promoted acculturation."[232] Men like John Ross (who would soon serve as the president of the constitutional convention and principal chief), John Ridge (son of Major Ridge), and Elias Boudinot quickly rose to prominence, in part due to their comparatively advanced education. These and other leaders tended to be more well-off than average Cherokees, "were no more representative of the Cherokees than the US founding fathers were of Americans," and, like the founders, often fought each other.[233] The aristocratic tendencies of these Cherokee leaders and their precarious situation as a nation in the 1820s make the 1827 constitution an even more remarkable document. Whatever they lacked in representativeness, the drafters of the constitution made up for in patriotism as they sought the survival of the Cherokee people and to cement some form of Cherokee political thought into constitutional law.

CHEROKEE CLAN IDENTITY AND ACCULTURATION

This chapter traces the adaptation of Cherokee society from its traditional mores into a centralized regime looking to stabilize itself in North America. In the 1700s, Cherokee membership depended upon belonging to a Cherokee clan, which in turn meant either having a Cherokee mother or being adopted into that clan. Over time, due to intermarriage, education, conversion to Christianity, and the accumulation of wealth in the hands of a few, Cherokees adopted a more patrilineal government structure in emulation, but not as a mirror image, of the United States. These new leaders passed laws that opened up citizenship to men and the descendants of men who had no clan and gradually began to erode Cherokees' matrilineal instincts, at least legally.

An individual belonged if they experienced clan membership—having a Cherokee mother or by adoption—as in the case of Chickawa, the formerly enslaved woman who became part of the Deer Clan via adoption. Cherokees valued outsiders who contributed something new to their nation and/or accustomed themselves to living as the Cherokees lived, like Christian Priber, who married a Cherokee woman and taught them new stories and skills. In both of these cases, Chickawa, who was Black, and Priber, who was white, were accepted into Cherokee society because they shared in and contributed to common Cherokee experiences.

In the next chapter, I detail the Cherokee Constitution of 1827, the achievement that both codified the new wave of Cherokee nationalism into the sort of document that whites understood and valued and that whites also used as an excuse to expedite removal. The implicit congressional understanding in this period was that the Cherokee way of life needed improvement: that Cherokee culture was deficient in a civilized world. Christian missionaries—many with genuinely good intentions and hearts for Indigenous peoples, whom they saw as poor and suffering—dedicated their efforts to *uplifting* the Indians and making them in the model of white American citizens.[234] A majority of congressmen, however, generally saw being Cherokee as "savage," miserable, and generally wasteful, and found it useful to paint them as such to obtain support for Indian removal.[235]

THE NEW CHEROKEE REPUBLIC
1827–1866

HARRIET RUGGLES GOLD was born in 1805 to an affluent and influential family in Cornwall, Connecticut.[1] Her father had helped found the Foreign Mission School there. In 1817, a young Cherokee man named Buck Watie, son of Oowatie, was invited to continue his education in Cornwall. His teachers praised Buck as a model of acculturation and intellect, who around this time adopted the name Elias Boudinot for himself after the president of the American Bible Society.[2] Harriet met the young Elias and the two soon formed a close relationship, united in their passion for education and the evangelization of the Cherokee people.[3]

Elias had converted to Christianity in 1820 and thereafter received the aplomb of both his teachers and the white benefactors of the Foreign Mission School. That same good feeling toward model student Boudinot and his cousin, John Ridge, also enrolled at the school, soon soured when Ridge married Sarah Bird Northrup, a young white woman, in 1824. Those same benefactors who had praised the converted, educated Cherokee men now burned them in effigy and defunded the school. Two years later, in the spring of 1826, Elias and Harriet were married themselves and settled down to live in the Cherokee Nation.[4]

In response to the growing trend of Cherokee men marrying white women, the Cherokee Nation in 1825 passed a law stipulating that "the children of Cherokee men and white women, living in the Cherokee Nation as man and wife, . . . are hereby acknowledged, to be equally entitled to all the immunities and privileges enjoyed by the citizens" of the Cherokee Nation descended from the mother's side.[5] Boudinot himself affixed his signature to the bill as clerk of the National Council. By this new law, Elias and Harriet Boudinot's six children were counted as full and equal Cherokee Nation citizens despite their mother having no clan affiliation. Since maternal clan membership traditionally conveyed Cherokee belonging, this law contributed to the gradual erosion of traditional mores in favor of a system where the legal benefits of fatherhood were more pronounced.

While the 1827 Cherokee Constitution "inaugurated a new era of Cherokee history," the changes in Cherokee society that led to its drafting were gradual and nuanced.[6] Far from being the product of a united Cherokee Nation, the constitution sparked its share of intense resistance—for example, a traditionalist named White Path led a group of Cherokees who publicly confronted their politicians, demanding a return to the old ways—for the compromising way that the document attempted to fit Cherokee principles and practices into a United States–inspired legal framework.[7] The early Cherokee Republic found itself wrestling with "a co-narration of 'law,' both ancient and modern."[8] Yet the leaders who met in the summer of 1827 in convention, despite their differences and the growing gulf between themselves and the Cherokee people, desired to protect the communal lands guaranteed by treaty and their national sovereignty.[9] Part of their efforts, however, included rearticulating belonging in the Cherokee Nation in a way that would significantly affect the practice that had brought Chickawa and her descendants into the tribe.

Chickawa had previously become a member of a Cherokee clan via adoption. Her children, because she was a woman, inherited her clan affiliation.[10] Harriet Gold, however, had no clan affiliation; Cherokee legislators welcomed her children into full citizenship by virtue of them having a Cherokee father instead. This chapter examines these changes in detail, and presents the adoption of the 1827 Constitution of the Cherokee Nation as the first durable shift in Cherokee citizenship policy. That constitution reveals both policy and foundational Cherokee ideas. The policy ideas, ideas that tell how foundational ideas translate into political reality, are reflected in the laws and the design of the constitution itself. The foundational ideas implicit in the constitution require deeper analysis. In order to "get our knowledge of simple things from composite things," I begin by analyzing the 1827 Cherokee Nation Constitution to gather what sort of policy ideas are immediately present.[11]

THE CONSTITUTION OF THE CHEROKEE
NATION (1827)

Addressing his fellow citizens at New Echota shortly after his election as principal chief under the new republican government, John Ross told them that the "organization of the new Government, the revision and amendments of the old laws, so as to make them in unison with the principles of the constitution, will require your attention; & it cannot escape your wisdom, that the laws should be short, plain & suitable to the condition of the people, and to be well executed."[12] These "fellow citizens," leaders in the Cherokee Nation, had a task before them even more herculean than drafting their new constitution: they intended to continue merging the "old laws" with new principles. At the same time, they were determined to find new ways to resist increasingly vicious pressures from their American neighbors, especially Georgians, to vacate their land.

The constitution itself is a remarkable document. The innovation and energy that went into its crafting convey both a deep sense of urgency and meticulous care. On the surface, this constitution resembles the United States Constitution. The educated elite among the Cherokees found much to praise in the form of the US Constitution and adapted it to suit their own purposes.[13] A closer reading, however, reveals distinct differences from the United States in how these Cherokee leaders intended their government to function.

The men who drafted their constitution gave top priority to legally protecting their communally held lands.[14] Article I made explicit that Cherokee lands were theirs, to "remain the common property of the Nation," in perpetuity.[15] While this provision protecting boundaries is certainly not unique—the Georgia Constitution of 1798 contained similar language—the explicit articulation of holding land in common is. In the years prior to the convention, political leaders wrestled with implementing penalties for individuals leaving Cherokee territory—Cherokees moving away from the Nation would forfeit ownership of communally held lands.[16] The new constitution affirmed this policy: for those who physically left, their rights and privileges as citizens of the Cherokee Nation ceased. The constitution made it further clear that citizens of the Nation "shall possess no right nor power to dispose of their

57

improvements in any manner whatever to the United States, individual states, nor individual citizens thereof."[17] This latter provision, understood to be the case in existing state constitutions, was made explicit here to combat perpetual misguided attempts by whites to deal with individual Cherokees to acquire land. Individual property, however, such as improvements on the land, were owned privately and protected.

The governing institutions themselves were modeled on the US government; yet the balance of power tipped in favor of the legislative branch. The 1827 constitution set up a government that relied heavily on the General Council, the members of which were responsible for selecting the officials in the other two branches. The General Council was their bicameral legislature, consisting of the Council and the Committee; representatives from both were selected from multimember districts for brief terms. According to Article IV, Section 1, the General Council was responsible for electing the principal chief and Article V, Section 6 provided the Supreme Court with three justices, each of whom the General Council appointed to finite terms. The structure of and power afforded to the General Council reflected the tradition of making decisions through consensus, rather than by coercion.

The new constitution afforded citizens many similar legal rights to those listed in the US Constitution. Article V, Sections 14 and 15, ensured that citizens had a right to a speedy, fair trial by an "impartial jury" and the right to be "secure in their persons, houses, papers, and possessions from unreasonable searches and seizures."[18] Cherokee lawmakers had been keen on securing these legal guarantees since as early as 1810.[19] What Americans would consider the *missing rights*, however, are perhaps most interesting here.

Notably, the constitution did not list a right to free speech or freedom of the press. This was, as William McLoughlin put it, "no accident."[20] The first Cherokee written newspaper, the *Cherokee Phoenix*, initially under the direction of Elias Boudinot, was a government publication, designed to inform and represent a united Cherokee people, not a divided tribe, as many Americans thought them.[21] According to Chief John Ross, "the public press" must be supported by the people and kept from containing "scurrilous productions" and "sectarian principles on religious subjects."[22] "As the Phoenix is a national newspaper," wrote Boudinot, "we shall feel ourselves bound to devote it to national purposes," which meant, among other things, presenting the Cherokee Nation, in an intentional way, as politically unified to neighboring whites.[23]

Other enumerated rights differed from those articulated in the US Constitution, but mirrored state constitutional provisions, such as the treatment of religion in the 1780 Massachusetts Constitution. Article VI, Section 2, of the Cherokee document prescribes a religious test to hold office, stating that "no person who denies the being of a God, or a future state of rewards & punishments shall hold any office in the civil department of this Nation." Article VI, Section 10, reinforces this religious test by proclaiming that "religion, morality, and knowledge" are essential to good government, the "preservation of liberty, and the happiness of mankind." These lines were controversial. John Ridge wrote that, upon learning Christianity, his "heart received the rays of civilization and [his] intellect expanded."[24] Yet many traditionalists lacked Ridge's enthusiasm.[25]

Cherokees had traditionally believed that consensus was the only legitimate way to structure government, "from the bottom up."[26] With this new constitution, however, Cherokees who increasingly found themselves governed by an aristocracy of pro-acculturation Christian elites now experienced the culmination of those elite efforts. This is not to say that traditional practices and beliefs were completely stifled.[27] Far from it. The vagueness of the wording regarding religious belief in the constitution is itself one indication of compromise. Where the Massachusetts Constitution was bold, for example, the Cherokee Constitution was cautious, not identifying Christianity by name but instead requiring belief in "God, or a future state of rewards & punishments" to hold office. Furthermore, "ministers of the Gospel," an explicit reference to Christian missionaries and local converts who also served, were prohibited from serving as principal chief or in the General Council, perhaps to alleviate traditionalist fears.[28]

Yet perhaps the most important alteration to the old ways articulated in the new constitution was the legal definition of citizenship. The aforementioned constitutional provisions reshaped or reaffirmed Cherokee *practices* and *policies*—what Cherokees could legally do. The statements on citizenship policy, however, changed what it meant to legally *belong* to the Nation; they attempted to change who could *be* Cherokee. Traditionally, those who experienced clan membership and Cherokee culture belonged. Acculturation brought with it new ideas, including a *liberal nationalism* that encouraged racialized legal language that determined belonging by race. These ideas mingled with traditional mores during this period, creating a policy system that favored Cherokee blood while excluding Black persons who may also have had Cherokee ancestry.

A NEW ARTICULATION OF CITIZENSHIP

Article III, Section 4, stated that "the descendants of Cherokee men by all free women, except the African race . . . as well as the posterity of Cherokee women by all free men . . . shall be entitled to all the rights and privileges" of the Cherokee Nation. Section 7 further qualified that voting rights were extended to "all free male citizens . . . who shall have attained to the age of eighteen years." A free male citizen—descended from either a Cherokee mother *or* father, excepting Black persons—therefore, could, in one sense, enjoy the fullest range of political motion in the new republic.

This legal definition of tribal citizenship challenged the traditional practice of favoring matrilineal decent. The constitution, following the legal trend of the previous decade, granted the "right of inheritance to widows and orphans" and admitted the "children of white women and Cherokee men to citizenship in the nation."[29] The wording of the text also potentially opened the door for illegitimate children to become citizens themselves—even the children of white women via Cherokee men, who had no clan membership.[30] The constitution, in fact, did not mention clans at all.

Women, children, and Black persons were not given the franchise, as was the case in many states at the time.[31] The official removal of women from the political sphere was a far cry from the traditional political structure in which honored women played a pivotal and complementary role in town decision-making.[32] The *Cherokee Phoenix* after 1827 published several articles on "female delicacy" that promoted an idealized vision of femininity as incorruptible, tender, and "highly acculturated to white values."[33] The editor, Boudinot, himself promoted such images in an effort to inspire his fellow citizens toward genteel virtue: a woman ought to be "softened and refined by the influence of womanly feeling—whose passions are strong, but chastened and directed by delicacy and principle."[34] Such a being did not belong in an arena of vulgar politics.

In developing this new articulation of citizenship, Cherokee citizens found themselves in the midst of "two complementary processes: political centralization and the internalization of western notions of race and nation."[35] The stages by which Cherokees had begun to think of themselves as a distinct racial group since the latter half of the eighteenth century—in addition to considering themselves bound by kinship, language, culture, and spirituality—had culminated in a presentation of legal, race-based citizenship in their first constitution. This policy alienated many traditionalists in the Nation, who held fast to the old ways of determining tribal belonging.[36]

Those of African descent also felt the brunt of this emergent racial consciousness.[37] Nationalism decreased in some ways the authority of the clans and changed the way new members could be admitted formally into the tribe. Legally, the manner in which Chickawa, formerly enslaved in Georgia due to her race, entered the Nation was no longer viable. Tiya Miles recounts the story of Shoe Boots, a Cherokee warrior who requested Cherokee Nation citizenship for his three Afro-Cherokee children, the product of a master-slave union with an enslaved woman named Doll, in 1824.[38] The Council replied that Shoe Boots' children could be counted as citizens of the Nation but forbade Shoe Boots from "begetting any more Children by his said slave *woman*."[39] A few weeks later the Council passed a law outlawing Cherokee-Black marriages. The continual practice of race-based chattel slavery in the Cherokee Nation, in emulation of its neighbors, had habituated many to the notion of a racial hierarchy that the law ought to protect.[40] After all, among the men who drafted the constitution, the twelve listed on the 1835 Cherokee census owned by that date 355 slaves. Chief John Ross' own household included 19 enslaved persons.[41]

Despite the changes that all of these policies represented for traditional Cherokee practices, however, they also indicate a desire to maintain, by rearticulating, a standard for exclusive membership in the tribe. Article I, Section 2, which provided the conditions under which Cherokee citizens might have their citizenship revoked, reinforced this exclusivity: whenever any citizen "shall remove with their effects out of the limits of this Nation, and become citizens of any other Government, all their rights and privileges as citizens of this Nation shall cease." The Nation would not, and politically could not, tolerate dual citizenship:

citizens of the Cherokee Nation needed to be invested in the physical Nation itself. The risk to their lands was too great.

Cherokee legal practice thus shifted from one that predicated membership on belonging to a Cherokee clan to legal citizenship based on descent from a Cherokee mother or father. Yet, to reiterate, the 1827 constitution did not mark a sudden and overwhelming transformation of beliefs and practices across the board. The old ways still held powerful sway in a Cherokee Nation that was, in the 1820s and 1830s, numerically dominated by non-English-speaking traditionalists.[42] From the core of this cultural debate arose factions that would vie for control of the Nation in the turbulent years to come.

BLOOD CITIZENSHIP

The 1827 Constitution of the Cherokee Nation reveals several important policy ideas—ideas about how those on the Cherokee Council and those authoring the constitution thought that their newly articulated republican government should function. This constitution reaffirmed the spirit of several important old practices, like protecting communally held lands, maintaining a standard of exclusive citizenship, and preserving the public importance of spirituality. It also articulated newer policies based on the model of American civilization, like individual rights, especially in civil and criminal courts. In addition, the structure of government itself was officially transformed. Impersonal institutions replaced clan units as arbiters of the law. "Despite [these] major changes in the structure of Cherokee government since the days of town councils," however, "political ethics remained relatively unchanged."[43]

A great many Cherokees carried old political traditions into the 1820s and beyond, believing, among other things, "that leaders should represent a consensus" and cherishing "a passionate attachment to the earth."[44] Yet the gradual cultural turn away from the "gendered division of labor that empowered women and men as autonomous producers" of the diverse resources needed to survive and toward a more patriarchal society proved unnerving to some.[45] Thus, the policy ideas presented in the 1827 Cherokee Constitution reflect a mixture of attachment to traditional political norms and attempts to "introduce white peoples' habits" among the people.[46] Table 1 displays major policy ideas present in the 1827 Cherokee Constitution.

Table 1. Major Policy Ideas in the 1827 Constitution

Citizenship	Legal belonging determined by having a Cherokee mother or father, by birth or adoption, excepting descendants of Black persons.
Individual Rights	Individuals have the right to a speedy and fair trial, legal counsel, a trial by a jury of their peers, and protection from unreasonable searches and seizures.
Land	All lands shall be held in common by the Nation as a whole; individuals have no right to dispose of the land or improvements as they see fit.
Faith and Spirituality	Individuals have liberty of conscience; however, officeholders must believe in a state of eternal reward or punishment. Ministers of the gospel cannot hold office.
Government Structure	Independent legislative, executive, and judicial institutions, separate yet ultimately controlled and determined by the legislature.

Laws passed in the preceding twenty years, as many Cherokee leaders worked to centralize their government, remained in force as well, contributing to the new institutional order. Among these were the laws outlawing the practice of clan revenge in 1810, discouraging and then banning polygamy in 1819 and 1825 respectively, and regulating the treatment of Black persons.[47] These latter provisions included laws passed in 1824 stipulating that all Black persons "coming into the Nation on any pretense whatsoever, shall be viewed and treated, in every respect, as intruders," and prohibiting marriage between Blacks and either Indians or whites living in the Nation.[48] Likewise, the eight legislative districts created in 1820 remained in operation.[49]

The tenets of Protestant Christianity, spread notably in this period by Moravian, Baptist, Congregationalist, and Presbyterian missionaries, continued to compete and merge with traditional beliefs as well.[50] The constitution shows a very subtle struggle between Christianity and Cherokee spirituality in its attention to religious belief as essential for "good government, the preservation of liberty, and the happiness of mankind."[51] Christopher Teuton and Hastings Shade suggest that Cherokee society has always encouraged an essential spirituality, cultivating in people a concern for harmony and balance in their attempts to "stand in the middle."[52] Christianity had brought institutional hierarchy, the consolidation of many spirits into a single God, the idea of original sin, and salvation through Jesus Christ. [53] These ideas, coupled with the American preference for male-run households, jockeyed for position among Cherokee leaders as they designed their new legal system.

The Cherokee Nation had also to deal with the problem of emerging liberal nationalism. The United States was, at the same time, dealing with this problem in their own peculiar way. Liberal nationalism is the idea that liberal principles can unify a nation—that disparate ideas usually kept separate can be held together: political obligations, individual autonomy and rights, cultural membership, and a recognition of political equality, among others.[54] In societies "defined by common descent, culture, language, and/or history," citizens come to share a sense of mutual acceptance, cooperation, and support, which, when infused with liberal nationalism, may assume an "exclusivist" form of government.[55] The Cherokee Nation, in its own unique way, infused liberal principles with traditional ideas, creating a liberal regime dedicated to the preservation of exclusive tribal belonging.

Taken as a cohesive whole, the Cherokee Nation was debating their vision of the good life itself: while certain foundational ideas remained the same, like how Cherokees related to the land, their commitment to spirituality, and their desire for exclusive citizenship, these ideas were exposed to radical challenges. The core principle of citizenship, exclusive to sustain the integrity of the tribe, remained firm, yet the articulation of this idea into law was rife with new layers of racial prejudice, gendered hierarchy, and nationalism. Figure 3 displays the new Idea Pyramid, specific to how citizenship was treated in the 1820s.

The Cherokee Nation government sustained the basic premise of this new policy era—incorporation of whites, deemphasis on clan membership at the national level, prejudice against Black persons—for the next forty years, only altering the law in a major way when forced to by the Treaty of 1866.[56] The remainder of this chapter describes the intervening period. Major culturally critical events like the Trail of Tears, the Act of Union, and the decade of peace and growth leading up to the Civil War did not usher in a new era in the development of citizenship law—although they did certainly shape Cherokee culture.[57] The period between 1827 and 1866 was characterized by Chief John Ross' extraordinary efforts to hold the Cherokee Nation together

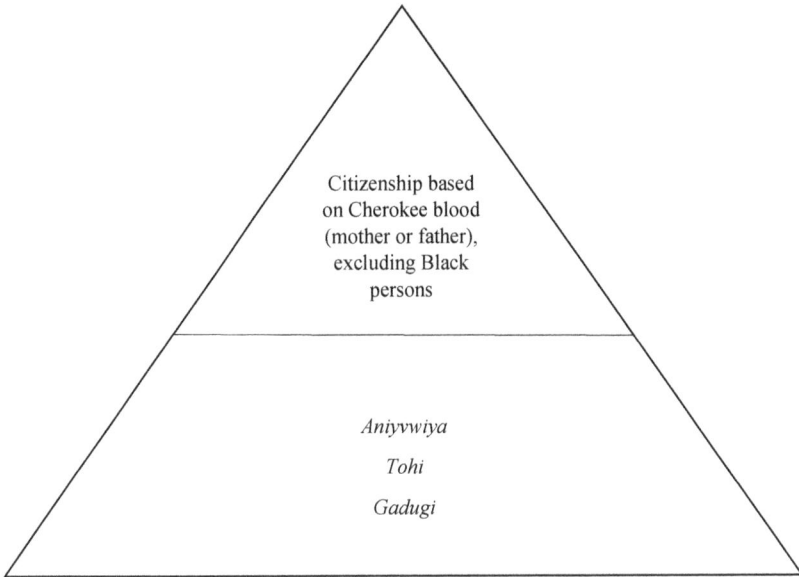

Figure 3. Foundational and Policy Ideas about Cherokee Nation Citizenship, 1827

as removal, acculturation, betrayal, and violence threatened to tear them apart.[58]

CHALLENGES TO THE NEW CHEROKEE REPUBLIC

Reactions to the new Cherokee Constitution were varied within the Nation and negative among their neighbors outside of the Nation. Georgians were especially incensed. The *Cherokee Phoenix*, as the mouthpiece of the Nation, attempted to assuage their concerns:

The Cherokee Constitution has produced a very mistaking idea in the minds of many persons, especially such as endeavor to take every advantage of the Indians. To say that the Cherokees have declared themselves independent of the United States and violated, in their constitution, their connection with the General Government, would be doing them very great injustice: for the thought of such independence has never entered into their minds, as we already have had occasion to declare . . . This constitution was adopted for the good of the Cherokee People, as

65

their condition made it evident that they could not improve otherwise in legislation. . . . We do not claim rights which do not belong to us, much less are we so blinded as to suppose, that we can within ourselves change our relation with the General Government. Rights, however, we have, secured to us by treaties, and will the people of this enlightened land, emphatically called the land of freedom, deprive us of these few rights?[59]

Georgians, however, like John Forsyth, governor of Georgia from 1827 to 1829, were unmoved. In the debates over the Indian Removal Act two years later, Forsyth, at that time a senator, would argue that the Cherokee Constitution represented a blatant attempt to erect a new state within the jurisdiction of another state, something that could not occur "without the consent of the Legislatures of the States concerned," as stated in the US Constitution.[60] "The intrusive sovereignty of a petty tribe of Indians," Forsyth argued, did not carry actual political weight.[61]

Georgians declared that the "United States [had] obtained, by treaty, the power to legislate over the Cherokee, and transferred [that power] to Georgia" when Congress gave Georgia specific geographical boundaries in 1802.[62] The United States had obtained such power, according to Forsyth, at the signing of the Treaty of Hopewell (1785), wherein the Cherokee Nation granted Congress the right to legislate for them; Forsyth and other Georgian congressmen argued that this treaty amounted to an abdication of legislative authority, and thus of sovereignty.

The reality behind these arguments was, however, that the people of the Cherokee Nation had proved adept at *civilizing*, the goal of the prevailing United States policy of the previous thirty years.[63] "Civilizing" Indians in this period meant instructing them on how to build cities, farms, schools, churches, and seats of government in emulation of American culture as a normative good. It also meant Christian evangelization. This civilization policy was effective in the Cherokee Nation, but not in the way that US officials had hoped. Congressmen had planned that Indians would fully assimilate into American society—and give up their large areas of communally held land to new settlements in the process.[64] Part of the reason that the federal government avoided dealing with many serious border problems in the early period was because many tribes fled west on their own to avoid altercations with white settlers.[65] Since they wanted land, the United States was content to let Indians leave and permit settlers to inhabit the remains. When civilizing Indigenous peoples resulted in the substantial westernization of many tribes—including the Cherokees, who formed a constitutional government—the United States found that eastern Indians became politically entrenched and better able to legally defend their land titles.[66]

Faced with this unintended consequence of civilization policies, Georgians in the late 1820s doubled down on the idea that the Cherokee people were not at all *civilized* and decided, as John Forsyth had, to paint them as backward and violent: "You might as reasonably expect that wild animals, incapable of being tamed in a park, would be domesticated by turning them loose in the forest."[67] The *Cherokee Phoenix* reprinted an article from a Georgia newspaper, the *Georgia Statesman*, to similar effect: "Though much has been said about the Cherokee civilization, we are of opinion that many strides must be taken before those Indians may with truth be termed a civilized people.... A system of thievery, by which property is run into the white settlement, is said to exist even around New Echota; and frequent murders are committed without the perpetrators being apprehended or brought to trial!"[68] In response, the editor of the *Phoenix* retorted that the *Georgia Statesman* was perhaps "not aware that the instigators, leaders and principals, of this system of thievery are whitemen [*sic*], citizens of Georgia."[69] The response did not even attempt to address the dubious references to clan revenge, which had been formally outlawed in 1810.[70]

Outside of Georgia, others were grappling with the potential ramifications of the new Cherokee Constitution. United States Indian agent Hugh Montgomery, in an April 16, 1828, letter to the chiefs of the Cherokee Nation, wrote that the "subject of your having formed a Constitution, and Constitutional Government, has Raised a Considerable Clamour, particularly in the adjoining States."[71] In his letter, Montgomery relayed a brief message from President John Quincy Adams regarding the creation of the new constitution: "Convene the Chiefs, and inform them, that [President Adams] wishes them, destinctly [*sic*] to understand that this act of theirs, cannot be considered in any other light, then as Regulations of purely municipal Character—And which he wishes them *distinctly* to understand, will not be Recognized, and [as] Changing any one of the Relations under which they stood to the

General Government, prior to the adoption of said Constitution."[72] In
other words, Adams punted, suggesting both that the new constitution
did not change anything and that he would not do anything about it.
Montgomery cautioned Cherokee leaders to "cultivate the friendship of
the surrounding states" and avoid strife caused by any overt assertions of
sovereignty that would be sure to stir up anger in their white neighbors.[73]
He also offered his own interpretation of President Adams' message: the
Cherokee Nation ought to understand their constitution as akin to a
town charter, a statement of municipal regulations, not an assertion of
national sovereignty on a par with a contemporary nation-state. The
Treaty of Hopewell, argued Montgomery, relinquished sovereignty of
the latter kind—the kind that enjoys the freedom to treat with foreign
nations and conduct themselves totally as it sees fit.

William Hicks, interim principal chief, and John Ross, at the time
serving as second chief, responded in earnest. Their response was a deft
rebuttal of the idea that their constitution achieved nothing:

> We freely and with pleasure coincide with the Executive, in the
> opinion that our relation and connection with the General Gov-
> ernment, is not changed, but remains the same as it was before the
> Cherokee Constitution was adopted. That instrument contains a
> special article, which states, that all lawful treaties between the
> United States and this Cherokee Nation shall be the supreme law
> of the land. This proves, the view of this Nation as to its connec-
> tion with the General Government without any shadow of doubt-
> ful construction. Your explanation of 'Municipal Regulations,'
> however . . . is inapplicable to the true situation of this Nation
> that claims for itself & always maintained sovereign jurisdiction
> over its territorial limits . . . This Nation by its own Legislature
> authorized and recommended the adoption of a Republican
> Constitution, which has been done. It had no relation or con-
> nection to *a State* to ask of it, its consent being connected and
> related to the United States *alone* by treaty. And as this Nation
> never surrendered her right to self Government or the exercise
> of its internal and domestic regulation, it was needless to ask for
> it from the General Government, to whom, as a generous nation,
> our improved Legislation for ourselves could not possibly afford

any misapprehension, or a subject of disapprobation.—As to your views of certain passages of our treaties with the U States, we do not deem it necessary at this time, to reply to them.[74]

The *Phoenix* echoed Ross and Hicks' enthusiasm, stating that the "words of the President contain no intimation that the Cherokees ought to be prohibited from forming a Constitution, but on the contrary, that this Constitution can be recognized by the General Government," so long as its provisions do not alter the existing relationship between the United States and the Cherokee Nation.[75] Cherokee leaders were ecstatic: aware that what they had accomplished was novel—the first Indigenous tribal nation within the bounds of the United States to develop a constitutional republic—Hicks, Ross, and Boudinot rejoiced at what they understood as the support, or at least willingness to let them be, of President John Quincy Adams. Adams' inaction, however, would in a few months be replaced by a president all too willing to involve himself in Cherokee affairs.

Cherokee leaders, aware of the tendency of Americans to dismiss or ignore their sovereignty, did not rest after their constitutional accomplishment. The Nation continued to refine their citizenship laws in an effort to stave off internal conflicts (e.g., land or property disputes) among citizens. In October 1829, Chief Ross signed a bill terminating the citizenship status of any white citizen who had previously married a Cherokee citizen who, at the death of their Cherokee spouse, had no children; that is, whites who had become citizens through marriage, whether men or women, could not remain citizens while childless and single. The General Council further stipulated that, in the above scenario, even if said white citizens did have Cherokee children, they would lose their citizenship if they then married other white people and would be classified as intruders if they remained in the Nation thereafter.[76] Two weeks later, Chief Ross signed another bill that would have far-reaching implications. The General Council decreed that "if any citizen or citizens of this Nation shall treat and dispose of any lands belonging to this Nation without special permission from the National Authorities, he or they, shall suffer death," the ultimate loss of citizenship.[77] Such an act now officially amounted to high treason, although Cherokees had understood that to be true for many years.

Georgians, however, were not to be deterred.[78] In December of 1829, the state legislature passed a law extending jurisdiction, both civil and criminal, over the Cherokee Nation's territory. They further attempted by this act to "annul all laws and ordinances made by the Cherokee nation . . . as if the same had never existed." This act not only dismissed Cherokee sovereignty but refused to grant political rights to Indians in Georgia courts. Cherokees were given a faux choice: remove or plan to be removed by enrolling for emigration. Georgia was determined to make life so difficult for Cherokees that they would willingly give up their land and go west.[79]

Georgia lawmakers followed up this act with another a year later, in 1830, that permitted Georgia officials to arrest and send to labor camps whites living among the Cherokees without a license or permit issued by the governor of Georgia. The barefaced greed in the text of this bill provides a partial explanation for Georgian actions. The bill provided, in multiple sections, the governor with the ability to summon and regulate guards for "the protection of the gold mines" in the Cherokee mountains. Theda Perdue provides a further explanation: "Fearful that Congress might fall under the control of antislavery forces, [Georgians] saw two immediate ways to block such a threat. One was to replace Indians with free white voters . . . The other solution was to embrace" state sovereignty, as strictly interpreted from the US Constitution.[80] Georgia dared the federal government to step in, a step they were sure that new president, Andrew Jackson, would not take. Indeed, Jackson told Cherokee leaders that "the government was powerless to prevent the state of Georgia from exercising sovereignty over them" and publicly stated that he would not enforce any treaties that conflicted with Georgian pretensions.[81]

President Jackson thus "was committed to removing Indians from east of the Mississippi—if not from the face of the earth"—and gave the Cherokees, a sovereign nation, no serious diplomatic voice in Washington.[82] With small chances of negotiating with a president who had made clear from his first annual message to Congress his intentions toward tribes in the East, and with Congress unilaterally passing laws affecting their lives without representation—by that point, Congress had passed the Indian Removal Act: a partisan affair in the Senate (28–19) and a narrow regional affair in the House (102–97)—Cherokees turned to the courts for relief from Georgian oppression.[83]

The first Cherokee case to reach the Supreme Court in this period came in 1831. *Cherokee Nation v. Georgia* was concerned with whether Cherokees "could approach the Supreme Court as a court of original jurisdiction based on their treaty rights."[84] Chief Justice John Marshall answered "no," demeaning Indigenous governments as "domestic-dependent nations" that lacked true sovereignty.[85] The Cherokee Nation, according to Marshall, had no legal standing as a foreign nation. Samuel Austin Worcester, however, a Congregationalist missionary in the Cherokee Nation and friend of Elias Boudinot who had worked on the *Cherokee Phoenix* and the translation of the New Testament into Cherokee—and who was arrested for refusing to submit to Georgia rule while living among the Cherokees—did have standing. In July 1831 the Georgia Guard arrested Worcester, along with ten other missionaries who refused to take the oath of allegiance Georgia required to remain on the land.

In *Worcester v. Georgia* (1832), the Supreme Court ruled that "Georgia law was not valid within the Cherokee Nation."[86] Key to this decision were the conclusions that federal law held in territory under federal control and tribal nations retained the attributes of sovereignty that they did not expressly relinquish.[87] Georgia, however, refused to relent, defying the decision, an action that Jackson supported.[88] The Cherokee Nation was thus buffeted by the actions of the president and Congress and by the inability of the Court to itself act despite, practically speaking, siding with the Cherokee Nation in their struggle against Georgia.

At the same time, internally, the Nation suffered from the lack of a common vision for the future. Cherokees had always valued consensus: those who disagreed with the majority customarily withdrew and allowed the group to continue despite their personal qualms. Western education and individual economic self-interest, however, had challenged that sentiment. Freedom of speech and of the press, tenets of civilization preached by missionaries and taught in American schools, were powerful notions, especially to those in the Nation unhappy with both their treatment by Americans and the perceived distance between themselves and their political leaders. This "rising middle class" had begun to resent "the economic [and political] power of Principal Chief Ross, Chief Justice John Martin, and councilmen Joseph Vann and Lewis Ross," among the richest men in the Nation who also wielded great political power.[89]

Chief Ross had two overarching goals during his long tenure as chief: keep his nation united and protect Cherokee lands. Each goal appeared hopeless at different points in the 1820s and 1830s. Cherokees were divided, not only among the acculturated elites, who had begun to think differently from one another about removal, but between those elites and the greater number of Cherokee traditionalists, who retained old tribal practices. Yet another group, the Old Settlers, had already chosen to emigrate west voluntarily and assembled their own laws in Indian Territory.[90] Individual Cherokees, like those who voluntarily moved west, demonstrated that they could give up living on their ancestral lands, something traditionalists could not do. The greater part of the tribe held firm to their homeland and to their preferred manner of living there. While the three branches of the US government debated and ruled upon their fate, Chief Ross encouraged his people by reminding them that they had rights that could be used to defend themselves against Georgia. "With this vain hope held out to them the Indians refused to consent to remove."[91]

Elias Boudinot, long a proponent of both Cherokee sovereignty and acculturation, had become disenchanted by the US government's attitudes toward the Nation.[92] He had also lost hope of ever living alongside whites peacefully. The racism he experienced upon marrying Harriet Gold from the same people he had tried so hard to emulate and appease left him convinced that whites and Indians could never truly integrate on a large scale.[93] He had dedicated much of his public life to attempting to convince whites that the Cherokees were indeed civilized and worthy of their own sovereign government. This belief remained but transitioned into a belief that could also consider removal a viable option—to save the Nation from destruction at the hands of Georgians or the federal government. He was thus discouraged by Ross' insistence on remaining in the East in the face of overbearing pressure from both Georgia and the US federal government to move and was among those who sought to *save* their people by signing away Cherokee lands in 1835.

In 1837, Boudinot wrote that the "controversy among the Cherokees themselves" was "founded upon the question of a remedy, to extricate the Cherokees from their difficulties."[94] The "first rupture" among the Cherokees occurred over preserving the "land of our fathers" against white encroachments. Some believed that a new policy was needed: a policy that sought to preserve the Cherokee Nation by moving west. "Contending uselessly against superior power" was futile and would lead to their total destruction. Boudinot argued that Chief Ross had chosen destruction and charged him with "having deluded [the people] with expectations incompatible with and injurious to, their interest." Boudinot and his fellow pro-removal advocates therefore took matters into their own hands "to save a *nation* from political thraldom and moral degradation." Remaining and subjecting Cherokees to the laws of the states would "rivet the chains and fasten the manacles of their servitude . . . The final destiny of our race, under such circumstances, is too revolting to think of."[95]

Boudinot, Major and John Ridge, and like-minded Cherokees—a decided minority soon to be known as the Treaty Party—consented to the Treaty of New Echota without the participation of the Cherokee Council or Chief John Ross.[96] Signed on December 29, 1835, the treaty was negotiated at a conference held by one Reverend John Schermerhorn, who preached to a partisan crowd in favor of removal. This scheme became known as the "Christmas Trick"; Chief Ross, who was in Washington at the time, believed that the US government would never accept such a document. But pro-treaty Cherokees John Ridge and Stand Watie, Elias Boudinot's brother, came to Washington themselves as part of a rival Cherokee delegation, carrying with them the new treaty. The new treaty gave up Cherokee lands in the east for $5 million and new territorial borders west of the Mississippi.[97]

US officials used this unrepresentative treaty to justify and enforce westward removal. The signers wrote Ross and the General Council that they were motivated by the "misery of our people accumulating every day" and sought amelioration while Ross was in Washington.[98] This treaty exacerbated the growing rift among Cherokee leadership. While the Treaty Party headed west, Ross and the vast majority of the Cherokee Nation's citizens remained, fighting the disingenuous treaty until they were violently removed. Factions with different immediate political and cultural interests had formed over the issue of removal. The "Old Settlers" had voluntarily relocated to Indian Territory well before 1835, and the Treaty Party, who supported removal, soon followed by 1838. According to scholar Daniel F. Littlefield Jr., these first two groups numbered roughly 6,000.[99]

The Ross Party, fundamentally opposed to removal, was later forced to relocate and made to march west in 1838–39. Their enslaved Black persons went with them, suffering alongside their Cherokee masters.[100] The Cherokees who marched numbered approximately 16,000.[101] A quarter of these captives died. George Hicks, who had been educated at the same Moravian Mission School as Boudinot and John Ridge but who nevertheless opposed removal, described the journey in 1839:

> Winter has been very cold & we have necessarily Suffered a great [deal] from exposure, from cold & from fatigue. Our people, a great many of them were very poor & very destitute of clothing & of the means of rendering themselves comfortable. We done all in our power to remedy their destitute situation & contributed very much to their comfort by supplying them, so far as we could, with clothing Blankets & shoes, but still we have Suffered a great deal with sickness & have lost since the 21st of October last about 35, a great proportion of them were aged & children. . . . We look to the Almighty for strength & protection to enable us to reach the place of destination—As yet we are hardly half way . . .[102]

Formerly enslaved woman Eliza Whitmire, then a child of roughly five years old, later vividly recalled "General [Winfield] Scott's order to remove the Cherokees" west:[103] "The Cherokees, after being driven from their homes, were divided into detachments of nearly equal size, and late in October 1838, the first detachment started, the others following one by one. The aged, sick, and the young children rode in the wagons, which carried the provisions and bedding, while others went on foot. The trip was made in the dead of winter, and many died from exposure from sleet and snow, and all who lived to make this trip, or had parents who made it, will long remember it, as a bitter memory."[104]

At the time of the removal, "a considerable number of the tribe fled into the mountains of Tennessee and North Carolina and refused to emigrate."[105] The United States and North Carolina were not as interested in those "remote, mountainous, and uninviting" regions and so did not press the issue as fiercely as Georgia had to the south.[106] After General Scott marched out the majority of the Cherokee people, this remnant took pains to become "inoffensive and inconspicuous" while "buying property on which they could live without disrupting white settlers."[107] Historian John R. Finger reports that some of these Cherokees considered joining their brethren between 1839 and 1841 but that love of their homeland and fear of the intertribal fighting in the West kept them in place. By 1843 the government of North Carolina had at least tacitly recognized the presence of the Eastern Band of the Cherokees and let them remain; they eventually developed their own laws and government.[108] The Eastern Band of the Cherokees has dwelt there ever since.

AN ACT OF UNION

By the time the Ross Party relocated in Indian Territory, there already existed a council and settled laws. Ross called for unity—and to implement Cherokee constitutionalism out west—to which western Cherokees replied in June 1839 that if "your original laws, created beyond the Mississippi, [were] to be brought here, brought to life, and have full force," it would be "entirely repugnant to the government and laws of the Cherokee Nation" and would "thereby create great dissatisfaction."[109] These same western Cherokees had previously objected to "receiving emigrants except on terms; they took the position that the land set apart by the Treaty of 1828 belonged to them" and they had not wanted to share it.[110] Animosity against Chief Ross had grown, as many who had voluntarily removed believed that Ross had given Cherokees false hope that they could defend their lands and sovereignty in the East. The Old Settlers and Treaty Party members in Indian Territory were weary of the intentions of the great number of Cherokees marching west to join them.

Shortly after Ross called for unity between the eastern and western Cherokees, Treaty Party leaders Major Ridge, John Ridge, and Elias Boudinot were murdered. The assassinations were part of a carefully planned and coordinated effort that stemmed from more than "just disputes over the sale of Cherokee lands and the removal; they had roots in older personal feuds" and traditions.[111] Cherokees had long held that those disposing of their lands without a general consensus deserved death. The law passed by the General Council ten years earlier in 1829, drawn up by John Ridge himself, also stipulated that the penalty for treating or selling Cherokee lands without the consent of Cherokee authorities was death.[112] With the brutal punishment of these men, the "animosity between pro- and anti-removal Cherokees flared into violence" that lasted decades.[113]

The calamity that followed saw Ross and his defenders brace for the vengeance of Elias Boudinot's brother, Stand Watie, who was bent on raising a company of men to kill Ross, and the western Cherokees' newly resolute attempts to resist incorporation.[114] Yet about 2,000 people still assembled at the Illinois Camp Ground on July 1, 1839, to draft documents necessarily to form a united Cherokee Nation.[115] Nearly two weeks later, those gathered drafted and signed an "Act of Union between The Eastern and Western Cherokees," wherein they "solemnly and mutually agree[d] to form . . . one body politic, under the style and title of the Cherokee Nation."[116] As Ross had long desired, the "two branches of the ancient Cherokee family" were once more, on paper at least, politically unified.[117]

More than this, the Act of Union was also a reassertion of the most fundamental rights of sovereignty: the Cherokee Nation was a "separate and distinct Nation," in possession of all essential attributes of sovereignty, which they had never surrendered via treaty agreement. The act declared their resolve to uphold the rule of law as a single nation that was not dissolved but only relocated. Sequoyah himself, under the name George Guess, signed the act as "President of the Western Cherokees" and would go on to sign the new 1839 constitution as well.[118] George Lowrey lent his signature as "President of the Eastern Cherokees." Yet, while this Act of Union was important for the governance of the Cherokee Nation, it did not completely heal the deeper wounds that had formed between factions.

The July convention at the Illinois Campground also exerted its power over the far less numerous and vilified Treaty Party members, unilaterally pardoning the assassins of Boudinot and the Ridges while stripping the surviving faction members of the ability to hold national office for five years.[119] By March of the following year, Treaty Party members still held out hope that "sufficient evidence may be obtained against

[John] Ross of having been the sole cause of the murders" committed by his followers.[120] John Alexander Watie, brother to Stand Watie and the late Boudinot, informed the former in the same letter that another attempt had been made on the life of one Jack Hawkins, another Treaty Party member, who managed to escape. The violence continued.

The early 1840s saw the Ross and Ridge-Watie factions battle each other for the ear of the US government in Washington, hoping alternately to receive support for their control over the Cherokee Nation.[121] The turbulent conditions in the Cherokee Nation compelled Stand Watie to "assemble a body of armed men at Old Fort Wayne," near the Arkansas border, which Watie justified as necessary to defend himself "against the aggressions of the Ross party."[122] Yet despite these serious divisions, those who did assemble managed to host a second successful constitutional convention.[123] Drafted and ratified in 1839, this document would frame their government institutions for the next half century.

A NEW CONSTITUTION IN 1839

Out of the horrors of removal and internal violence came a new constitution similar to the one that had preceded it in 1827. The 1839 Cherokee Constitution is in essence a rearticulation of the provisions made in the 1827 constitution, with a few notable alterations. One of the biggest differences lay in the separation of powers, specifically in the manner of electing the principal chief. Formerly, the General Council elected the chief executive, but now the principal chief was to be elected by "the qualified voters on the same day and at the places where they shall respectively vote for members to the National Council."[124] The popular election for chief was an alteration made to appease western Cherokees, who were apprehensive of the political control of their eastern kinsfolk, and particularly of John Ross.

Citizens, according to the 1839 constitution, included: "The descendants of Cherokee men by all free women except the African race, whose parents may have been living together as man and wife, according to the customs and laws of this Nation . . . as well as the posterity of Cherokee women by all free men. No person who is of negro or mulatto parentage, either by the father or mother's side, shall be eligible to hold any office of profit, honor, or trust under this Government."[125] Cherokee leaders in convention in 1839 continued both their trend of gradually permitting

a greater number of whites into full citizenship and their racial prejudice against Black persons. Citizenship therefore flowed through the
Cherokee bloodline—unless that bloodline mixed in ways Cherokee
leaders disapproved of.[126] In that latter sense, Cherokee law during this
period, eliminating as it was the national power of clan relationships, also
imposed limitations on Cherokee blood itself to determine membership.
Since Cherokee blood could not overcome racial prejudice, Cherokee
blood was not fully able to determine citizenship either.

Table 2 displays the major policy ideas present in the 1839 constitution. Notable here is the same articulation of individual rights as in the
previous constitution, along with the same absence of the right to free
speech or the press. Otherwise, the same dedication to faith and spirituality remained, including religious tests for office, with one exception. Conspicuously absent was the clause prohibiting ministers of the
gospel from holding public office. Cherokees like the Reverend Jesse
Bushyhead, a Baptist minister and chief justice of the Cherokee Nation,
had already been closely involved in Cherokee politics for many years:
as many prominent Cherokees became involved with the missions and
were ordained ministers themselves, the prohibitions on merging ministers and politics faded away.[127]

Cherokee leaders would add to these citizenship provisions in a few
key ways over the next twenty years. In September 1839, the National

Table 2. Major Policy Ideas in the 1839 Constitution

Citizenship	Citizenship determined by having a Cherokee mother or father, by birth or adoption, excepting descendants of Black persons.
Individual Rights	Individuals have the right to a speedy and fair trail, legal counsel, a trial by a jury of their peers, and protection from unreasonable searches and seizures.
Land	All lands shall be held in common by the Nation as a whole; individuals have no right to dispose of the land or improvements to the United States or its citizens.
Faith and Spirituality	Individuals have liberty of conscience; however, officeholders must believe in a state of eternal reward or punishment.
Government Structure	Independent legislative, executive, and judicial institutions, separate yet judiciary totally controlled by the legislature; independent executive.

Council passed two major laws regulating marriage within the Nation. The first was "An Act to Prevent Amalgamation with Colored Persons," which created harsher punishments—up to fifty "stripes" for women offenders and one hundred lashes for men—for intermarriage with Blacks.[128] The second came on September 28 and required all white men or citizens of the United States to obtain a "written license for that purpose" from a circuit or district court in the Nation in order to marry a Cherokee woman.[129] The two must then be married by either a minister of the gospel, "[an]other authorized person," or a judge.[130] This act further stipulated that abandonment of the aforementioned wife would result in a loss of citizenship for the man, which entailed removal from the Nation.

While they were establishing their government in Indian Territory, Cherokee leaders also passed a number of laws further restricting liberties of Black persons living in the Nation. In November 1840 the National Council decreed that "it shall not be lawful for any free negro or mulatto, not of Cherokee blood, to hold or own any improvement within the limits of this Nation."[131] Neither could enslaved persons own any capital or livestock. In October 1841, the National Council made it a crime to teach "Negros to Read and Write," whether they be freed or enslaved. The next year, in December 1842, Chief Ross signed another bill expelling all free Blacks, "excepting such as may have been freed by our citizens," from the boundaries of the Nation—this to combat Black persons entering Indian Territory to run away from their masters or those seeking life outside the reach of the United States. A more general version of this act was passed in 1844 to expel criminals, settlers, and other squatters who had come from elsewhere in the United States—in effect, nearly all noncitizens.[132]

In 1843, the Council passed "An Act admitting to the right of Citizenship certain Creek Indians" that permitted Creek families who had "emigrated from the east of the Mississippi river, in the several detachments of Cherokees that removed in 1838" to enjoy all the privileges of citizenship in the Cherokee Nation.[133] These "Creek Indians having been received by the Cherokees in their Nation East," and due to their shared experience of removal, could be counted among full Cherokee citizens. The qualifications, in this instance, were not Cherokee blood, but rather shared experience; the method was legislative intervention into citizenship policy that amended *blood as culture* to include those who shared in certain experiences as identified by legislators.

Around the same time, the Cherokee, Creek, and Osage Nations, who had suffered removal together and who were now close neighbors in Indian Territory, signed a compact. This document, which the Cherokee government officially approved and confirmed on November 2, 1843, was intended to establish peaceful relations, secure rights, and promote the general welfare. To that effect, the tribes promised "Peace and friendship," proclaimed that "Revenge shall not be cherished, nor retaliation practiced, for offenses committed by individuals," and provided for avenues of collaboration should any breaches of the law take place.[134] Notably, Article I, Section 9, provided that "any citizen of one Nation may be admitted to citizenship in any other Nation, party hereto, by consent of the proper authorities of such Nation." This arrangement opened the door for greater fluidity in terms of membership between nations that viewed alliance as the best way to defend themselves against the United States.

Of the remaining citizenship laws of this period, two types remain of note. In the first case, the National Council passed numerous laws granting or re-granting, depending on the situation, citizenship to white men who had married Cherokee women, so long as they remained together living within the boundaries of the Nation.[135] Of the second kind was a law reinforcing their commitment to punish selling, gifting, or otherwise signing away Cherokee lands without the consent of the proper government authorities: "Any person or persons, who shall, [agree to cede, exchange, or dispose in any way, or any part or portion of the lands belonging to or claimed by the Cherokees] . . . are hereby declared to be outlaws: and any person or persons, citizens of this Nation, may kill him or them so offending, at any time and in any manner most convenient within the limits of this Nation, and shall not be held accountable to the laws for the same."[136] This law, in contrast with those passed in the 1820s, instead of regulating punishment for the crime of high treason (giving land to whites), deregulated the punishment for this crime in a manner that harkened back to clan revenge and the ancient practice of killing those suspected as witches.[137] Traitors who gave away land were too dangerous to be kept alive.

It was also during this period that the US Supreme Court handed down its first decision on the issue of native adoptions of non-Indians in *United States v. Rogers* (1846). Here, the Supreme Court dealt with the question of whether a tribally adopted white person convicted of murdering an Indian "could be excluded from the provisions of an act of Congress that exempted Indians who had committed crimes against other Indians from federal courts."[138] William S. Rogers argued that, since he was an adopted Cherokee citizen, he exercised the rights and privileges of full citizens, which included the federal court exemption. Chief Justice Roger Taney disagreed, offering his own construction of "Indian" "based almost solely on racial criteria."[139] Rogers did not count as a Cherokee citizen and was therefore not exempt from being tried in federal court. In so ruling, Taney denied the Cherokee Nation's ability to determine who could be counted as a Cherokee, evident in Article 5 of the 1835 Treaty of New Echota. Taney's ruling "set the precedent on tribal adoption of non-Indians and the racial character of much federal Indian law" since.[140]

CIVIL WAR AND CONTENTIOUS PEACE

Throughout the 1840s and 1850s, as Cherokees settled into their new territory, the Nation found itself changing demographically.[141] Even greater tensions emerged as the acculturated progressive population grew and the number of traditionalists shrank. According to Daniel F. Littlefield Jr., to be a "full-blooded" Cherokee meant something more than racial pride; "it indicated a distinct social, political, and economic attitude" opposed to the impositions and relishes of white civilization.[142] Traditionalists generally did not own slaves and largely disliked the practice. Slave owners among the Cherokees tended to be those with mixed ancestry for whom the practice had been beneficial as well as part of their family heritage. This tension between progressives and traditionalists came to a boil by the time Confederates asked the Cherokee Nation to join the Southern cause.[143] While Chief Ross advocated neutrality, these factions paved the way for the eventual Cherokee-Confederacy alliance in 1861.[144] Social violence and the Confederacy's insistence, coupled with the fact that the other tribes in Indian Territory had joined, eventually caused Ross to relent. The Cherokee people, however, did not go wholeheartedly into the fray.[145]

Partly because of its location in the northeast corner of Indian Territory, the Cherokee Nation, amid its own infighting, was swept up into the Civil War. Many in the Confederacy, especially Arkansas governor Henry Massie Rector, wanted to shore up their western borders by securing the Cherokees as allies in the wars to come. When secession was brought up in Arkansas, Governor Rector appealed to Chief Ross as "natural allies in war and friends in peace," jointly invested in the "application of slave labor."[146] But although Governor Rector tried to instill in Ross a fear of Lincoln and the Union, Ross determined to remain neutral in whatever conflict the United States were contemplating. While Governor Rector pressured him to join the Confederacy, Chief Ross found himself caught at home between the pro-Union Keetoowah Society, comprising mostly traditionalists, and the pro-Confederacy Knights of the Golden Circle.[147] A militant branch of the Keetoowah Society, called the "Pins" or "Pin Indians" because they "wore crossed straight pins on the left lapel of their hunting jackets," were bent on preserving the old ways against increasing acculturation; their tools were "war and blood revenge."[148] These organizations represented social divisions that had been brewing for many years through the tensions brought on by mixing Cherokee and American social values and practices.[149]

As it was in the United States, slavery in the Cherokee Nation was often viewed as a political problem rather than a moral one. In the Nation, "even the full-bloods, who had little stake in the institution, would resent [abolitionist missionaries interfering] . . . in their internal affairs."[150] Indeed, prominent Cherokee political figures, like Baptist minister and chief justice Jesse Bushyhead, who was also a part of Chief Ross' inner circle, were slaveholders themselves.[151] Some, like Rudi Halliburton Jr., claim that the Cherokees never seriously grappled with the moral ramifications of slaveholding and therefore created no serious abolition societies.[152] Others, like Theda Perdue, contend that the *Cherokee Phoenix* editor's penchant for sharing articles positively portraying abolitionist arguments and African colonization efforts reveals a broader support for the antislavery movement.[153] And indeed, the presence of abolitionist missionaries like Baptist Evan Jones (whom pro-Confederacy Cherokees accused of influencing Chief Ross), whom many Cherokees admired, appear to have "tempered criticism of abolitionism."[154]

As the Civil War drew closer, abolitionist missionaries in the Nation were often ostracized and Cherokee politicians avoided the troubles of addressing the abolitionist cause.[155] In 1860, John Rollin Ridge (journalist, novelist, and son of the murdered John Ridge) wrote that abolitionist missionaries were "no longer preaching the gospel, but Abolitionism. They are no longer attending to the legitimate business on which they came, but are interfering with an institution which has existed for many years among the Cherokees, and which is as firmly rooted in their midst as it is at this moment in South Carolina or Alabama or Mississippi."[156] Slavery largely divided Cherokees because the institution was a product of white culture and white civilization.[157] Cultural preservation was often of greater concern than the morality of human bondage. After all, "the abolitionists put the laws of God above those of men," and whites had long used "morality" to cajole, threaten, and dispossess Indigenous peoples while demeaning their traditional practices.[158]

In May 1861, "Confederate forces annexed the Indian Territory as a military district" and by October of that year Albert Pike, Confederate liaison to Indian Territory, had convinced each of the Five Tribes to join the Confederacy.[159] That December, Union troops began to move in force through Cherokee territory, causing many Cherokees to defect to the Union side. Chief Ross himself followed suit, eventually fleeing to Philadelphia. By the end of the war, a majority of the Nation, including most traditionalists, had joined the Union. The war, however, had been disastrous for the Cherokee Nation, both in terms of physical damage and social division. The conflict dispersed and decimated the "Southern Cherokees," then under the charge of Stand Watie.[160] Watie had held out "with a third of his people when the other two thirds renewed their allegiance to the Union."[161]

When at last Watie surrendered his Confederate command in 1865— he was the final Confederate brigadier general to lay down his arms— the rush began between the Ross and Watie factions to carve out for themselves a beneficial peace treaty with the United States.[162] The eventual treaty, the Treaty of 1866, largely conformed to the wishes of the Ross Party—that the Cherokee Nation remain one united community— but also made significant changes to Cherokee Nation citizenship law.[163] The Treaty of 1866 essentially revoked and then restored many provisions of previous treaties, but at least one important thing had changed: the definition of citizenship. The new treaty defined citizenship of the Cherokee Nation as belonging to all native-born Cherokees, all Indians and whites legally adopted by members, all freedmen liberated by acts of their masters, and all free Black persons residing therein.[164] The terms of the treaty, and the new legal definition of Cherokee citizenship, were set to affect those who could be declared residents of Cherokee territory within six months of the signing. This latter clause of the treaty would become the basis of an intense legal, social, and political conflict that has continued into the twenty-first century.

THE FIRST DURABLE SHIFT IN CHEROKEE CITIZENSHIP

This chapter chronicles citizenship in the Cherokee Nation as it developed from the 1820s up through 1866. The 1827 Cherokee Nation Constitution proclaimed a shift in citizenship policy at the national level that had been developing for some time: the articulation of Cherokee blood as a means to keep citizenship exclusive. At a glance, Cherokee leaders during this period shifted, created. and sustained national policies that heavily favored *blood as ancestry*. The Cherokee Nation Constitution and laws of the 1820s, after all, ensured that, legally speaking, the children of Cherokee mothers *or* fathers could be counted as citizens regardless of clan affiliation. Upon closer inspection, however, *blood as ancestry* in this period was *not* a simple prioritization of Cherokee blood. There was an unmistakable racial prejudice against those with Black ancestry, a prejudice that could be used to effectively cancel out the legal power of Cherokee blood to determine citizenship status.

Traditional practices, however, also retained authority.[165] Despite the increasing efforts of Cherokee leaders to legally prevent the citizenship of Black persons (and Black-Cherokee marriages), on at least one notable occasion the Cherokee Supreme Court ignored the law in favor of traditional mores. In 1833, Chickawa's legal white owner came to claim her. The Deer Clan "appealed to long-standing tribal custom that persisted despite the apparent primacy of the Cherokee nation-state" and secured her continued freedom.[166] The court, ruling in favor of the Deer Clan, violated the constitution and laws of the Cherokee Nation to uphold the traditional clan practice of adoption—a policy of *blood as culture*. It may be tempting to think of clan mores as favoring *blood as culture* policies and the Council as favoring *blood as ancestry* policies, but this oversimplification is complicated by certain citizenship laws passed in the 1840s. The Council in 1843 admitted into full citizenship "certain Creek Indians," who had undergone removal alongside the Cherokee people—an apparent move favoring a policy of *blood as culture* to welcome Indigenous peoples who had shared in the same experiences into Cherokee Nation citizenship.[167] Citizenship policy between the 1820s and 1866 was therefore a complex mixture of *blood as ancestry* and *blood as culture* as the Cherokee people attempted to define the contours of their sovereign nation.

The next chapter covers in detail the Treaty of 1866. This treaty imposed on the Cherokee Nation a new articulation of citizenship, a major shift in policy, dictated by United States officials to solve the freedmen crisis after the Civil War. Before 1866, people could obtain Cherokee Nation citizenship through clan practice (clan adoption, birth to a Cherokee mother) or by an act of the Cherokee Nation's government (birth to a Cherokee father, strictly regulated intermarriage); people could also be excluded through these methods. Treaty agreement became a third path to Cherokee Nation citizenship, one that legally trumped legislative acts of the Cherokee Nation (and clan practice) in the United States court system. The shift in Cherokee Nation citizenship policies toward a strong preference for *blood as ancestry* (with important and revealing exceptions noted above), begun in the 1820s, proved durable as Cherokee leaders sustained this general policy through removal, a second constitutional convention in 1839, and the Civil War, only changing their citizenship requirements when required to do so by the Treaty of 1866.

CITIZENSHIP BY BLOOD AND TREATY
1866–1907

WILLIAM JEFFERSON WATTS was a descendant of those Cherokees who, wanting to avoid removal, left the Nation in the early 1830s, dispersing across the several states and territories. These people were not, however, Watts declared, "ignorant of the treaties and their birth-rights."[1] Watts and his family moved to the Cherokee Nation, now in Indian Territory, in 1871, where he resided and opened a business. Watts, like many others, regarded the 1870 act of the National Council stating that "all such Cherokees as may hereafter move into the Cherokee Nation and permanently locate therein as citizens thereof, shall be deemed as Cherokee citizens" (provided that these enroll with the chief justice of the Supreme Court within two months and make "satisfactory showing to him of their being Cherokees") as an open invitation to return to the Cherokee Nation.[2] The subsequent mass immigration, however, "became so great that the Cherokee authorities became alarmed that their country might be overrun."[3] As a result, it became nearly impossible for anyone to enroll as a citizen, regardless of the legitimacy of their claim. The Nation lacked the infrastructure to handle the influx of claimants to citizenship.

Overwhelmed, the National Council in 1874 passed, and Chief William Potter Ross signed, the "Sweepstake Act," rejecting the citizenship claims of certain families.[4] This act authorized the principal chief to request that the US Indian agent remove those listed from the Nation and authorized sheriffs to "sell after fifteen days' public notice . . . all improvements of persons declared by the National Council to be noncitizens of the nation and subject to removal as intruders."[5] Watts himself was thus removed from citizenship in the Cherokee Nation, after having been previously approved by the chief justice. The Watts family, however, resisted the decision, calling it a breach of their fundamental rights, and appealed to the United States for help.

After the Civil War, the Cherokee Nation faced a citizenship crisis on three fronts. The first conflict lay between the Nation and the ever-growing hoard of white settlers: "'homesteaders,' 'sooners,' and 'boomers' . . . who carried aspirations of building a life for themselves and their families on the 'Unassigned Lands' of Indian Territory."[6] These migrants harbored the same disregard for Cherokee sovereignty as many prominent US agents and politicians, reckoning the profits of trespass well worth the cost. A second conflict arose internally as the Nation wrestled with newcomers to the West claiming Cherokee citizenship by blood. Many Cherokees were thus denied citizenship at various points during this period. The aggrieved sought the intervention of the United States, whose agents were often more than willing to usurp Cherokee authority and take control of the situation.

A third conflict emerged between the Nation and the multitude of freedmen who sought tribal citizenship after the six-month deadline in the Treaty of 1866 had passed (and in some cases who were rejected despite having lived in the Nation prior).[7] Chief John Ross himself had fought against incorporating freedmen during the treaty negotiations, and his sentiments were echoed in many corners of the Nation by those who did not want the Nation to accept individuals without Cherokee blood, by those prejudiced against freedmen, and by those who feared that the United States was dictating who could be called Cherokee.[8] These groups were not mutually exclusive.

Unlike the 1827 constitution and surrounding policies—Cherokee innovations that significantly altered Cherokee citizenship—the United States forced Cherokee Nation authorities to rearticulate their citizenship provisions post–Civil War and then refused to recognize their authority over the matter. The Cherokee Nation found itself dealing with immigration on a massive scale and a United States keener on acquiring land than protecting tribal sovereignty. Although the 1866 treaty stipulated that the US Indian agent agreed to remove from the Nation "such persons, not lawfully residing or sojourning therein," on many occasions, as Watts detailed, the agents refused, believing the Cherokee authorities wrong, biased, or simply unable to execute justice.[9] The result was, in the opening decade of the twentieth century, the disassembling of tribal governments.

THE TREATY OF 1866

Since a great number of tribal nations had forged alliances with the now-vanquished Confederacy, the United States gathered tribal representatives and peace commissioners at Fort Smith, Arkansas to hammer out new treaty arrangements in September 1865.[10] Both northern and southern Cherokee factions sent representatives—the former still led by Chief John Ross, the latter by Elias Cornelius Boudinot, son of the murdered Elias Boudinot, and Stand Watie—ready to fight for a fair treaty. Each faction, however, understood the term "fair" differently. For Chief Ross, the goal was peace and unity. The southern Cherokees, however, demanded "nothing less than the division of the Cherokee Nation," citing irreconcilable differences and a hatred for Ross' leadership.[11]

Dennis N. Cooley, President Andrew Johnson's new commissioner of Indian affairs, decried all Cherokees as "bona fide rebels" and refused to recognize Chief Ross as the legitimate leader of the Cherokee Nation at the Fort Smith conference.[12] Each party signed a peace treaty in September 1865, yet these documents simply ended open hostilities. The factional split within the Nation remained as each side demanded official recognition from Washington. United States negotiators informed each party that "in any new agreement, the Cherokees would have to make peace with the United States and other Indian tribes, free their slaves, and adopt them into the tribe."[13] The representatives reconvened in Washington in 1866 to hopefully bring closure to their conflict.

The southern Cherokees received "an extremely cordial reception in Washington," due in part to their willingness to include in any treaty provisions that would allow railroad expansion through the Nation.[14] The southern faction was also determined to secede and form their own government. Delegate J. W. Washbourne wrote fellow political leader Joseph A. Scales on June 1, updating him on the situation:

> The Ross delegation has been dismissed by the Commissioner because they would not agree to a division . . .

The President has ordered that a treaty be made with us for our pro rata share of the nation. This is positive. On the 22d May [they] were drawing up a treaty. It is probably signed before this. Ross is going to try to beat us in the Senate. His only show is what it was when you left. He will be beaten there. He is trying to make [favorable] public sentiment through the N.Y. Tribune. . . . His day is done. Ours is rising fast and bright. . . . I have been appointed to write to Gen Watie to urge him at once to organize the Southern Cherokee Government in the Canadian District. In God's name be swift about it.[15]

The repeated attempts by the southern faction to paint Ross as an illegitimate leader seemed to be working, especially since the lead negotiators for the United States had stakes in railroad companies and land speculation.[16] Yet the Ross Party's appeals to the Senate and public presses ultimately proved fruitful and forced the hands of the negotiators and Andrew Johnson, who most likely did not wish to be seen as dealing exclusively with a secessionist faction that had been loyal to the Confederate cause before, during, and after the Civil War.[17]

While their newspaper campaign and appeals to sympathetic senators succeeded in getting Johnson and Cooley to dismiss the southern Cherokees' treaty plans, Ross and his councilors did not get everything they wanted either. Ross wanted the United States to concede that the Cherokee Nation had always been loyal and could therefore receive reimbursements for all the damages suffered during the Civil War as allies of the Union.[18] He also refused to give land to the railroad companies and would not agree with Iowa senator James Harlan's territorial plan. (In 1865, Senator Harlan and his cohort planned to establish a single consolidated government over Indian Territory, puppeteered by the United States.)[19] Kansas Senator James Henry Lane spoke for many in the Senate in his impassioned support for the bill and of their plan to send freedmen into Indian Territory: "In my opinion, nothing can be better calculated to clear the political arena of the question of what shall be done with the black man than to pass this territorial bill, open up this country for him, and he will flock in there and become a useful member of society."[20] The territorial bill and the plan to send freedmen into the Cherokee lands angered Ross, who opposed granting Cherokee Nation citizenship to freedmen.

During the negotiations, the United States and Cherokee Nation proposed four different plans for how to handle the freedmen and their descendants. The first would establish "a segregated district within the Nation for colonization by the freedmen."[21] The second, a favorite among Cherokees, would remove the freedmen altogether, at the expense of the federal government, to grant them colonies outside the Nation. The third solution called for adopting the freedmen into the tribe on an equal footing with other Cherokee citizens, a policy favored by the United States. The fourth option, suggested by Senator Harlan in 1865, would "open the entire Indian Territory to Negro colonization."[22] Ultimately, Ross supporters were willing to adopt freedmen into the tribe (but not as full citizens entitled to share in per capita payments) and give them their own land for *separate* use. Southern Cherokees wanted the United States to deal with the problem and take freedmen elsewhere.[23] The United States wanted the Cherokees to assume the responsibility of caring for their own formerly enslaved peoples and many from the surrounding areas too.

The resulting Treaty of 1866 was a messy compromise.[24] For his part, Ross had succeeded in keeping the Nation unified: gravely ill, he signed the treaty on July 19 as "Principal Chief of the Cherokee Nation."[25] Ross died on August 1; the Senate approved the treaty on August 11. The southern Cherokees' attempt to formally divide the Nation had failed. The United States, however, succeeded in obtaining a number of its desired outcomes. While Ross was able to prevent the inclusion of large land grants for railroads, the treaty did include provisions for rights-of-way for two tracks, "one going north and south and one east and west through the Nation."[26] The United States would also not pay for damages incurred during the war. The new treaty also required that the Cherokee Nation incorporate as citizens all freedmen liberated by acts of masters and all free Black persons residing therein—although Ross limited this provision by stipulating that it only applied for up to six months after the treaty was signed.[27] Defeated, Elias Cornelius Boudinot lamented to Stand Watie on July 25:

> We have been beaten; that is to say we have not been successful
> in securing an absolute separation. . . . I incline to the opinion
> that the better policy would be to accept what [Ross] put in their

treaty as it does not commit us to anything, and gives us a good chance to renew the demand for a division at a more favorable opportunity.

The treaty grants a general amnesty, declares confiscation laws void, and gives the Ross party no jurisdiction over us in civil and criminal cases before the courts. They shoulder all the responsibility of the negro matter. We get none of the money. I haven't time nor patience to explain.[28]

At John Ross' passing, the National Council called upon his nephew, William Potter Ross, to fill the vacant role of principal chief. All too familiar with the turmoil in the Nation after a long and brutal war, William Ross—who had fought on both Confederate and Union sides in the conflict—called for unity and cautioned against factionalism in his first public address as chief.[29] In particular, Ross advocated complying "in good faith with all [of the Treaty of 1866's] provisions" that the Cherokee people might "render harmless those articles of the treaty which, regardless of our constitution, changes its provisions and clearly contains [sic] the germs of future strife and division."[30] Indeed, several articles of this treaty would prove divisive to a recovering Nation.

Among those divisive treaty articles, United States officials sowed the seeds of allotment in Article 20, which stated that "whenever the Cherokee national council shall request it, the Secretary of the Interior shall cause the country reserved for the Cherokees to be surveyed and allotted among them, at the expense of the United States," thereby placing the allotment of Cherokee communally held lands on the table in any future conversations. The Nation was also "significantly diminished in its territorial holdings—namely the Cherokee Strip and the Cherokee Neutral Lands in Kansas—due to the treaty terms" in Article 17.[31]

In his address, the new Chief Ross proposed amendments to meet the demands of the United States in accordance with the treaty. He began by calling for the repeal of confiscation laws, which allowed the Cherokee Nation to confiscate property left unattended for two years and which had resulted in the loss of the houses and other property of many soldiers and refugees who had been absent during the war (this particularly affected the southern Cherokees, many of whom had refused to return until they were guaranteed political power and protection).[32]

This met the demands of treaty Article 3. Article 11 granted "the right-of-way through [Cherokee] lands to such railroads as may be authorized by act of Congress," and Cherokee cooperation in building the same. "I am favorable," Ross declared, "to granting the aid asked for, . . . I am opposed to a grant of lands to railroad companies for sale and settlement by a white population."[33]

The Canadian District was set aside for use by southern Cherokees, most of whom were members of the old Treaty Party, its leaders relatives of John Ridge and Elias Boudinot. The new treaty granted these Cherokees amnesty and promised reunification without prejudice. The southern Cherokees, however, distrusted William Ross as they had distrusted his uncle before him and many refused to return to the Nation with another Ross in power. Both sides of the agreement were promised justice in their dispute via the oversight of the US district court in Arkansas, which now had jurisdiction over the Canadian District to ensure that Cherokees would not seek vengeance on one another there.

To deal with the contentious Article 9 regarding citizenship, Ross called for a new census to accurately account for all Cherokees, "whites who are citizens by adoption, and of all Blacks admitted to the full rights of Cherokee citizenship" living in the Nation.[34] Article 9 of the treaty ran as follows:

The Cherokee Nation having, voluntarily, in February, eighteen hundred and sixty-three, by an act of the national council, forever abolished slavery, hereby covenant and agree that never hereafter shall either slavery or involuntary servitude exist in their nation otherwise than in the punishment of crime, whereof the party shall have been duly convicted, in accordance with laws applicable to all the members of said tribe alike. They further agree that all freedmen who have been liberated by voluntary act of their former owners or by law, as well as all free colored persons who were in the country at the commencement of the rebellion, and are now residents therein, or who may return within six months, and their descendants, shall have all the rights of native Cherokees: *Provided,* That owners of slaves so emancipated in the Cherokee Nation shall never receive any compensation or pay for the slaves so emancipated.

This article provided for the entry into full legal Cherokee citizenship of *all* free Black persons, not merely those formerly enslaved by the Nation, as long as they resided within the Nation before the six-month deadline. Ross, also noting that the treaty demanded amendment of Cherokee education laws, which forbid Black persons from being educated in the Nation, called on the Council to "establish schools for the benefit of colored children" and to enact provisions for the care of "destitute orphans" of all races.[35] While the National Council moved quickly to turn the treaty provisions into law, they remained ever wary of losing their authority.

CITIZENSHIP BY BLOOD AND TREATY

From 1866 on, the Cherokee Nation's leaders "exacted the political, economic, and legal machinery" to carve out for themselves a "third space of sovereignty" that lay "within the United States and yet outside of it."[36] The heart of the citizenship question in the Nation after the Civil War was a battle over sovereignty: Did the Cherokee Nation have the sovereign authority to, in the words of Principal Chief Dennis Bushyhead in 1883, "count and claim its own children for itself and to be let alone while doing so"?[37] The 1866 treaty marked a major shift in citizenship policy because it suggested that the Cherokee Nation did not have that full authority, or at least had such authority only in certain cases. Cherokee leaders responded to the crisis by asserting their sovereignty in the face of major opposition.[38]

After Chief Ross' admonition, the Cherokee Nation amended their constitution in November 1866 to meet the treaty's demands, including articulating a new definition of citizenship. The new citizenship law stated that "all native born Cherokees, all Indians, and whites legally members of the Nation by adoption, and all freedmen who have been liberated . . . as well as free colored persons who were in the country at the commencement of the rebellion, and are now residents therein, or who may return within six months from the 19th day of July, 1866, and their descendants . . . shall be taken, and deemed to be, citizens of the Cherokee Nation."[39] Alarmed at US attempts to dictate who could be considered Cherokee, the National Council opted for a strict interpretation of the six-month provision in the Treaty of 1866 that acknowledged citizenship only for those who returned to the nation within six months of the signing.[40] Six months, however, was not enough time for all those displaced by the war to return to Cherokee territory. For years after the treaty, scores of freedmen and their families migrated back. The National Council routinely denied them citizenship.[41]

Article 15 of the treaty added another important provision, allowing that "friendly Indians might be settled upon unoccupied lands in Cherokee country."[42] One year later, in April 1867, the Cherokee Nation entered into an agreement, brokered by the United States, with the Delaware Indians, whom the United States was keen to remove to Indian Territory. This agreement saw the Delawares "become members of the Cherokee Nation, with the same rights and immunities and the same participation (and no other) in the national funds, as native Cherokees," their children being in all respects regarded "as native Cherokees" too.[43] Article 15 was invoked again in 1869 when the Shawnee Indians entered a similar agreement, relocating to the Cherokee Nation and also becoming citizens in the process.[44] Table 3 displays the paths to legal citizenship in the Cherokee Nation as of 1866.

The United States, however, frequently proved to be an obstacle in how Cherokee leaders implemented their policies. US officials were aided by those in the Nation who were willing to help them by publicly challenging Cherokee Nation authority over matters of jurisdiction or citizenship. Individuals like Elias Cornelius Boudinot and William Jefferson Watts welcomed United States intervention in Cherokee matters to further their own economic interests. Others, such as Dennis Bushyhead and missionary John B. Jones, fought to ensure that the Cherokee

Table 3. Paths to Legal Citizenship in the Cherokee Nation, 1866

Cherokee Blood	Treaty Agreement
Born of a Cherokee mother or father/adoption.	Formerly enslaved persons and free Blacks living in the Cherokee Nation within six months of treaty signing (1866).
Marriage to a Cherokee citizen, provided the couple reside in the Cherokee Nation.	"Friendly Indians" relocated to the Cherokee Nation (1866).
Act of the National Council.	Compact between Cherokee, Creek, and Osage Nations (1843).

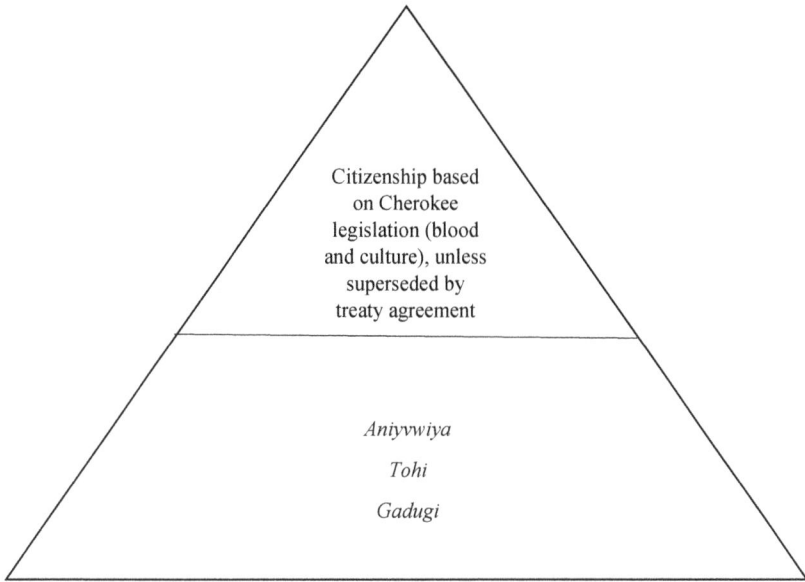

Figure 4. Foundational and Policy Ideas about Cherokee Nation Citizenship, 1866–1907

Nation itself retained its sovereign power to decide in important matters like citizenship. Figure 4 displays the idea pyramid, updated to reflect the situation in the Nation after Civil War. Since the United States imposed the rearticulation of citizenship in the treaty, the foundational ideas at the bottom of the pyramid have not changed. The policy idea, however, has changed: from restricting citizenship to blood Cherokees to both blood Cherokees and those deemed citizens by the terms of the treaty.

The Treaty of 1866 significantly changed the legal articulation of Cherokee citizenship. In years prior, people could obtain Cherokee Nation citizenship through clan practice (clan adoption, birth to a Cherokee mother, kinship) or by an act of the Cherokee Nation government (birth to a Cherokee father, strictly regulated intermarriage, admission of certain Indians); people could also be excluded through these methods. As Tiya Miles writes, the boundaries between these systems often blurred: sometimes kinship trumped written law, as some Cherokees identified as kin those whom the law did not or would not recognize.[45] Treaty agreement became a third path to Cherokee Nation

95

citizenship, one that legally trumped legislative acts of the Cherokee Nation (and clan practice) in the United States court system. The new law stipulated that formerly enslaved peoples, many with no blood relation, had to be included as legal citizens. The second-story idea shifted, yet the foundational idea—that citizenship should be kept exclusive—endured. Since the Cherokee Nation had not designed this policy on its own, there was now a tension between policy and foundational ideas. While US officials saw the treaty as a means to finalize the end of slavery and simultaneously deal with the issue of freedmen in Indian Territory, many in the Cherokee Nation actively resisted the redefinition of their tribal citizenship.

THE CHEROKEE FREEDMEN

From the end of the Civil War, "the freedmen question was constantly before the Cherokee public."[46] While the Cherokee Nation fought with the United States over the authority to identify and maintain its own citizenry, freedmen and their families struggled for the rights of citizenship, which included a share in tribal lands and communal funds. United States officials ultimately "refused to recognize the authority of the [Cherokee Nation] commissions regarding the freedmen" and in doing so "made serious inroads upon Cherokee autonomy."[47]

After emancipation, freedmen living in the Cherokee Nation lacked the political organization to demand much other than the practical benefits that came from citizenship in the Nation, like part of the federal payouts for land acquisitions.[48] As W. E. B. Du Bois wrote, "[the] mass of the freedmen at the end of the war the lacked the intelligence so necessary to modern workingmen" and were unable in many cases to earn a living for themselves.[49] Without citizenship status, it was difficult enough to earn wages, let alone provide for families; their biggest concerns were food and shelter.[50] Scattered during the Civil War, taken prisoner or by their masters to other states, freedmen had a difficult enough time surviving, let alone understanding the need to return six months after a treaty they knew nothing about had been signed.[51] While Chief William Ross, in an 1873 address, advocated for leniency in the six-month provision, the Nation soon found itself overwhelmed with claimants and could not deal with all of them adequately.[52] Many Cherokee freedmen, interviewed decades later, described the unease and confusion present after the war had ended and their subsequent fight for survival.[53]

Since the Civil War had torn apart Black kinship associations, many flocked to Fort Gibson, a Union fort, seeking a new life.[54] These individuals had had no formal education in the Cherokee Nation: according to Morris Sheppard, a Cherokee freedman, "We never had no school in slavery, and it was agin the law for anybody to even show a Negro de letters and figures, so no Cherokee slave could read."[55] In such a position of need, freedmen struggled to form something resembling a political community. Refugees trickled back into Indian Territory months or years after the deadline for citizenship had passed. Further complicating the issue, many people once held in bondage in the south also ran to the Cherokee Nation, hoping for better treatment than they had received in the southern states.[56]

Union soldiers shaped much of the initial experience of freedom that these formerly enslaved peoples had. Chaney McNair, born in bondage in 1852—and enslaved at the end of the war by prominent Cherokee leader William Penn Adair—recalled that the Union soldiers propelled much of the direction of Cherokee society in the late 1860s by either moving, stealing from, or employing formerly enslaved persons.[57] Chaney Richardson spoke of the same behaviors attributed to the soldiers and lamented the resulting hardships of abuse and neglect.[58] The United States government, however, in many cases provided the only hope of survival for freedmen—especially Fort Gibson, which "offered a source of refuge for them"—who found themselves unwanted by Cherokees and the surrounding states.[59] "I got free while I's in Kansas," Chaney McNair recalled. "After the War was over, we colored folks all had to go back to prove up; tell where you come from, who you belong to, you know, so we get our share of land. . . . If all the slaves come back they give 'em Cherokee citizenship, but we had to be back by '66."[60]

Many individual freedmen decided, for different reasons, that the Cherokee Nation would make the best home. Eliza Whitmire recounted the confusion that abounded after the war had ended, as most had no idea what to do once freed: "Some of the slaves went back and worked for their old masters for several years, rather than try to make a living, after being set free."[61] Likewise, Cora Gillam, owned by Cherokee masters before and during the war, described the situation for many formerly enslaved peoples in Indian Territory: "When slaves got free, they didn't have nothing but their two hands to start out with. I never heard of any master giving a slave money or land. Most went back to farming on shares. For many years all they got was their food."[62] The scattered, disheveled communities were thus unable to coalesce into cohesive associations for many years after the Treaty of 1866 went into effect. By the time stable freedmen communities were established, like Foreman in what would become Sequoyah County, Cherokee Nation leaders had already resolved to enforce strict interpretations of their treaty with the United States.[63]

Freedmen's decisions to return and belong to the Cherokee Nation were born not of a firm theoretical conception of citizenship but rather of a need to acquire basic necessities. The requests made by freedmen of both US and Cherokee governments after 1866 often included little more than the means to survive.[64] These peoples desired recognition in order to meet the needs of everyday life. Throughout the 1870s, freedmen groups continually made pleas to the Office of Indian Affairs to grant them Cherokee citizenship so that they could work and earn a living.[65] When the Cherokee Nation passed an act refusing to share government payments with freedmen in 1883, many reacted by again petitioning the US government so that they could have a share in the bounty.[66]

The reactions of Cherokees to living among their former slaves as free peoples were mixed. Some, like Phyllis Petite, described their former Cherokee masters as kind because they allowed their former slaves to continue to live with them, taking care of them and their families.[67] Patsy Perryman described both the social stigmas faced by freedmen in the Cherokee Nation after the war and how children were often responsible for dealing with the US government on behalf of their parents. Children, including Perryman, took to the new education system more quickly than their elders. Perryman herself wrote multiple letters to Washington during the land allotment period on behalf of her parents, who could neither read nor write to secure monies or land by themselves.[68]

Moses Lonian was born into slavery in the town of Salina, Cherokee Nation, in 1857. Louis Ross, treasurer of the Cherokee Nation and Chief John Ross' brother, owned most of the land around Salina, "including the old salt wells, and was considered a very rich man."[69] In addition to the salt mines, Louis Ross also owned Moses' parents, whom he had purchased from a white man named Lonian in Arkansas, along with roughly 147 other slaves. "I [was] with William P. Ross [Louis Ross' nephew] when the slaves were set free," Moses reported, Louis having lent him to William at some point.[70] In 1862, Union soldiers tore through the Cherokee Nation, taking newly freed Moses and other slaves north to Kansas, where they directed them to Fort Scott. Moses' family settled in nearby Anderson County and there survived the rest of the war.

"Louis Ross had not been a very kind master to his slaves," and, once emancipated, Moses' father took for his family the name "Lonian," that of his original white master, instead of "Ross."[71] Name changes were common among formerly enslaved peoples, many of whom did not like the idea of retaining the names of their Indian masters. This practice, and Moses' father's decision to change their name, "cost his children their rights in the Territory, as we were classified as doubtful when we came back, because we bore the name of a white master."[72] Moses returned to the Cherokee Nation in 1888.

The situation of the freedmen and their requests to become part of the Cherokee Nation provided US officials an opportunity to bring the Cherokee Nation closer to the norms established by American politics. The Cherokee resistance to incorporating the freedmen, and the freedmen's pleas to the United States for help, gave US officials an excuse to condemn the Cherokee Nation as insubordinate, unjust, and ineffective—a condemnation that eventually led to the dissolution of the Cherokee Nation itself. Intermarriage had, of course, already put strain on the practice of defining Cherokeeness by blood. But the imposition of a foreign power, the United States, brought down a heavy legal hammer on top of Cherokee politics, further reshaping the Cherokee Nation in the United States' image.

In 1869 the National Council empowered the Cherokee Supreme Court to sit as commissioners to pass judgment on citizenship claims.[73] Yet, while Cherokee leaders asserted their authority to define their own citizenship, they quickly found that they could not handle the chaos of hundreds of people pouring into Cherokee Territory.[74] Lacking the infrastructure to handle these claims, often officials either hastily denied many freedmen or kept them in limbo. Cherokee officials referred those rejected claimants to the commissioner of Indian affairs along with a request for their removal—a provision present in long-standing treaties. This status quo, however, proved untenable. As early as 1871, inundated with pleas from freedmen and their families, the Office of Indian Affairs ordered Union agents in Indian Territory not to remove freedmen whom Cherokee leaders classified as intruders.[75] The Union Agency instructed freedmen and others struggling with the Cherokee Nation for citizenship to come directly to US officials instead, further undermining Cherokee authority.[76]

The laws passed between 1824 and 1866 provide ample evidence that Cherokee nationalists sought a community where Black individuals were specifically enslaved, oppressed, or otherwise unwelcome.[77] The testimony of formerly enslaved people once held in bondage in the Cherokee Nation further illuminates the marginalization these families suffered.[78] In addition to racial prejudice, anthropologist Circe Sturm argues that the Cherokee resistance to incorporating the freedmen was "motivated largely by economic factors," and certainly many Cherokees loathed the idea of sharing federal money and land. Yet Cherokees also had deep-seated cultural and ideological reasons for resisting the imposition of American values.[79]

CHEROKEE CLAIMANTS

In 1867, Chief William Ross, as interim chief, proposed four goals for building the Cherokee Nation back to its prewar strength: "increase our means, multiply our numbers, enlighten our people and fortify our position" with regard to Cherokee lands.[80] Out of Ross' second goal came the National Council's call for Cherokees around the United States to return to the Nation a few years later in 1870. Ross himself, however, was replaced in 1867 by newly elected Principal Chief Lewis Downing, a Baptist Minister and good friend of Evan Jones, the Baptist missionary who had stuck with the Ross Party during the removal crisis.[81]

Downing had served as military chaplain of companies F and S of the Cherokee Mounted Rifles during the war. The members of this regiment were predominantly traditionalists who owned no slaves, most likely all members of the Keetoowah Society. Downing, after the war, opposed discriminating policies aimed at the Confederate faction of the Cherokees, and his unifying sentiments crystalized into the Downing Party. John B. Jones, son of Evan Jones, threw his political weight behind

Downing, including his considerable influence among traditionalists, who gravitated to the party as a result. Downing was elected chief in 1867 with the support of most Cherokee factions. "The Downing party thereafter controlled the political affairs of the Cherokee Nation until Statehood save for the regime of Chief Dennis W. Bushyhead" from 1879 to 1887.[82]

William Ross had stood for election in 1867, but dissatisfaction with his candidacy developed in the ranks of the original Ross Party. The "breakaway group, comprised mainly of full bloods who had formerly followed John Ross, put forth Lewis Downing" instead.[83] The Confederate Cherokees, hating the Ross family, supported Downing; "to them there was no difference between him [William Ross] and his uncle," John Ross.[84] Fights broke out across the Nation during the election as old factions realigned. The National Party, which came to comprise predominantly acculturated progressive Cherokees, supported William Ross in 1866 and again in 1872.[85]

Regardless of party affiliation, however, supporters of both Downing and the National parties understood their rights and the guarantees of previous treaty agreements and defended their communal landholdings with one accord. Land had been held in communal tenure since before anyone could remember. A Cherokee citizen could cultivate as much land as they wanted and tribal laws protected them in their right of occupancy as long as they actively used the land and lived upon it. The Cherokee people, thanks to their cultural mores, especially *gadugi*, had a "natural gift for collective enterprise" that allowed them to prosper in such a system.[86] Much of the latter part of the nineteenth century saw Cherokee leaders articulating a defense not only of communal landholdings but of the character of Cherokee citizens themselves.

One thing that William Ross and Lewis Downing faced in common were continual threats made in Congress to institute a territorial government over Indian Territory. By 1870, Chief Downing had presented several petitions to Congress against one such proposed territorial bill, arguing, among other things, that such a bill was but a malicious attempt to induce the Indians to give up their lands: "We need not remind you that the establishment of such a government over us would work our certain and speedy extinction by subjecting us to the absolute rule of a people foreign to us in blood, language, customs, traditions, and interests, who would speedily possess themselves of our homes, degrade us in our own estimation, and leave us a prey to the politicians and land speculators, thus destroying the unity of our race and producing national disintegration."[87]

After Downing's death in office in 1872, Ross, again selected by the National Council as interim chief, continued to fight against Congress' territorial plans. These territorial plans threatened to take away Cherokee lands by abrogating treaty agreements that guaranteed to the Cherokees Nation the right to their lands in fee simple and to organize themselves on their lands as they saw fit. "If existing treaty obligations are worthless," Ross argued, "what more strength and sanctity will belong to [congressional] statutes?"[88]

On March 5, 1872, William Ross stood in front of a congressional committee, arguing against one of the many proposed territorial bills Congress toyed with in the years following Civil War. The Cherokee Nation, as a sovereign nation, Ross declared, did not want to be absorbed into a larger territory but rather asserted its authority as a distinct regime. While the Cherokee Nation was opposed to congressional control, it was not, Ross asserted, "opposed to progress and improvement." Their institutions, including and especially their communal landholdings, had developed in ways "suited to their condition," the result of authentic self-government in action:

They [the tribal nations in Indian Territory] hold the title to their respective reservations in common, but not their houses, farms or personal property. These are held in severalty. Whether wise or unwise, their systems are adapted to their condition. None among them are landless, and none need be homeless vagrants while living, to be dumped in the "Potter's Field" of civilization when dead. . . . They are not paupers fed from the hand of charity, but are entirely self-sustaining. The money paid to them annually is no gratuity, wrung by taxation from the sweating brow of the white man, but is the interest of your national obligations for lands obtained from them at your own prices, and which were seldom, if ever, equal to their true value. They ask not for these changes [the loss of land and sovereignty]. They dread them.[89]

Ross' reference to the Potter's Field was no mere rhetorical flourish: the allusion to Matthew 27:3–8 and Acts 1:18 directed knowing Americans toward the early Christian socialist tradition, further detailed in Acts 2:42–47, in which those Christian communities lived "together and held everything in common. They sold property and possessions to give to anyone who had need. . . . They broke bread in their homes and ate together with glad and sincere hearts." The Potter's Field was used to bury paupers, indigent people, and criminals, purchased with the money Judas received for betraying Christ—money that the chief priests considered "blood money," unsuitable for anything but purchasing tainted land. Ross' meaning was clear: Americans' lust for Indian lands amounted to a betrayal of not only treaty agreements but also of traditional core Christian communal ethics. He appealed to Americans' "Christian civilization," as his uncle Chief John Ross had so many times before in his fight against removal, to uphold their treaty obligations and recognize Cherokees' inherent right to self-government.

Faced with such congressional pressures, Cherokee leaders sought to reevaluate and reinvigorate their citizenry that they might strengthen their position as a nation. In November 1870, to bring "strength to our reduced numbers," as William Ross put it, the National Council passed an act to benefit the Nation that welcomed Cherokees who returned to live there permanently with full citizenship.[90] The wording of this bill implied that said Cherokees living apart from the Nation were not full citizens and would not be considered thus unless they physically lived in and had a stake in the Nation.

Yet, finding themselves inundated by citizenship claimants, the National Council moved to throw out previously decided-upon claimants in 1874 with "An Act to Remove Certain Persons herein named Beyond the Limits of the Cherokee Nation." Ross signed the controversial bill that December. Previous treaties had stipulated that the United States promised to remove from the Nation anyone whom the Cherokee Nation labeled an intruder. Men like William Jefferson Watts were incensed: Watts and his family, including his brother Solomon Watts, had accumulated considerable wealth, believing their claims to be genuine. Watts turned immediately to the United States for protection of his property against what he called an "unconstitutional" act.[91]

Watts and others in his situation formed the Cherokee Citizenship Association dedicated to protecting the rights of various classes of claimants: those admitted under the 1870 act but later decided against by the council; those with prima facie certificates of citizenship furnished by the US agent prior to August 11, 1886; those with positive proof of Cherokee blood; and those who had enough circumstantial evidence to gain a suit before an impartial court.[92] By the late 1880s, Watts claimed that there were roughly 9,000 claimants in Indian Territory, most of them living in the Cherokee Nation. The Citizenship Association rerouted all rejected or ignored citizenship petitions by their members to the Office of Indian Affairs, whose agents routinely sided with claimants against the Cherokee Nation.

The Cherokee Nation arrested Watts in 1877 for violating the intercourse law by selling merchandise without a permit. Since he was categorized as a noncitizen, his store was closed and he was placed under guard for a month. Watts' case was eventually submitted to the district court in Arkansas, where Judge Isaac C. Parker discharged him for want of jurisdiction, releasing Watts' home and store back into his possession. The Cherokee Nation, however, did not readily submit to US authority in the matter. Soon, Watts' improvements along the Arkansas River were sold at a sheriff's sale for $15 under the 1874 confiscation act; these were valued at $2,000.[93] Watts, again dispossessed of his improvements in the Cherokee Nation, sent word to Commissioner of Indian Affairs Ezra A. Hayt, who ordered the principal chief in 1880 to restore Watts' property to him immediately.

During this back-and-forth, US agents maintained that while the Cherokee Nation could declare certain people noncitizens, once they did so, they had no jurisdiction over them and could in effect do nothing but petition the United States for removal. Acting Commissioner A. B. Upshaw stated that, by declaring certain persons a "noncitizen or intruder, the Cherokee Nation has no jurisdiction over his person or property, and consequently the action and proceedings of its authorities in selling said property and dispossessing him of it, are not warranted . . ."[94] Intruders were the purview of the US government, which had promised to deal with them (but often did not). Upshaw decided that the Cherokee Nation must give intruders time to sell off their property and thus did not have the authority to confiscate improvements. Cherokee leaders were thus faced with a catch-22.

A few years later, the United States Supreme Court decided in the case of *Eastern Band of the Cherokee Indians v. United States and Cherokee Nation, Commonly Called Cherokee Nation West* (1886). In this case, the court ruled that, since the Cherokees in North Carolina had "refused to join their countrymen in the removal to the lands ceded to them west of the Mississippi," they could claim nothing belonging to the Cherokee Nation in Indian Territory.[95] These people had, in effect, legally cut themselves off from the common fund of the Cherokee Nation. The Cherokees in North Carolina were considered "citizens of that state," not of the Cherokee Nation. If Cherokees wanted to enjoy the common property of the Cherokee Nation, they must be admitted into full citizenship of the Cherokee Nation by that government pursuant to its laws.[96] Yet, at the same time, US agents and commissioners refused to respect those laws. The commissioner of Indian affairs declared that "if injustice should be done in any case, the removal of any person unjustly denied admission to citizenship should be refused."[97] The standard of justice here was not the decision of the National Council, however, but rather what US officials believed the correct decision should have been.

WHITE SQUATTERS OVERRUNNING THE NATION

The Treaty of 1866 had permitted the construction of two railroads. Yet Congress went further in the years that followed, promising railroad corporations millions of acres of Indian land contingent on the extinction of the Indian title. Chief William Ross was livid in his protest to Congress: "These soulless corporations hover like greedy cormorants over this territory, and incite congress to remove all restraint and allow them to swoop down and swallow over 23,000,000 acres of the land of this territory, destroying alike the last hope of the Indians and the honor of the government . . ."[98] To achieve their aims, as Georgia had done decades earlier to effect removal, anti-Indian partisans continued to depict the Cherokees and other tribal nations as "backward" since they would not give up their land. Enemies of the Cherokee Nation targeted their preference for holding land in common, in a public domain belonging to the Nation, not owned by individuals.

After the Civil War, Cherokee leaders found themselves not only having to defend their sovereignty and lands but also having to defend the ways in which they lived communally *on* the land. Since antiquity, Cherokees had in many ways taken the fact that they held lands in common for granted. The particular Cherokee cosmovision emphasized harmony and balance, concepts that made the practice of communal landholding a natural one that enabled them to fulfill communal sharing obligations and offered them free range of movement. In contrast to American greed, indulgence, and extreme poverty, Cherokee communalism, leaders like Chief Bushyhead argued, prevented those social ills by guiding citizens toward supporting the common good.[99] Americans like political economist Henry George were then prodding the United States to acknowledge the "delusion" that "private property in land is necessary to the proper use of land, and that again to make land common property would be to destroy civilization and revert to barbarism."[100] This did not mean, historian Andrew Denson writes, "that reformers looked to the Indian Territory for examples of proper systems of landholding" but rather that parallel American debates over economic philosophy "helped tribal leaders find new ways of defending common lands and Indian nationhood."[101]

The policy of holding land in common flowed naturally from the idea that citizenship in a political community is an activity, not merely a legal statement of fact. Holding land in common, and therefore citizenship in such a regime, requires an *active* participation, habituated toward practically concerning oneself for the common good. Americans generally argued that "selfishness," or self-interestedness properly understood as a desire to consistently obtain more wealth, was the chief cornerstone of American civilization.[102] Communal land tenures inhibited the accumulation of vast wealth. Cherokee leaders countered that the practice of communal landholding not only practically solved certain critical social ills, like homelessness and extreme poverty, but also constituted the best way to habituate republican citizens toward civic virtue, defined as an active concern for the health, safety, and well-being of the whole people.[103] These Cherokee statesmen ultimately argued that citizenship in a nation was not merely a means to an end (as US citizenship was for Americans a means to accumulate wealth, enjoy protected liberties, etc.) but rather an end in and of itself.

In 1883 a group of eastern humanitarians, led by Senator Henry L. Dawes, began meeting regularly to discuss the "Indian problem."[104] They observed the influx of white settlers into Indian Territory and the lack of stable law enforcement therein; since the Cherokee Nation and other tribal nations could not prosecute crimes where an American was involved, lawlessness spread like wildfire, especially among white squatters. Most, like Dawes, paraded their desire for Indian lands under the guise of philanthropy. The *real* impediment to Indigenous *civilization* was communally held lands, which prevented them from catching the strain of capitalist fever infecting Americans. It was the Cherokees' fault that their Nation had become a haven for lawlessness. Dawes put his argument succinctly in 1885:

The head chief [of the Cherokees] told us that there was not a family in that whole nation that had not a home of its own. There was not a pauper in that nation, and the nation did not owe a dollar. It built its own capitol, in which we had this examination, and it built its schools and its hospitals. Yet the defect of the system was apparent. They have got as far as they can go, because they own their land in common. It is Henry George's system, and under that there is no enterprise to make your home any better than that of your neighbors. *There is no selfishness, which is at the bottom of civilization.* Till this people will consent to give up their lands, and divide them among their citizens so that each can own the land he cultivates, they will not make much more progress. But there is another lesson; they are intensely afraid of the United States. They distrust this Government. They lean away from us, although they are in our midst. Although they own territory, and have a population capable of becoming a State of this nation, instead of becoming part and lot with us, they are leaning away from us. Why? Those who want to take away the Indian's land without his consent can find a lesson in this. When we made our last treaty with them we provided that a railroad should run through their territory. When we chartered the Missouri, Kansas and Texas Railroad to run through there, we foolishly put into the grant that whenever the Indian title becomes extinct this railroad shall have a strip 20 miles wide.

The Indian has been made to believe that the United States is
after that land, and that if they have anything to do with the
United States it will get that land from them, and so you cannot
treat with these Indians. They won't have anything to do with
you. They prefer to be isolated because they cannot trust us. We
have tried to get their land, and there is no possibility of treating
with them till that delusion is got out of their minds. These five
nations will stand off and be isolated under a system that has got
its growth. I give this illustration to show what a tribe of Indians
can do if they are firmly fixed in their homes, and also to show
how the United States, in order to accomplish this new policy,
must have the confidence of the Indian growing out of the fact
that we don't lie to him.[105]

Dawes based his argument on the assumption that the Cherokees
would not give up holding land in common only because they did not
trust the United States. Cherokees' mistrust of the United States was
well earned, but a genuine belief that communal lands led to a good
life and encouraged *gadugi*, not spite, bolstered Cherokees' reticence.
Cherokees had to contend with not only the rush of settlers that by
1890 outnumbered them but also with moralistic arguments about the
necessity of greed for civilization, for *progress*. In essence, Americans
believed that good citizenship required property ownership and an
acquisitive nature.[106]

Cherokees, on the other hand, valued their communal tenure and
were willing to defend their mores. William Ross argued that their
system created no "landless paupers" or "absent landlords" to brutally
eject them: the Cherokees had among them poverty but not starvation
since the independence brought by access to natural resources like
"wood, water, land, [or] homes" might be had by all.[107] Principal Chiefs
Joel B. Mayes and his brother Samuel Houston Mayes, chiefs from 1887
to 1891 and 1895 to 1899 respectively, were particularly concerned with
presenting the ideal citizen (incidentally modeled by the Cherokees) as
unable to lead a good life under the auspices of private land monopolies.[108] Chief Joel Mayes in 1891 presented his case, arguing that the best
form of republican government cultivated the mores necessary to share
lands among citizens, reducing poverty and homelessness:

The constitution and laws of the Cherokee Nation makes its domain the common property of the Cherokee people; wisely intending that all should reap a benefit from the same and making the homes of our people inaliable [*sic*]. There is no doubt but this is the true system of government for the protection of the poor and helpless in the continued possession of their homes. Hence we have no paupers. There is not a citizen of the Cherokee Nation but who can have a place he can call home; a piece of land that he and his posterity can hold in perpetuity. This no doubt is the best form of government, not only for the Indian in his helpless condition in wrestling with the Anglo-Saxon race for his existence on the face of this earth, but the best government for all mankind.[109]

To nurture the mores necessary to sustain such a system, Joel Mayes argued, a people needed to institute laws preventing citizens from monopolizing portions of the land, more than their own needs warranted. The National Council had the authority to pass laws that they deemed "expedient and proper to prevent citizens from monopolizing improvements with a view of speculation," including forcing those who fenced off more land than they needed to pay those who would otherwise use the land in their own need.[110] Greed fought with the Cherokee hospitality ethic, with *gadugi*, for supremacy. Stamping out the former was a crucial step toward cultivating a virtuous citizenry.

Joel Mayes did not mean that the Cherokees exercised *charity* as the Americans did (which usually meant almsgiving), but rather that Cherokees engaged in a "comprehensive, pervasive transfer of food and material goods among neighbors" who all understood that hospitality meant giving and receiving for the benefit of all.[111] Individualistic Americans, like Senator Dawes, saw in this system dependency, a state anathema to the American image of a self-made man, proudest of achievements made alone. And while it was the case that some Cherokees did become wealthy, these did not reach the extremes found in the rapidly industrializing United States. Neither, however, were poor Cherokees as destitute as the impoverished in the rest of America.[112] The Cherokee system, in general, did not produce the extremes of rich and poor; much of this was due to a lack of individual acquisitiveness.

This is not to say that the Cherokee Nation was a middle-class utopia; this was not Priber's "Kingdom of Paradise." Joel Mayes himself, in his defense of the Cherokee system, cautioned that "evils will creep into the best institutions that man can devise."[113] Many Cherokees attempted to cordon off large tracts of land to become wealthy by monopolizing natural resources or tried to hoard the earth's fruits for themselves. Poorly or unenforced laws also led to the degradation of a citizenry. A "republican" form of government, like the Cherokee Nation, had to stand upon the pillars of education, faith, and hospitality to sustain itself in respect for the law and for each other's humanity.[114]

Yet the Cherokee Nation was not permitted to exist, thrive, or fall based on its own merits, in a vacuum. The dazzling riches some Americans were capable of obtaining ultimately won the hearts of those in Congress who presumed to decide the fate of the Cherokee Nation. The oft-tossed-about idea of *Manifest Destiny* bore with it a particular religious fervor that captured both the American heart and the American mind. Removal westward, as Chief John Ross had predicted in 1836, was never going to be enough for a people bent on spreading their political ideals across the globe.[115]

Undeterred by the Cherokee Nation or the half-hearted attempts made by the United States to escort them out, noncitizen whites continued to pour into the Nation. The most dangerous of these were those who advanced "some fantastic claim to citizenship, and who loudly demanded every privilege enjoyed by the Indians" despite the tribal authorities repeatedly denying them access.[116] Cherokee leaders soon found themselves operating a minority government in their own territory. The United States census of Indian Territory in 1890 listed 56,309 inhabitants in the Cherokee Nation: 29,166 were coded white, 5,127 were coded Black, and 22,015 were coded Indian.[117] While these individuals were classified based on their physical appearance, the numbers are telling. The Cherokees were slowly being squeezed out of their homes by all manner of people, whether arriving to hide from the law, to work honestly, to steal land, or to satisfy a legitimate claim to citizenship.

THE GREAT CITIZENSHIP CRISIS

The Cherokee Nation was faced with thousands of claimants to citizenship (a number that grew annually), eastern humanitarians who claimed to know what was best for their Indigenous neighbors, and a Congress that wanted to take over the land for development.[118] The 1880s in American history are often noted for being a time of great corporate corruption, railroad monopolies, and westward migration at the expense of the Indian.[119] In 1883, Chief Dennis Bushyhead addressed the federal government's continued attempts to dictate policy and practice to the Cherokee over their citizenship laws. The Cherokee government, claimed Bushyhead, "considering itself in the light of a parent to a family . . . had the right to count and claim its own children for itself and to be let alone while doing so."[120] This included the right to exclude the "unentitled" and "pretenders" who were not part of the Cherokee family.[121] Part of Bushyhead's exasperation came from US insistence on dealing with claimants as individuals, pretending "that the Treaty [of 1866] had been made with individual members, and not with the Nation as a whole."[122] Bushyhead articulated in his speech what many US agents either could not or refused to understand: that Cherokees viewed politics and the family as inseparable.

Without the appropriate infrastructure or help from the federal government, Cherokees were unable to keep up with the pressure of new claimants to citizenship, especially when the time came to receive payments for Cherokee lands sold to the United States. In 1883 the Cherokee Nation passed an act declaring that the money, some $300,000, could only be distributed among blood Cherokees.[123] The decision excluded freedmen and others from receiving any of the bounty. Desiring a share in the payment, many freedmen appealed to the Office of Indian Affairs, as they had done in the past. Indian Affairs, refusing to acknowledge Cherokee Nation's authority, used the situation to begin settling the issue of native sovereignty in the eyes of the federal government.[124]

Up until 1887, Cherokee leaders had successfully resisted American pressures for allotment and territorial assimilation. In 1887, Congress passed the General Allotment Act, better known as the Dawes Act, to turn Indians into private land holders. By allotting land to individuals in tribal nations, the thinking went, the total lands allotted would not equal the total acreage held in common by the tribes; the remainder would be left for white settlers and corporations to consume.[125] The Dawes Act, however, did not apply to the Cherokees, Choctaws, Creeks,

Chickasaws, or Seminoles because of prior treaty agreements. Nevertheless, the writing was on the wall.

Chief Joel Mayes cautioned the Cherokee people in 1889 against US officials' attempts to count them, stating that he "refused to appoint any one" to act with agents in charge of compiling tribal rolls.[126] While Chief Mayes was certain that "there [would be] no trouble in determining the citizenship of the Shawnees and Delawares," who had been incorporated in the 1860s, he was adamant that "bona fide colored citizens should be definitively known," to rule out illegitimate claimants.[127] Mayes did not anticipate a fair counting, especially when it came to the contentious issue of the freedmen and the hordes of settlers pretending to belong to the Cherokee Nation. Anticipating that the great eye of allotment would find them eventually, Cherokees actively resisted efforts to count them for years.[128] As a result, in addition to US census taker prejudices, the rolls compiled around this time are grossly imperfect.

The Dawes Commission, created in 1893, was tasked with negotiating with the Five Tribes for the extinction of their communally held lands. Many Cherokees, especially "full-bloods," resented this decision and resisted in every way possible short of war against the United States.[129] When the tribal nations refused to cooperate, Congress expanded the Dawes Commission to five members and renamed it the Commission to the Five Civilized Tribes. Henry Dawes himself joined on as the commission doubled their efforts and began to actually survey Cherokee lands. These commissioners, frustrated that the Cherokees did not see things their way, advised Congress to disregard treaty obligations and abolish tribal governments without their consent. Yet Congress refrained from doing so for the time being, opting for continued patience and negotiation.[130]

The insatiable American hunger for land, however, could not be delayed forever. Pro-allotment partisans, as had their forebears, argued that the Cherokees were "hopelessly venal" and corrupt without remedy save absorption into the United States.[131] Traditionalist Cherokees, Dawes argued, were in a state of "hopeless misery" due to their communal condition, which did not allow them to achieve the wealth of their American neighbors.[132] Dawes said this in spite of his previous admission that there existed not a pauper among them in the Cherokee Nation; this lack of pauperism, however, was due to Cherokees' redistribution ethic, *gadugi,* which discouraged the alleged selfishness needed to become a true American.[133] Americans also, in a fit of irony, criticized the Indigenous treatment of the freedmen, who in many cases had been ignored or relegated to second-class citizenship.

Americans, however, were not the only ones clamoring for allotment.[134] Some in the Cherokee Nation, according to author Robert J. Conley, had become so acculturated that they could not speak Cherokee and did not value traditional mores as their predecessors had.[135] One opinion letter, published under the name John Three Sixteen, argued that allotment would break up the "petty sort of foreign government in the midst of the United States" and end the "monopolistic evil that rests as a heavy burden and nightmare upon the large majority of our poor Indians and citizens."[136] John Three Sixteen also argued that allotment would end the "body of fossilized missionaries, who draw their sustenance from the various missionary boards of the sect occupying the territory"; these were opposed to allotment because, John Three Sixteen argued, it would make their jobs obsolete.[137] Tribal governance had become corrupt and unwieldy, and the only remedy, for those like William Jefferson Watts and a growing minority in the Cherokee Nation, was embracing American civilization.[138]

Factionalism again split up the Nation between those whose lifestyles mirrored their white neighbors and those who held to the traditional Cherokee old ways. The most famous of the latter group was Redbird Smith.[139] Born in 1850, Redbird Smith was raised on the ancient rituals, customs, and practices by his parents, Pig Redbird Smith and Lizzie Hildebrand Smith, who instructed him from an early age in the services and cause of the Cherokee people.[140] Pig Redbird Smith and Budd Gritts, a Baptist minister, took part in the reorganization of the Keetoowah Society in 1859; the constitution and laws of government that they drafted for the organization were meant to guide them as conservative Cherokees through changing political conditions and religious challenges.

Redbird Smith, historian Gregory D. Smithers, argues, "was a child of the Cherokee diaspora": an effort of Cherokees to understand and identify themselves over time in response to new situations and especially new locations.[141] How should the Cherokee religion be understood or adhered to in the latter half of the nineteenth century? In a reality where progressive Cherokees outnumbered traditionalists, did the old ways have a place?[142] Redbird Smith applied his parents' teachings and his education in Cherokee virtue to his counter-assimilation movement in response to allotment-era policies and the degradation of the Cherokee government. Cherokees' pride in their ancestral heritage was essential, Smith argued, so that "our posterity" might have a clear idea of Cherokee identity to guide them in their lives.[143] Indeed, Smith taught his followers that Cherokees were connected to their ancestors when they adhered to the ancient rituals and spoke their shared cosmovision. Redbird Smith's ambition was to unify all people of Cherokee blood by awakening their racial pride:

After my selection as a Chief [of the Keetoowahs], I awakened to the grave and great responsibilities of a leader of men. I looked about and saw that I had led my people down a long and steep mountain side, now it was my duty to turn and lead them back upward and save them. The unfortunate thing in the mistakes and errors of leaders or of governments is the penalty the innocent and loyal followers have to pay. My greatest ambition has always been to think right and do right. It is my belief that this is the fulfilling of the law of the Great Creator. In the upbuilding of my people it is my purpose that we shall be spiritually right and industrially strong. . . .

We are endowed with intelligence, we are industrious, we are loyal, and we are spiritual but we are overlooking the particular Cherokee mission on earth, for no man nor race is endowed with these qualifications without a designed purpose. Work and right training is the solution of my following. We as a group are still groping in darkness in many things, but this we know, we must work. A kindly man cannot help his neighbor in need unless he have a surplus and he cannot have a surplus unles [sic] he works. It is so simple and yet we have to continually remind our people of this.

Our Mixed-bloods should not be overlooked in this program of a racial awakening. Our pride in our ancestral heritage is our great incentive for handing something worth while to our posterity. It is this pride in ancestry that makes men strong and loyal for their principle in life. It is this same pride that makes men give up their all for their Government.[144]

The Keetoowah constitution was amended in 1889, making it more political in nature, which led to internal divisions between the Christian Keetoowahs and the Ancient Keetoowahs.[145] Despite this, each group was initially opposed to hasty action on the question of allotment. The Ancient Keetoowahs especially opposed allotment and, under the leadership of Redbird Smith, became known as the Nighthawk Keetoowahs because of their constant vigilance. As time passed and other tribal nations agreed to terms, the Keetoowahs split on how best to oppose allotment. Some believed that resistance was futile and attempted to make the best of their foregone conclusion that the Cherokee Nation had lost. The Nighthawk Keetoowahs, under Redbird Smith, however, refused to capitulate.[146]

All tribes but the Cherokee Nation consented to treat with the Dawes Commission by the late 1890s. On June 28, 1898, Congress passed the Curtis Act, which terminated the tribal tenure without Indian consent. Cherokee leaders, who had steadfastly refused to deal with them, were brought under the provisions of the act.[147] The Curtis Act gave the Dawes Commission authority to act without tribal consent, extended federal court jurisdiction over tribal lands, and allowed the United States to assume the tax payments of whites living in the Cherokee Nation.[148] Cherokees continued to resist while they had any ability to do so. When the Curtis Act abolished their institutions, Cherokee leaders attempted to secure a more favorable deal than Congress was willing to grant.

Chief Samuel Houston Mayes declared that his priority was to secure the continued existence of the Cherokee Nation and decried the destruction of the Cherokee Nation judiciary and other legal institutions. "I believe," Mayes said, "that the interests of our people would be better subserved . . . by an equitable individualization of the title to all our lands, to all the citizens of the Cherokee Nation."[149] The United States had broken its promises to the Cherokees, the basis of which lay in the treaties of 1835 and 1866. Chief Mayes lamented that "no one of you is more strongly opposed than I to the United States violating its solemn obligations with our people, without our consent, and I am ready to unite with you in every legitimate way to protect them."[150]

Chief Mayes appointed several men to meet with the Dawes Commission to hammer out an agreement. One of the Cherokee proposals attempted to broker a deal wherein they provided for those traditionalists who wished to remain living communally—to in effect allot for certain groups instead of individuals. They wanted to secure the ability of as many traditionalists as were willing to take allotments adjacent to one another and hold them as a corporation for their joint use.[151] The federal officials did not even consider this proposal. Other proposals included that freedmen should be limited to forty-acre allotments and should not share in the distribution of tribal funds; "the Dawes Commission embodied this proposal in the draft agreement."[152]

On January 31, 1899, a vote was held to determine what to do with the proposed Dawes Commission treaty: the conservatives lost by 2,015 votes in their efforts to reject all agreements with the commission.[153] This draft agreement, though accepted by the tribe, was nonetheless rejected by Congress as insufficient. An agreement was finally settled upon and adopted in 1902. In 1901 the Dawes Commission began working toward compiling the final tribal rolls to decide who got land allotments. The commission ultimately broke down those residing on Cherokee land into three categories: Cherokees, whites, and freedmen. All told, the counted inhabitants of the Cherokee Nation numbered 41,824 total, including 4,919 freedmen, 8,703 "full-bloods," and 27,916 "mixed-bloods."[154] There were over 1,000 freedmen who had previously been citizens, however, that the Dawes Commission excluded from its rolls due to a combination of clerical error, inability to produce proof of citizenship, and racial profiling. The final rolls closed and in 1907 the Cherokee Nation ceased independent operations as Oklahoma joined the Union.[155]

The Dawes Commission—what Theodore Roosevelt called a "mighty pulverizing engine to break up the tribal mass"—began eliminating the Cherokee policy of holding land in common and allowed the federal government to physically count and name Cherokee citizens.[156] Cherokees lost their ability to hold lands in common, their ability to determine tribal citizenship, and, by 1907, the entirety of their tribal governing authority. The Dawes Rolls determined who could be legally Cherokee from that point forward. Further complicating matters—factoring in the lack of cooperation from the Cherokee, the racial profiling of the census takers, and the inability to correctly place some people—the Dawes Rolls were a flawed list.[157] Not only did the United States assume control over Cherokee citizenship, they also miscounted some of the existing citizens; citizens based on kinship and communal knowing, rather than proved by legal documentation, were especially at risk of being overlooked.[158]

The federal policies of allotment and termination resulted in the third shift in Cherokee citizenship law. Of course, with these acts, Congress dealt major blows to Indigenous sovereignty across the board: what happened to the Cherokee Nation was part of a larger quest to eliminate all tribal governments and claim more land. US officials hoped through allotment that Indians would more fully Americanize.[159] Up until 1907, the Cherokee Nation faced social and political problems it lacked the infrastructure to handle. Powerless to stop the inflow of settlers and business that followed the railroads, the Cherokee Nation stood firm when it came to citizenship. Yet Cherokee citizenship was a changing concept throughout the period, as many acknowledged when the United States compiled an official roll of named citizens.

Critically, the final congressional action in the series of acts, designed to end the Cherokee Nation government and open the door for Oklahoma statehood, continued indefinitely both the tribe and Cherokee tribal government: "SEC. 28. The Tribal existence and present Tribal governments of the Choctaw, Chickasaw, Cherokee, Creek and Seminole Tribes or Nations are hereby continued in full force and effect for all purposes authorized by law, until otherwise provided by law."[160] While Congress' actions reduced their practical role, members of Congress did not cause the total elimination of the Cherokee Nation. Although the era of allotment and termination began with what seemed like the death of the Cherokee tribal government—historian Morris L. Wardell wrote in 1938 of the "passing of an Indian state," the Cherokee Nation, as "another step in the direction of a larger Union of American commonwealths"—Cherokee self-governance would continue in various forms until reestablished formally in the mid-twentieth century.[161]

THE SECOND DURABLE SHIFT IN
CHEROKEE CITIZENSHIP

This chapter chronicles citizenship in the Cherokee Nation as it developed from the 1860s up through 1907, the termination of tribal government. In this period, faced with the prospect of the United States dictating to Cherokees who could be considered Cherokees, the Nation did everything in its power to assert its sovereignty against the tide of American settlers and politicians bent on eliminating their way of life. As a result, Cherokees developed stricter policies for determining citizenship, rejecting even those with what had previously been considered valid claims at various periods. Cherokees also displayed a marked reluctance—and often blatant animosity—to admitting freedmen into full citizenship. The citizenship crisis was an *identity* crisis, but while the two were linked, each evolved in its own direction.[162]

While many were willing to accept the idea that freedmen could live in the Nation, Cherokee leaders resisted the idea that freedmen could share in Cherokee Nation funds when it came to per capita payments or land allotments: while freedmen might go to schools in the Nation and work for and beside Cherokees, they were not full citizens because they were not Cherokees by clan or by blood (distinctions that were already blurred) but rather by a forced adoption. As control slipped further from the Cherokee Nation's grasp, the United States used the freedmen's situation to undermine Cherokee interests, routinely siding with freedmen claimants to citizenship instead of the Cherokee leaders who demanded their removal. This created a power struggle that the United States never had any intention of letting Cherokee leaders win.

Despite the efforts of some Cherokee leaders to resist, the altered citizenship law—that non-blood-related freedmen were citizens—prevailed and helped create a new political reality for the Cherokee people in the post–Civil War era. This new reality forced Cherokee politics to wrestle with an influx of new citizens while contending with older struggles against American land grabs and divisive acculturation. Still, as evidenced by repeated efforts to suppress the number of new citizens, the Cherokee remained politically committed to the foundational idea that their membership ought to be exclusive, based now on some mixture of blood and experience. The second-story idea (the actual citizenship law) changed, but although the United States forced the Cherokee Nation into that position, the National Council and other leaders took agency where they could and restricted citizenship as much as possible.[163]

CHAPTER 4
ALLOTMENT AND TERMINATION
1907-1975

JOHN MANKILLER WAS born in the Cherokee Nation in 1889 to Jacob Mankiller and Susan Teehee-Bearpaw, members of well-established Cherokee families.[1] John was a young man when the Dawes Commission came through Indian Territory, breaking up communally held lands in preparation for Oklahoma statehood. John and his family were eventually assigned 160 acres in Adair County, land that came to be called Mankiller Flats. Congress took away from the Cherokee Nation government the authority to count and claims its own citizens for itself and replaced it with layers of bureaucracy that would govern the lives of Cherokee people for over sixty years.[2] Congress decided that those whom the Dawes Commission counted were legally Cherokees for all administrative purposes.[3] While John Mankiller was a citizen of the Cherokee Nation prior to allotment, others, like Francis Marion Dawson, had ties to the Cherokee Nation that were more controversial.[4]

Francis Dawson's family had been listed on the 1896 Cherokee Nation rolls. Around 1900, Cherokee Nation attorneys attempted to remove Dawson and his family from the tribe.[5] The Nation brought many witnesses before the Dawes Commission, including one (J. L. Clinkenbeard) who testified that Dawson had only one person who could allegedly verify his connection to the Cherokee Nation, a doctor from Arkansas. Clinkenbeard testified that Dawson had said that "he could give him [the doctor] four drinks of Arkansas whiskey and he would swear that black was white."[6] C. G. Braught, a Cherokee Nation citizen and Dawson's neighbor for many years, also testified that Dawson had arranged with the court to have each of his family members listed on the Dawes Rolls for one hundred dollars apiece. Despite this evidence, the Dawes Commission ruled that, because Francis Dawson and his family had appeared on the 1896 rolls, they were officially citizens of the Cherokee Nation and could not be removed.[7] Many Cherokees, like John Mankiller, whose family had been known for generations, were accurately counted. Others, however, like Francis Dawson, were counted despite the protests of Cherokee officials.

The early decades of the twentieth century present a quandary for studying citizenship in the Cherokee Nation, since the official government apparatus ceased to function.[8] The Cherokee Nation had no formal citizenship policy. These were the years of congressional control over the Cherokee people: forced onto allotments, many were trapped in place; others left. Still others resisted by attempting to create an Indian state or by integrating Cherokee values into the dominant American society. Yet this era still bore witness to the "longevity, continuity, and resilience of Cherokee political, intellectual, and cultural life" despite the lack of a governing body.[9] While the Cherokee Nation entered a long period of "political dormancy" in 1907, "Cherokee *nationhood* remained very much a part of how Cherokees from this period continued to understand themselves and the multiple worlds in and across which they moved."[10] Understanding the forces which moved during this period is critical, therefore, to the development of citizenship in the Cherokee Nation as it would be later articulated in the 1970s and beyond.

THE DAWES ROLLS

Allotment, Daniel Heath Justice writes, "remains the great rupture in this history, far more traumatic for us than either Removal or the events that followed the Civil War, for in those circumstances the Nation was gravely injured but still largely physically intact, both in terms of land and population."[11] Before allotment, the Cherokee Nation had the authority to determine its own citizenship requirements, save for the citizenship provisions of the Treaty of 1866, which they could not abridge. After allotment, Congress, and federal courts, "determined that Congress has the power 'to supersede that [self-]determination when necessary for the administration of tribal property, particularly its distribution among the members of the tribe.'"[12] The work of allotment began with the compilation of the Dawes Rolls by a congressionally appointed commission to count those living in Indian Territory. Their ultimate goal was the dissolution of tribal governments, the breakup of communally held lands, and the final assimilation of the American Indian.[13]

The Dawes Commission found the work that they had planned to accomplish far more difficult than they had anticipated. Tribal nations had kept their own citizen rolls, but these, as in the case of the Cherokee Nation, had been complicated by the incorporation (or rejection) of whites, other Indians, and freedmen—and especially by hordes of squatters. In many tribal nations, the recognition of citizenship usually rested upon family or neighborhood knowledge: local Cherokees *knew* who was Cherokee and who was not.[14] Many traditionalists were either extremely reluctant to enroll or refused outright, actively fleeing from attempts to count them. The commission was also faced with opportunistic tribal leaders who, seeing the writing on the wall, wanted to get the best personal deal out of allotment for their friends and families that they could. Still others pretended to be Cherokee Nation citizens to get their share of the land bounty. The commission thus had agents in every corner of the Cherokee Nation working against these difficulties. Reformers, notes American Indian studies scholar Tom Holm, were probably surprised that "the most stubborn resistance to their measures came from American Indians who throughout the nineteenth century were considered to be the prime candidates for allotments": the so-called Five Civilized Tribes and the Cherokee Nation in particular.[15]

The Cherokee enrollment came last out of the Five Tribes; the Dawes Commission began the process in 1901, checking their work against the tribal census of 1896.[16] Redbird Smith related his experience when the agents came to count him: "When the Dawes Commission was here for the purpose of making the enrollment for final settlement by the allotment of the land, I stood up for my rights. I stood for the treaties and agreements that were made by my fathers with the Government of the United States; and I was at home enjoying myself in peace when I was arrested and taken to prison. I and several other Indians were arrested and taken together to the Muskogee jail for standing up for our rights— my old treaty with the United States Government—as I have always stood for it without violating any part of it, nor have I violated any law."[17]

Smith spent a night in jail and the following morning was made to enroll against his will. While Smith and other Cherokees resisted enrollment, whites of all persuasions desperately attempted to partake by petitioning the Dawes Commission.[18] These applications the commission judged against the standard of extant Cherokee Nation citizenship laws: whites who had married into the tribe after 1877 were generally denied enrollment as suspicions mounted as to their motivations.[19]

The final Cherokee Nation rolls included 36,619 Indians, including 27,916 "mixed-bloods" and 8,703 "full-bloods."[20] In addition, the commission included 286 whites and 4,919 freedmen, bringing the final total up to 41,824.[21] These individuals were made citizens of both the United States and the state of Oklahoma by 1907. Counting the Cherokee people was one thing; securing allotments for each eligible person was another. Births and deaths complicated the process further, as the commission primarily relied upon documented evidence—evidence that many Cherokee families did not normally keep.[22] The selection of allotments occurred mostly in 1904 but was prolonged by Cherokees having to go to federal courts to be declared executors of their deceased relatives' estates—to therefore claim the allotments that would have been theirs.

While Cherokee leaders convinced the commission to make concessions throughout the process, "the final product grossly misrepresented Cherokee society in significant ways."[23] Commissioners divided and rearranged Cherokee households to look more like American nuclear families, thus splitting up kinship relations that had lived together for generations. Eliza Brown, for example, was an elderly Cherokee woman at the time of allotment who shared an extended household, including multiple buildings, with her husband, their grown daughters, her brother, and her sister.[24] The Dawes Commission separated Eliza and her husband, James, from her siblings (e.g., placed them on a different enrollment card) when it came time to divide up the land. The separation of different generations from one another fed into the wave of anti-traditionalist sentiment that surrounded the process: traditionalists were, after all, those most likely to live in traditional household arrangements.

Furthermore, historian Angie Debo reported, some Cherokees did not actually receive any land at all.[25] The agreement with the Cherokee

Nation in 1902 fixed the individual share at 110 acres of average land. When allotment began on January 1, 1903, it became clear that the Cherokee Nation did not have enough land, so Congress provided that "each citizen who failed to receive his share should be paid $651.20 to invest in land" instead.[26] By 1910, officials had identified 1,522 Cherokees who were to receive payment instead of land. Additionally, "new borns" who had "won their right to enrolment in 1912 received no land."[27]

The Dawes Rolls and allotment accomplished many things; among the most serious were the breakup of communally held lands and of Cherokee kinship groupings.[28] Citizenship in the Cherokee Nation had for roughly ninety years been signaled by an amalgamation of clan practice and Cherokee Nation legislation.[29] The Treaty of 1866 added a new dimension whereby the federal government could supersede Cherokee Nation authority to determine citizenship. With allotment, Congress created a new layer of bureaucratic regulation that determined who could be considered Cherokee: a federal policy of *blood as ancestry*.[30] Progressive reformers, through Congress, designed this system to stamp out traditional kinship associations and more fully Americanize Indigenous peoples by declaring that their *Indigenous status* depended on how much Indian blood they had. Biology, according to these reformers, conveyed belonging. Under this regime, Rose Stremlau writes, identity became a "statement rather than a way of life."[31]

The Cherokee Nation government went dormant. The clerk of the Cherokee Supreme Court had made the last entry in the official ledger in 1898; formal use of Cherokee written law ended that day.[32] Yet, Rennard Strickland argued, "the values central to law—the shared consensus of common ideals, the command to do the right thing"—remained the same, even without an operational government.[33] Just as each prior shift in citizenship policy did not necessarily mirror a widespread cultural rejection of certain foundational ideas, so too did Cherokee people continue to preserve their cultural traditions together as citizens of Oklahoma, albeit in different ways.[34] Figure 5 shows how the Dawes Commission policy supplanted the Cherokee Nation's ability to identify citizens by their own reckoning.

In addition to altering the legal definition of citizen, allotment had a disastrous effect on the land itself.[35] Rose Stremlau has written in detail

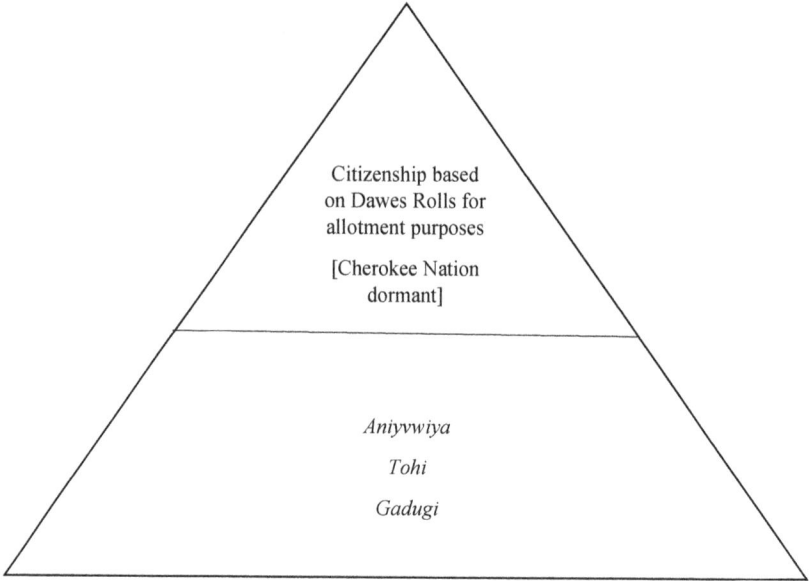

Figure 5. Foundational and Policy Ideas about Cherokee Nation
Citizenship, 1907–1975

of how rapid development in Oklahoma was not only destructive of
Cherokee mores but also bad for the environment:

> The quick development of the region led to the mismanage-
> ment of natural resources. Efforts to regulate use and conserve
> resources were not enacted until the early 1930s, by which point
> the damage was done. For over two decades since allotment, tim-
> ber stands had been cut bare and soil was overfarmed, causing
> the deterioration of the ecosystem. This led to diminishing wild
> resources. Groves of surviving nut-bearing trees shrunk because
> they could not adapt to the denuded land. Game could no lon-
> ger thrive in the sparse woods, and animal populations declined.
> Soil runoff reduced the fish population by filling fishing holes
> and muddying rivers.[36]

The Cherokee practice of holding land in common—and the lack of
collective exploitation of that land—had kept the land healthy and fer-
tile. The consequences of Oklahomans (and Americans in other states)

rapidly stripping natural resources from the earth were keenly felt years later, during the great Dustbowl in the 1930s.

RESISTANCE TO ALLOTMENT: THE SEQUOYAH CONVENTION

In 1905 a group of patriots led by Cherokees James A. Norman and Chief William C. Rogers, alongside Choctaw chief Green McCurtain, called for a constitutional convention to draft a document that they would submit to Congress for entry into the union of an Indian state. The proposed State of Sequoyah would encompass all of Indian Territory.[37] All tribal governments were to come to an end on March 4, 1906; while Indians were generally opposed to statehood efforts, the looming deadline set by the Curtis Act of 1898 forced them into action.[38]

The convention named Creek Chief Pleasant Porter convention chair and produced a document that struck the same progressive and populist tones as the eventual Oklahoma State Constitution. One of Chief Porter's goals was to hold a convention that would launch those involved into Oklahoma politics; thus, the Sequoyah Constitution contained many of the same restraints on elected officials that progressive Oklahomans wanted.[39] The Sequoyah Constitution contained no mention of communally held lands, nor of explicit Indigenous qualifications for citizenship. The most potentially controversial provisions came in Article III, Section 42, and Article VI, Section 3. The former stated that "all wild fish, game, animals, birds and fowls in this State are declared to be the property of the State"—a precursor for Article II, Section 36, of the Oklahoma Constitution, which provided that all citizens have the right to use "traditional methods" for the taking of fish and game. The latter stipulated that the General Assembly, in their first session, should extend to all women the right of suffrage.

Indigenous leaders soon realized that Congress, controlled by Republicans, was unlikely to admit the heavily Democratic Indian Territory into the union alongside Democratic Oklahoma. Despite this, Indian nation leaders campaigned heavily in favor of single statehood for their proposed Indian state. On November 7, 1905, an election was held where voters cast 56,279 votes in favor of the Sequoyah Constitution and petition to Congress; 9,073 votes were cast against.[40] Congress, however, refused to consider any Sequoyah statehood bills. The Sequoyah

Convention, according to Angie Debo, "was a most impressive demonstration of the political vitality that still existed in the Indian citizenship."[41] Cherokees, without the governing authority of their laws, fought against the destruction of their regime, even if that meant accepting statehood alongside their tribal neighbors and the loss of their own distinct governing authority.

Congress, meanwhile, continued its campaign against tribal governments in its reaction to the United States Supreme Court rulings in the Cherokee Intermarriage Cases.[42] These cases dealt with the distribution of tribal property to intermarried whites ahead of allotment. These cases originated when Cherokee Indians "by blood" filed claims against the enrollment of 3,627 white persons who tried to participate in allotment of Cherokee lands. The court of claims ruled that whites who had acquired Cherokee Nation citizenship by marriage prior to November 1875 had equal per capita rights to those of Cherokees by blood and could receive allotted lands (but not Cherokee funds). Whites who had intermarried between November 1875 and November 1877 had no right to Cherokee property or funds unless they had paid a $500 fee to the Cherokee Nation. The court also held that white men who abandoned Cherokee wives automatically forfeited all rights as Cherokee Nation citizens.[43] Chief Justice Melvin W. Fuller, writing for a unanimous court, affirmed the decision of the court of claims in every respect: "the Cherokee Nation had virtually unencumbered authority to qualify the rights of citizenship that it had bestowed."[44] Congress, however, with the support of President Roosevelt, moved to provide intermarried whites the power to dispose of their improvements prior to allotment and was about to grant those same people allotments but for practical reasons decided against this—for fear that there might not be enough land to allot.[45]

Ultimately, legal scholar Stacy L. Leeds argues, the failure of the State of Sequoyah may have been a blessing in disguise.[46] The resulting state would have entered the Union as an equal member, subjected to all United States laws; it would not have preserved tribal governance under a different name. "Unlike the Oklahoma model which conditioned statehood on surviving tribal rights," Leeds writes, "the State of Sequoyah would have come into the union on the understanding that the Five Tribes would no longer exist as political entities."[47] Furthermore, a State of Sequoyah would have in some ways vindicated Progressive reforms, enabling reformers to proclaim that their policies had succeeded—that "tribal governments could be terminated and that former tribal citizens could become citizens of the United States" and fully participate in the American polity.[48] Had Congress paid it more attention, they may have discovered that Progressive reforms might actually have been better satisfied by allowing the tribal governments in Indian Territory to coalesce into another state among many.

RESISTANCE TO ALLOTMENT: TRADITIONALIST REACTIONS

Indian Territory and Oklahoma were merged into one on November 16, 1907. In the preceding decades, Congress had established itself as firmly in control of tribal governments and tribal nations. While the Supreme Court upheld the Cherokee Nation's ability to count and claim its own members—barring certain treaty provisions (e.g., the Treaty of 1866)—Congress had the final voice in tribal citizenship matters. These events, and the termination of Cherokee Nation communal landholdings, continued to alienate many of the more conservative Cherokees, who "withdrew in passive disapproval from a movement in which they felt they had no part."[49] The new government over Indian Territory was therefore established largely without their participation.

By 1902, "full-blooded" Cherokees had dwindled to number around 6,500, compared to the over 21,000 "mixed-blood" Cherokees.[50] Many traditionalists refused to enroll or accept their land allotments, rallying around figures like Redbird Smith of the Nighthawk Keetoowahs in their opposition to acculturation and American promises.[51] US Indian agents were ultimately authorized to choose allotments for those who refused, but many traditionalists in turn refused to recognize the authority of the land titles, just as they had rejected the American education system.[52] As a result, most could not understand English or the new Cherokee leadership, most of whom had become fluent in that language, losing their own along the way. A prominent Progressive politician, Michael Cunniff, toured and praised post-allotment Oklahoma in 1906: "the breaking up of tribal relations in Indian Territory and the admission of the Indians to citizenship and to individual ownership of land" had led to its transformation into idyllic farmlands and productive mines, as well as great economic opportunity.[53] He was especially pleased by the fact that, when he walked through the city streets, "you have to be told that [someone] is Indian."[54]

Cherokee novelist John M. Oskison captured the traditionalist sentiment in 1917 when he lamented how Cherokees had become forced to fumble with the English language, a tongue never intended to convey Indigenous ideas.[55] Many Cherokees saw English as utilitarian, not uplifting, and so traditionalists had little use for it.[56] The old and the young no longer spoke the same words, nor could many understand each other. When allotment came for the Cherokee Nation, "the old Indians were not asked" since it was assumed that they would disagree and, even if they did agree, that they would not be of any use.[57] The alienation these people felt during the allotment period led many to desire an "escape from the society dominated by whites and mixed-bloods who, to them, were white in their thinking."[58]

The prospect of United States citizenship, coupled with a new state forming in Oklahoma after the seeming destruction of their government, left many confused and afraid: "They lived in a constant fear of dispossession, not knowing that they were protected by the patent they refused to accept or, failing that, that they owned an allotment somewhere. And surrounding them with hungry eyes upon their land were the onrushing white men. Even at the best, the neat rectangular survey disrupted their simple agriculture and deprived them of the free range for their livestock."[59] One popular proposed remedy was emigration to Mexico, where many believed that they could purchase land and establish a community to live in a regime governed by the old ways.[60] There, they thought, Cherokees could live safely and *communally* on lands beyond the reach of greedy Americans. The precedent did exist. Nearly one hundred years earlier, in 1817, The Bowl had led Cherokees into Spanish-controlled Texas out of disgust with treaty arrangements back east.[61] While the Texas Cherokees did have an arrangement with the Mexican government, after Texas independence the Cherokees were driven out, fleeing to Indian Territory to join the Old Settlers in the 1830s. Chief John Ross himself had written to Joaquín María de Castillo y Lanzas of Mexico in 1835 to inquire about moving the main body of Cherokees to that country instead of Indian Territory.[62] Ross was, however, unsuccessful in brokering any such deal.

To preserve their old ways, traditionalists in 1895 led by Bird Harris—
brother of Cherokee Principal Chief C. J. Harris—began negotiating
with President Porfirio Díaz of Mexico to purchase a tract of land in
Sinaloa.[63] This group was so concerned about Congress extinguishing
their way of life that they were willing to part with their precious lands
in Indian Territory in the hopes of keeping their traditions alive elsewhere. This planned move soon fizzled out as Cherokee leaders soured
on the idea, leaving the mass of traditionalists leaderless and unable to
effect an emigration on their own without resources.[64] Their desires a
matter of public record, some ambitious men took notice and used the
promise of emigration to Mexico to seduce traditionalist Cherokees to
give up their lands and other assets to them in Indian Territory.[65] Allotment, however, diluted such schemes as greedy men were able to swindle
Cherokees out of their land via that system without much difficulty.

Allotment itself prevented many emigration dreams from coming
to life. The nature of allotments, according to scholar Henry E. Fritz,
condemned reservation Indians to poverty by trapping them on land
that they could not sell or alienate.[66] Indians were forcibly given the
"perilous gift of American citizenship" only to be despoiled as individuals under federal and Oklahoma state laws.[67] Emigration seemingly an
impossibility, Cherokee conservatives turned toward the idea of creating a traditionalist commonwealth in some isolated part of the Cherokee Nation. Sympathizers with this plan argued that the Treaty of New
Echota of 1835 guaranteed an Indian commonwealth, where certain
Indians who wished to could remain living communally as their ancestors had done.[68] However, Federal officials refused to entertain the idea
of Indians continuing to live communally, no matter how small the
group.

The Nighthawk Keetoowah Society nevertheless continued to fight
for the creation of a traditionalist commonwealth. The plans went so
far as to the erection of schoolhouses and other public buildings along
the southern border of the Cherokee Nation. In 1921, over one hundred traditionalists prepared to move to this proposed commonwealth,
the brainchild of Cherokees like Ed N. Washbourne, a leader among
the Keetoowahs, who argued that "the best people in the world are the
fullblood Indians. They are honest to a man. They are not honest like
the halfbreeds or the whites, just here and there . . . They can colonize

because they are not jealous of one another as whites or halfbreeds would be and they are not suspicious that someone will run off with the funds. They will build up an ideal commonwealth within the State of Oklahoma and subject to the state laws and soon every fullblood Cherokee Indian will be these and under the protection of the Nighthawks."[69] Philanthropist Dr. Charles Sumner Young, from California, pledged to help the Keetoowahs create their dream commonwealth. Working closely with Keetoowah Chief Sam Smith (son of Redbird Smith) and William C. Rogers, Young came to Oklahoma and created the Clara Barton–Sequoyah Foundation to oversee the project but died in 1926, after which time, his estate was divided and the money dried up. The financial logistics died with Young, who was buried at the site.[70]

ADAPTATION AFTER ALLOTMENT

By their agreement with the United States, the last election in the Cherokee Nation was held on July 1, 1902. The agreement also stipulated, among other things, that the US secretary of the interior would take possession of all Cherokee schools and would create town sites to give preferential treatment to squatters, that the *Cherokee Advocate* would be sold, and that the Cherokee Nation would exist no later than 1906, except for purposes of signing allotment deeds.[71] That same year, seventy-six-year-old Cherokee Nation citizen, writer, and statesman DeWitt Clinton Duncan told a Senate committee what it was like trying to survive after allotment: "I am in that fix, Senators, you will not forget now that when I use the word 'I' I mean the whole Cherokee people. I am in that fix. What am I to do? I have a piece of property that doesn't support me, and is not worth a cent to me, under the same inexorable, cruel provisions of the Curtis law that swept away our treaties, our system of nationality, our every existence, and wrested out of our possession our vast territory. . . ."[72] In their final election, the Cherokee people elected as principal chief William C. Rogers, who was predominantly responsible for signing deeds transferring land titles to individual allottees.[73] Rogers served as chief until his death in 1917; the United States retained him as someone with ostensible legitimacy who could guide Cherokees through their transition into life as American citizens. However, other leaders, like Redbird Smith, continued in their resistance to acculturation.[74]

ALLOTMENT AND TERMINATION

Redbird Smith's great ambition, Emmet Starr wrote, was "distinctly not" to "reestablish the old and discarded regime of the Cherokee Government, but to awaken a racial pride" to inspire well-off Cherokees to aid and care for their less fortunate brethren.[75] Redbird Smith's organization, the Nighthawk Keetoowahs, under the direction of Sam Smith, continued his mission to sustain Cherokee cultural mores after his father's death in 1918. The Nighthawk Keetoowahs maintained that the Cherokee people had much to offer the rest of the world: when the United States had become involved in the Great War in 1917, Redbird Smith "issued an edict to all the fires of the Nighthawk Keetoowahs" urging those who were eligible to sign up for the draft without hesitation and not to take advantage of their draft exemptions.[76] All but two eligible members heeded his call to arms, including John E. DeLozier, who was killed in action in France in 1918.[77] "Various Keetoowah organizations kept alive a Cherokee sense of being a people," Andrew Denson writes, "a sense that a distinct tribal community existed despite political reorganization and the loss of land."[78]

In 1920, Sam Smith, reflecting on the state of the Cherokee people, especially given their participation in the war, wrote a letter to Levi Gritts, imploring him to assume the mantle of principal chief of the Cherokees. By 1920, Smith hoped for a better relationship with the US government; he saw that the time was ripe for again distinguishing a political leader of Cherokees' own choosing to continue as a distinct community:

Pursuant to a well defined plan and program of the Nighthawk Keetoowahs of Full-blood Cherokee Indians, you have [b]een designated by the Council of said Society to serve our suffering cause in the capacity of CHIEF OF THE CHEROKEES.

. . . [B]eginning with the trying times of the year Nineteen Hundred, these people were overwhelmed with what seemed to them an attempt on the part of the United States government to divest them of what they considered their vested rights; they were all too suddenly divested of the rights and prerogatives of self determination in their National Governmental affairs, with the result that they eventually crystalized into a recalcitrant attitude. They looked askance upon every movement of the government, taking the position that every move now, meant exploitation of what little they have left of a once vast holdings.

This unfortunate position was largely justified . . . by the fact that a large number of their own blood, who had been fortunate enough to have received the advantage of literary training, now became the allies of the unscrupulous and exploiting hordes . . . who seem to destiny itself to have designed to always precede the wholesome citizenry . . .

. . . the loyal and unequivocal response of not only our Full-blood Nighthawks but of all the American Indians, to the Nation's call to Arms and Service in our recent World Struggle; all contribute to rehabilitate the Indians' self respect and confidence in themselves, as well as confidence in the integrity of purpose in their behalf on the part of the Government of the Unitd [sic] States.

. . . There is carried with this, a new psychological angle so far as the Full-blood Indian is concerned. For the first time in history he realizes through the attitude of the United States Government, that his material effects and his manhood as a National asset; that he is part and parcel of the body politic of a great Commonwealth. He is alert to the responsibilities of his new position. He is expecting participation in the administration of his affairs. . . . Within a decade the restricted period shall terminate and during that same space of time all our Claims against our Government may be adjudicated and finally settled.[79]

Smith argued that the people needed a representative who not only cared for them but who could also effectively lead them through the looming crisis brought on by the end of the allotment restriction period. Someone needed to deal with the Five Civilized Tribes' agency and with the commissioner of Indian affairs. The United States, however, appointed their own chiefs to serve as figureheads and sign documents: A. B. Cunningham in 1917, followed by Ed Frye in 1923 and Richard Choate in 1925.[80] Although some, as Wilma Mankiller put it, "erroneously assumed that the Cherokee Nation had ceased to exist" due to the absolute political control of the United States, cultural as well as legal life remained in that body despite American suppression.[81] Grassroots efforts to unify the people, like Smith's, continued. Cherokee leaders formed an executive council to conduct business and hold meetings with both Oklahoma and the United States and pursue their legal claims. The US government, meanwhile, refused to officially recognize the organization and "continued to operate with its own system of presidential appointees."[82] That system, however, was insufficient for the task, and under this type of administration Cherokees were swindled and cheated out of their lands and homes. Many sensational stories of "graft and kidnappings and murders of allottees whose tracts contained oil and mineral wealth attracted public attention," but these were not the norm.[83] Most Cherokees who lost their lands or money lost these through legal, albeit unethical, means: their abuse was part of the routine (mis)management of their allotments.

Congress passed the Indian Citizenship Act in 1924, which "conferred US citizenship on noncitizen Indians."[84] During the debates in the House of Representatives over the Indian Citizenship Act, Representative—and Cherokee Nation citizen—William Wirt Hastings (D-OK) spoke of the end of Indian affairs, stating that "during the present session of Congress everything has been done that has been possible to wind up the affairs of the Five Civilized Tribes."[85] Congress' optimistic appraisal of the situation, however, was not borne out by the reality in Oklahoma. While the act made Indians everywhere citizens of the United States, many states refused to acknowledge Indigenous peoples as full and equal citizens, especially when it came to jury duty, testifying in court, and voting, rights that would not be protected for decades.[86]

The Institute for Government Research released in 1928 the Meriam Report, the results of an investigation into the living conditions of Indigenous peoples.[87] This and subsequent, similar reports found the Cherokees and other Indians "menaced by famine" and "prolonged drought" while at the same time "the general financial depression made it impossible for them to secure work."[88] Confronted with this information, government officials were forced to recognize the failure of allotment policies to improve economic conditions among Indigenous peoples. While allotment may have required many to live in a manner more closely approximating white Americans, it did not provide the economic freedom many

Americans claimed would be open to Indians once they owned their lands in severalty.[89] Traditionalists were hit particularly hard because of the restrictions placed on their allotments: the land could not be alienated for twenty-five years. These restrictions, meant to protect traditionalists from "land grafters," also rendered them trapped and immobile. They could not sell their land to raise capital and so many sank into poverty and faced starvation.[90]

In 1944, author and poet Ruth Muskrat Bronson dramatized the consequences of allotment through the eyes of a fictional character, Jim Runningwolf:

Jim Runningwolf is typical of much of the Indian population. He doesn't know how to farm. His people were hunters. But he sits on his allotment wishing someone would come along and show him what to do. The Indian Agent comes along.

"You are not using your land," he says to Jim. "Why don't you let me lease it for you to that white farmer who was looking it over the other day?" All right with Jim. The government has always insisted it knew best anyway. So Jim Runningwolf and many others like him become petty landlords living in idleness on an annual rent barely sufficient to hold off starvation—never enough to lift the shadow of malnutrition from their households.

Then there is the problem of heirship. When Jim Runningwolf dies there will be four daughters and one son to inherit his one hundred and sixty acres. No one of the five heirs has enough money to buy out the other four. The usual way a white family handles such a situation is for the family member who wants to keep the farm to mortgage the land for enough to buy out the other heirs. The Runningwolf heirs can't do this for this land cannot be sold because Jim Runningwolf is a ward. So, in the absence of a will, the only thing to do would be to partition his land among the five heirs. In a country ill adapted to agriculture, thirty-five acres are not worth much money, so the land will probably not be partitioned. Instead, the government will go on leasing the land, dividing the lease money among the heirs down through the generations.[91]

Thus did the United States government keep Cherokees and other Indigenous people dependent on the United States during the time of allotment.[92]

FEDERAL POLICY SHIFT

In what Vine Deloria Jr. called "perhaps the only bright spot in all of Indian-Congressional relations," the Wheeler-Howard Act—or Indian Reorganization Act—of 1934 declared Congress' intentions to end allotment period policies and permit tribes to organize for political and economic reasons.[93] During the 1920s, thanks in part to the Merriam Report, there was a growing sense among reform groups that Indian life needed to be drastically improved.[94] Reform movements culminated in the Reorganization Act that sought to "revive traditional tribal institutions and integrate them with a program" for economic rehabilitation.[95] Yet, while Congress was willing to grant more autonomy to tribes, there was doubt among US officials that Indians were ready for self-government: the allotment and termination periods had sunk many into extreme destitution and the lack of strong internal government had bred corruption.[96]

In 1933, President Franklin Roosevelt appointed sociologist John Collier commissioner of Indian Affairs. Collier was sympathetic toward the plight of Indigenous peoples and actively fought against the injustices of allotment. Collier and his solicitor, Felix Cohen, cowrote the bill that became the Wheeler-Howard Act to, as Collier put it, end the allotment system "with its train of evil consequences."[97] The Indian Reorganization Act ended allotment practices, providing that "hereafter no land of any Indian reservation, created or set apart by treaty of agreement with the Indians . . . shall be allotted in severalty to any Indian."[98] It also authorized the secretary of the interior to restore to tribal ownership the remaining surplus of lands of any reservation previously opened to sale. This act provided for the self-government of their reservations by Indian residents. Thereafter, the Indian Bureau began to recognize tribal groups as eligible for government services, including New Deal programs for rehabilitation.[99]

Thirty years into the allotment era, many people had internalized the idea that DNA, or blood quantum, indicated identity.[100] Identity was often used as a statement instead of being conveyed by an activity or set of lived experiences. Tribal nations thus wrestled with multiple competing definitions of identity as they reorganized in the wake of Wheeler-Howard. Two years later, Congress extended the principles of the Wheeler-Howard Act to Indians living in Oklahoma with the Oklahoma Indian Welfare Act of 1936.[101] A decade after that, Congress passed the Indian Claims Commission Act, which permitted a pseudo-Cherokee government to bring lawsuits before the Indian Claims Commission and allowed Cherokees to participate in federal programs.[102] Presidentially appointed Chief Jesse Bartley Milam (Milam was elected by a grassroots Cherokee movement in 1938; Roosevelt and Truman later confirmed his appointment) called a tribal convention in 1948 to select an executive committee to attend to other political matters, like choosing attorneys to prosecute cases.[103] He also began purchasing property to be held in trust for the Cherokee Nation—roughly 21,000 acres.[104] Upon Chief Milam's death, President Truman assigned the office of principal chief to William Wayne Keeler, an oilman, who would be heavily involved in Cherokee politics for the next three decades.[105]

In the 1940s, amid growing unrest, a group of Cherokees identifying themselves as Keetoowah people, descendants of the Old Settlers—believing that "Kituwah" or "Keetoowah" was the original name of the Cherokees—sought and received congressional recognition as a separate tribal organization.[106] Congress officially recognized the group as the United Keetoowah Band of Oklahoma (UKB) in 1946; in 1950 a constitution and bylaws, plus a corporation charter, were ratified. The tribal nation claimed to include descendants from *true* Cherokees who had worked to preserve traditional mores.[107] Their membership originates from a list of members identified by a resolution dated April 19, 1949—certified by the superintendent of the Five Civilized Tribes agency.[108] From the beginning, the UKB imposed a one-quarter Indian blood quantum minimum upon its members in their effort to maintain a racially Cherokee community.[109]

Under Keeler's leadership, however, the Cherokee Nation leaned in a different direction. When it came to identifying Cherokees, Keeler's regime gradually built a policy that considered those with even the smallest degree of Cherokee blood to be citizens, reflecting the state of their de facto leaders, a policy more lenient than their neighbors.

The federal government, however, still operated under a system that identified those with at least one-quarter Indian blood as Cherokee.[110] As he engaged in state-building, Keeler surrounded himself with a "white-Cherokee elite," which came to dominate business and political life in eastern Oklahoma.[111] Through their influence, the executive committee sought greater control of Cherokee political affairs, creating the "Five Civilized Tribes Intertribal Council" and later, in 1952, the Cherokee Foundation Inc., which "operated much like a charity organization" to help those in need.[112]

The momentum of this New Deal–era federal policy had slowed, however, after World War II ended, when bureaucrats believed tribal governments were outdated in the new world order.[113] Collier had resigned in 1944 and the Eisenhower administration renewed attempts to terminate tribal organizations and acculturate Indigenous peoples. Termination and relocation policies constituted a new plan to end the "government's trust relationship over Indian lands" and relocate native residents to new homes in urban centers.[114] Wilma Mankiller, who was relocated under the federal relocation program as a little girl, explained that the "government wanted to break up tribal communities and 'mainstream' Indians," so they moved them to where they might become more *American*.[115] House Concurrent Resolution 108 in 1953 "announced Congress' purpose to end tribal wardship" and "sever federal obligations to tribes" to further facilitate assimilation.[116]

The Meriam Report had shown Indians in a "desperate situation" and that allotment policies and mismanagement had created "no progress of any kind" on tribal reservations.[117] Rather than assimilating Indigenous peoples into the American culture, allotment and its abuse had left Cherokees and others poor and destitute. President Truman had in 1950 appointed Dillon S. Myer his commissioner of Indian Affairs—the same man who had been in charge of the Japanese internment camps during World War II—for the latter's experience in dealing with minority rights.[118] Myer's work, though he would leave office in 1953, set the tone for the next decade. The Republican wave after World War II sought ways to cut back on New Deal policies, including Indian welfare programs, among others, and decided that the best way to solve the "Indian problem"—and reduce expenses—would be to physically move them again.

To release Indians "from the confines of tribal communities," Myer and his successors in the Bureau of Indian Affairs encouraged *freeing* Cherokees from the communities that held them back from assimilation.[119] Cherokees lost access to federal services and protections. Large numbers of Cherokees had fled Oklahoma during the Great Depression, in what Chad Smith has called an "Economic Trail of Tears."[120] In the mid-1950s, the federal government started moving more Cherokees to big cities like Chicago, St. Louis, Los Angeles, and Detroit, to live as individual, economically independent Americans. The Mankiller family's poverty drove them to sign up for the relocation program in 1955, a traumatic event in the life of young Wilma Mankiller, who would vividly remember the racism she experienced in San Francisco and the pain of leaving their home for the rest of her life.[121] Local efforts to organize and aid the Cherokee people, however, continued in spite of these federal policies.

RESTRUCTURING THE CHEROKEE NATION

Historian Daniel M. Cobb writes that by the 1960s many Oklahomans "accepted the fiction that tribal authority had been subsumed by the state and that Cherokee history and peoplehood were, for all intents and purposes, things of the past."[122] The reality was very different: the Cherokee Nation, under the direction of federally appointed William Wayne Keeler, "was poised to reassert itself as a political and economic force," thanks in part to a $14.7 million settlement they had secured in 1961.[123] Most of the funds went to "Cherokee citizens by blood" (freedmen, left out of the distribution, sought legal remedy but were denied), while the rest was "left in the hands of the chief."[124] Keeler and his associates invested the funds into tribal programs, including the creation of the Cherokee National Historical Society (CNHS) in 1963 to operate the Cherokee Heritage Center.[125] The Cherokee Heritage Center was dedicated to keeping alive Cherokee art, theater, and traditions, and to maintaining important archives: "a site of knowledge sharing and the perpetuation of Cherokee culture."[126] The federal government also declared lands owned around Tahlequah, Oklahoma, "surplus" and returned it to the Cherokee Nation, which led to the construction of tribal office buildings, laying the groundwork for renewed government activities in earnest.[127] Keeler's efforts, however, were not the only works being done to restructure the Cherokee Nation in the 1960s.

Chief Keeler proved controversial, especially for many traditionalist communities, some of whom claimed that he "failed to understand the needs and desires of culturally conservative Cherokees and that his administration empowered the tribe's more acculturated members at the expense of traditional communities."[128] It did not help the cultural divide among Cherokees that Keeler was not democratically elected either.[129] A group of traditionalists led by George Groundhog created the Original Cherokee Community Organization (OCCO) in protest against their current governors.[130] Groundhog and his allies were opposed to Keeler's leadership and his business connections and, though they had little money, attempted themselves to cultivate traditional mores among Cherokees, arguing that their way was purer than Keeler's.[131] "Members of the traditional Keetoowah, Seven Clans, and Four Mothers societies" all soon began pushing for the popular election of the principal chief "in hopes of bringing to office someone who embodied their values."[132]

The OCCO had also organized in reaction to Oklahoma's restrictions on hunting and fishing that, OCCO leaders argued, suppressed Cherokees in exercising their natural liberties since hunting is at "the very core of Cherokee existence."[133] A group of young Cherokees challenged Oklahoma law by staging a "hunt-in" that resulted in the arrest of a man named John Chewie in 1966.[134] The state charged Chewie with hunting out of season and without a license. Chewie subsequently appeared in court in Jay, Oklahoma, admitting the charges and arguing that he was a "full-blooded Cherokee and he would not apologize for hunting on land that rightfully belonged to his people; nor did he have to be licensed like a dog by the state."[135] He had hunted to feed his family, Chewie claimed, a most natural thing that the state had no business restricting. On the morning of Chewie's court appearance, four hundred armed Cherokees showed up in Jay, waiting to hear the verdict. The case was held over for federal court, however, and no violence occurred that day. The case was eventually dismissed by the district court in Tulsa.[136]

The War on Poverty further fanned the flames of division. Federal money came to Oklahoma after the passage of the Economic Opportunity Act in 1964 to fund "programs for the poor, including Job Corps, Head Start, Neighborhood Youth Corps, and Legal Services."[137] The

Community Action Program, however, proved the most divisive. The guiding philosophy of the program was that those living in poverty ought to be empowered to "design, implement, and administer programs that affected their lives."[138] However, this did not mean, as many thought, that Cherokee communities would be empowered via renewed self-governance. The Office of Economic Opportunity (OEO) sent a task force to discuss the situation with the Cherokee Executive Council, who claimed that "it should possess exclusive power to administer all of the programs for tribal members" because of Cherokees' legal status as *Indians.*[139] The OEO, however, refused, arguing that monies had to be spread equally to those in a given region (selected by the government) and could not be given exclusively to Indian communities. The OEO, as United States agencies had before, determined "whether Cherokees had secured equitable representation in War on Poverty programs" based on legal identity and not on "definitions of community";[140] that is, the government again counted *blood* over *belonging.* Their accounting did not lead to the self-government promised by the program but rather heightened animosity between those in power and many traditionalists.

During the 1960s the global community was experiencing a wave of decolonization efforts, the culmination of international protests and demonstrations that had been going on since the end of the Second World War.[141] These protests—in America over the destruction of culture, the "loss of sovereignty attached to the reservations," the loss of "rights over protected lands," and the loss of "funding for health and education" services since the early 1950s—provoked determined responses among Indigenous organizations like the National Indian Youth Council in 1961 and the American Indian Movement (AIM) in 1968.[142] The Indian Civil Rights Act was also passed in 1968, which applied most of the US Bill of Rights to tribal governments. Principal Chief Keeler and the executive committee eventually created a system of community representatives: locally elected delegates who gradually "replaced the executive committee as the chief's advisors."[143] The emerging republic soon joined in with the chorus of Indigenous communities across the United States in urging Congress to restore to them the power of self-determination.

In a special message to Congress on Indian affairs in 1970, President Richard Nixon elaborated on his plan for Indian *self-determination.*[144] The "deprived and most isolated" condition of Indigenous peoples, Nixon said, "is the heritage of centuries of injustice." He argued that it was high time that federal Indian policies recognized the "capacities and insights of the Indian people. Both as a matter of justice and as a matter of enlightened social policy, we must begin to act on the basis of what the Indians themselves have long been telling us." Self-determination would therefore be a policy era in which the federal government made certain efforts to end the suppression of Indian self-government that prevented tribal nations from pursuing their own courses.

Congress passed the Principal Chiefs Act in 1970, which provided that the Cherokees and other tribes could popularly elect their own chiefs.[145] In 1971, for the first time since 1902, the Cherokees elected their own chief: Keeler, having served as appointed chief for so long, ran now and won.[146] Voter eligibility in this election was based on the Dawes Rolls. The Cherokees began once more to organize and implement a new government apparatus, obtaining approval from Congress in 1971. The decades without a functioning government, however, had exacted a heavy price: "Through a combination of allotment forgeries, embezzlements, misuse of notary seals, and other crimes, the overwhelming majority of land allotted to Cherokee citizens had found its way into white hands. The Nation's population had fallen to only 40,000 citizens, and federal government agencies had taken over responsibility for delivering services to individual Cherokee allottees."[147] The 1970 census revealed that many Cherokee people were living in abject poverty, without running water or electricity; the average adult had roughly five years of education.[148] Yet, as Wilma Mankiller later put it, "no one ever gave up the dream of a revitalized Cherokee Nation."[149] Organizations like the OCCO and CNHS, despite their differences, continued to work for Cherokees to provide a means to protect their rights.

Nineteen seventy-five was a landmark year for the Cherokee Nation. That year Congress passed the Indian Self-Determination and Education Assistance Act, which provided that tribes could contract with the Bureau of Indian Affairs to operate certain public programs for themselves. Keeler declined to run for reelection that year; he and his company, Phillips Petroleum, had been accused of making illegal contributions to Richard Nixon's presidential campaign. Keeler instead handpicked Ross Swimmer, a young lawyer, as his successor and backed his candidacy, even going so far as to restructure the election rules to allow Swimmer—who, under the rules, was too young—to run for principal chief. Keeler also restructured the filing deadline to allow Swimmer's application through.[150]

Upon Swimmer's election, the new chief moved quickly to form a group to work on a new constitution for the Cherokee Nation. Chief Swimmer characterized the reform movement in the Nation as "all over the place"—some people wanted to reinstate the 1839 constitution while others wanted something entirely different—so he took matters into his own hands.[151] The new Constitution of the Cherokee Nation was ratified in 1976. While this document differed from its predecessors in the nineteenth century, it was similar in its commitment to exclusive citizenship.

THE THIRD DURABLE SHIFT
IN CHEROKEE CITIZENSHIP

From 1907 to 1975 the Cherokee Nation government lay dormant, but that did not stop people from building a sense of nationhood where they lived. Out of the many moving pieces in this era, initial distinctions emerge: acculturation versus traditionalism. There were those who leaned into allotment and those who fled in its wake. Some tried to build a sense of Cherokee nationhood by integrating into American society, others by remaining in traditionalist enclaves.[152] Yet, despite these differences, Kirby Brown argues, Cherokee people continued to *stoke the fire* by holding on to that which united them: a desire to cultivate relationships and work for the common good; kinship; a shared history; and a drive to carry that honored legacy forward.[153] Many continued to find strength by living out *gadugi* obligations despite federal government attempts to undermine it.[154]

Politics, meanwhile, proved divisive. How could a dormant Cherokee Nation determine citizenship? The term "dormant," in this case, is important: the Cherokee Nation had not been destroyed. Perhaps "sleeping fitfully" is a more apt description. Despite their efforts to terminate the formal Cherokee Republic, the United States in fact perpetuated it by continuing to appoint chiefs with nominal authority. Moreover, Congress never disestablished the reservations during allotment.[155] The "dormant" Cherokee Nation, therefore, technically retained its legal boundaries. The Cherokee Executive Council, by the 1920s and 1930s, took shape and coalesced into a functional body that could act.[156] As New Deal policies afforded tribal nations more autonomy, however, the question arose: How would a Cherokee Nation that had suffered allotment and the Great Depression identify its members? In other words, how could a physically and ideologically divided Cherokee people establish a policy to keep citizenship exclusive?

Some sought remedy in US legal recognition. The United Keetoowah Band of Cherokee Indians, self-identified descendants of Old Settlers, created their own sovereign tribal government and required that members prove one-quarter Cherokee blood quantum to participate.[157] According to scholar Georgia Rae Leeds, UKB leadership argued that, because they lived among and could speak for local communities, they possessed greater legitimacy than Cherokee Nation appointees.[158] The Cherokee Nation, however, pushed back against strict blood quantum requirements for its citizens before ultimately landing upon descendance from someone listed on the Dawes Rolls as its metric in the 1970s. The political divisions, of course, were not clean. Some Cherokee Nation leaders were highly acculturated and fought against strict blood quantum standards for citizenship so that they, their friends, and their families could enjoy the practical benefits of citizenship and retain power—echoing the efforts of John Ross, Elias Boudinot, and John Ridge in the 1820s. Some were also traditionalists, like Crosslin Smith, recruited by Chief Keeler "to do reconstruction and build Cherokee Nation to get the general public of the Cherokee people involved" in the arduous task of self-government.[159]

US federal policy played no small part in these debates. Americans determined "Indianness" based on blood quantum; those with at least one-quarter Cherokee blood were Cherokees.[160] Confusing and contradictory US regulations had left viable a Cherokee Nation that they had intended to destroy; they also perpetuated racial categorization despite professed attempts to assimilate Indians. Membership in the Cherokee Nation, to federal officials, was a mere statement of biology. These policies and attitudes encouraged Cherokee people to view themselves in the same light. Before the concerted attack on their regime at the end of the nineteenth century, Cherokees had known who was Cherokee by how they lived their lives: whether people practiced *gadugi,* participated in traditional activities, spoke the language, or otherwise supported

Cherokee sovereignty and community. The wave of Progressive liberal nationalism that demanded the destruction of tribal governments also demanded the destruction of *cultural knowing*. Despite Progressives like Michael Cunniff (who did indeed have a vision of American citizenship as active, industrious, and innovative—a sort of Tocquevillian *commercial hero*) professing their desire to assimilate Cherokees into the American lifestyle, Americans instead encouraged Indigenous peoples to view citizenship as a statement, not as a way of life.[161]

David Wilkins and Shelly Wilkins have shown how, with few exceptions, before the new era of Native self-determination in the 1970s, "Native communities did not engage in disenrollment, banishment, or exclusion of bona fide members or even nonmembers very often, and when such expulsions or disenfranchisements were carried out only the rare individual was targeted, not entire families."[162] Since their major reconstruction efforts after the Indian Reorganization Act, Native governments began heavily using the language of the federal government, that of "blood quantum," or in many cases "fractions of blood," to determine membership or citizenship.[163] The influence of federal policies and attitudes in the early twentieth century has led to an increased focus on racial purity—tribal policies designed to prioritize race when determining authentic tribal belonging.

※

SELF-DETERMINATION AND THE DAWES ROLLS
1975–2017

REVEREND ROGER H. NERO, a Baptist minister, was a descendent of Cherokee freedmen and had lived as a Cherokee citizen during the termination period. Nero was one of the original enrollees listed on the freedmen portion of the Dawes Rolls—aged three at the time.[1] His family had received an allotment and had participated in cash land settlements over the next few decades.[2] Freedmen during the termination period had also participated in educational and housing benefits but had not qualified for federal benefits provided for other tribal members. On June 18, 1983, Nero and four companions, also freedmen, were turned away at the polls when they tried to vote in the Cherokee Nation election that year. They were turned away despite having voted in previous Cherokee Nation elections as recently as 1979. The officials who turned them away told them that freedmen no longer had the right to vote because they were not Cherokees by blood.

Nero responded by organizing a resistance movement, publicly stating: "We weren't allowed to vote because we were freedmen. They said that we didn't have Cherokee blood, but when I was born my birth certificate said that I was declared a citizen of the Cherokee Nation."[3] One year later, in 1984, Nero and other freedmen filed a class action suit against Principal Chief Swimmer, the tribal election committee, the United States, the Bureau of Indian Affairs, and a host of other individuals and agencies, alleging that the Cherokee Nation had systematically discriminated against them because of their race. Nero and his companions wanted $750 million in damages and to have the last Cherokee Nation election declared null and void.[4] "All we are trying to do is fight for our rights," Nero argued. "We want them to see us."[5]

Cherokee leaders, as they reconstituted their nation, wrestled over the definition of citizenship. The new constitution stated that "All members of the Cherokee Nation must be citizens as proven by reference to the Dawes Commission Rolls," including the Delaware and Shawnee agreements made in the 1860s.[6] "Many people," Wilma Mankiller recalled, "thought a requirement of one-quarter blood quantum should have been instituted," while others "objected to the inclusion of the Delawares and Shawnees" or the "exclusion of the Cherokee freedmen and intermarried whites."[7] While Mankiller argued that the Dawes Rolls referred to in the constitution meant only the Cherokee Rolls, Nero argued that the text of the constitution meant that all of the Dawes enrollees counted, including the freedmen. They were debating two different approaches to citizenship policy, *blood as ancestry* and *blood as culture*, through the lens of the Dawes Rolls.

After several years, Nero's case reached the Tenth Circuit Court of Appeals, which ruled in 1989 that the dispute between the freedmen and the Cherokee Nation was an intratribal affair; the United States had no jurisdiction.[8] The court held that the Cherokee Nation had the right to remain a "politically and culturally distinct entity," which prevented the United States from interfering. Since the integration of freedmen via the Treaty of 1866, the Cherokee Nation had consistently resisted full incorporation.[9] In the 1970s and 1980s, after decades of federal policies requiring that individuals prove Indian blood to be eligible for government programs, Cherokee Nation leaders leaned toward policies that acknowledged Cherokee blood as the true basis for citizenship. While the use of blood quanta did not have roots in historical precedent, restricting citizenship to those with Cherokee blood did.[10] As Cherokee Nation policies were debated and solidified, people like Reverend Nero were caught in the crossfire and lost their status as Cherokee Nation citizens. For the next thirty-odd years, Cherokees debated one another—and the Nation wrestled with the United States—over who had the right to declare who was Cherokee.

THE NEW CHEROKEE CONSTITUTION

In many ways, the Cherokee Nation established a government from the ground up in the 1970s. While guided by the lessons of history, the Cherokee people, as Ross Swimmer put it, had to relearn how to self-govern.[11] The 1975 constitution reflected a corporate model of government whereby officials acted as a board of directors overseeing tribal affairs. Swimmer viewed the Cherokee Nation "not necessarily as a government but as an organization" akin to a nonprofit with a budget of $10,000.[12] The new constitution reflected this outlook with its minimalistic approach to institutional structure.

The new government had three separate branches, legislative, executive, and judicial, yet these were structured differently than they had been in the previous 1839 Cherokee Nation Constitution. The legislative power was vested in the Council of the Cherokee Nation, a unicameral body consisting of fifteen members, all "members by blood" of the Cherokee Nation, each elected at large.[13] This unicameral body was more responsible for organizing the distribution of services than governing. At the time, with many Cherokee people scattered geographically, this Council fulfilled the need for reform and served as a rallying point for the reinvigorated Cherokee Nation, then some 40,000 strong.[14] Councillors served for terms of four years.

During the nineteenth century, and again after the Indian Reorganization Act passed in 1934, the federal government had pressured tribal nations to adopt unicameral legislative bodies. Given traditional Indigenous preferences for reaching consensus rather than submitting to simple majority rule, US officials urged unicameralism to make tribes come to decisions more quickly, without a lot of unnecessary deliberation, they argued. Swimmer maintained that a small unicameral legislature would increase energy in that body and serve as a means to improve the delivery of services to Cherokee citizens.[15] The primary function of this new Cherokee Council was therefore more administrative and less deliberative than the bicameral National Council of the past.

The principal chief, similar to the 1839 provision, would be elected by popular vote. Candidates for the office also needed to be members "by blood" of the Cherokee Nation; the office of deputy principal chief was created with the same stipulation. The judicial power was vested in the Judicial Appeals Tribunal, which consisted of three judges to be appointed by the principal chief and approved by the Council for terms set by the Council.[16] All elected officials had to possess Cherokee blood to run for office. The preference for Cherokee blood to participate in the Cherokee Nation government via elected office continued throughout the document, following the long trend of their constitutional history.

Notably, Article XIV provides the first mention in any Cherokee Nation constitution of clans by providing that "nothing in this Constitution shall be construed to prohibit the right of any Cherokee to belong to a recognized clan or organization in the Cherokee Nation." Since Congress' suppression of the old Cherokee government in the 1900s, Cherokees had drawn strength from and sought the protection of nongovernmental organizations such as the Keetoowah Society or the OCCO, among others.[17] Clan or organization membership here, however, did not by itself constitute legal citizenship in the Cherokee Nation.

Article II, relative to the Bill of Rights, referred simply to the Indian Civil Rights Act of 1968, which "shall apply to all members of the Cherokee Nation." The Indian Civil Rights Act made provisions of the US Bill of Rights applicable to tribal nations and included protections for speech and due process of law, among others. The Cherokee Nation, however, as it had in centuries past, still operated a national newspaper, named in the 1970s the *Cherokee Advocate*.

Article XV reserved to the Cherokee people the power of the initiative and the referendum to shape and alter tribal laws. The referendum was also the method by which the people could call for a new constitutional convention. Article XV, Section 9, required that the question of a constitutional convention be submitted to the people once every twenty years—a nod to Thomas Jefferson's famous prescription for democratic accountability. Section 10 of the same article, however, required that any amendment or new constitution must receive the approval of the president of the United States or his representative, thereby limiting the power of the Cherokee Nation to amend or supersede its governing document. This was necessary, Swimmer contended, to ensure that the United States supported the rebuilt republic.

Article III, Section 1, provided a new articulation of citizenship. Its statement, however, that "all members of the Cherokee Nation must be citizens as proven by reference to the Dawes Commission Rolls" left a few things open to interpretation. A textual reading of the clause might lead some to conclude that all the Dawes Rolls, including the white and freedmen rolls, counted. An originalist reading, however, might contend that only the Cherokee Rolls counted, especially since the ability to run for certain tribal offices depended on proof of Cherokee blood.

Swimmer, reflecting back on citizenship in the 1975 constitution, wrote,

> In 1975 we established, through the constitution, that one had to be either on—or a lineal descendant of—someone who was on the 1906 Dawes Commission Roll. And on the Dawes Commission roll there were approximately 41,000 Cherokees enrolled. So in order to be a member of the tribe one has to prove his ancestry back to a person on that roll. . . . That's somewhat arbitrary. . . . One of the reasons why we oppose blood quantum for membership is that there really is no way of determining what blood quantum is . . . [W]e treated membership as citizenship in a nation, not blood quantum.[18]

In a 1984 interview, Chief Swimmer defended the Cherokee Nation's articulation of citizenship against Nero's legal challenges:

> To run for office you must be a Cherokee by blood. I can't argue with that. I think it means what it says. The President of the US must be a natural born citizen. . . . The Cherokee Nation, good, bad, or otherwise, specifically says that to be an elected official you must be a Cherokee by blood. . . . The best evidence . . . has been a certificate of Degree of Indian Blood. . . . We provide services from the federal government using the federal government's guidelines. . . . Every program we get comes from the federal government and it comes with strings attached.[19]

Rebuilding the Cherokee Nation presented logistical problems when it came to determining citizenship. As Swimmer noted, the Nation was incentivized to adhere to the federal government's method for determining eligibility for certain programs—Cherokee Nation leaders decided that blood, but not one-quarter blood quantum, combined with a proven connection to someone listed on the Dawes Rolls, was a good method for determining Cherokee citizenship for legal purposes. The Dawes Rolls also made sense from a practical standpoint. They were an extant list of those living in the Nation. Congress had authorized the rolls and was therefore likely to presume that their own work was valid; avoiding federal challenges was another incentive for Cherokee Nation leaders in adhering to the Dawes Rolls to determine citizenship.

Figure 6 shows an updated Idea Pyramid, reflecting the official policy adopted by the Cherokee Nation in the 1970s and 1980s. To keep citizenship exclusive, leaders chose to strictly adhere to the Dawes Rolls but eschewed blood quantum restrictions utilized elsewhere by the federal government and other tribal nations, like the United Keetoowah Band and the Eastern Band of the Cherokees. Yet the exact relationship between citizenship and blood in the constitution was vague: over the next few decades, the Council would tend toward using blood in determining full citizenship, as the ability to run for elected office and receive certain benefits depended on *blood as ancestry*.

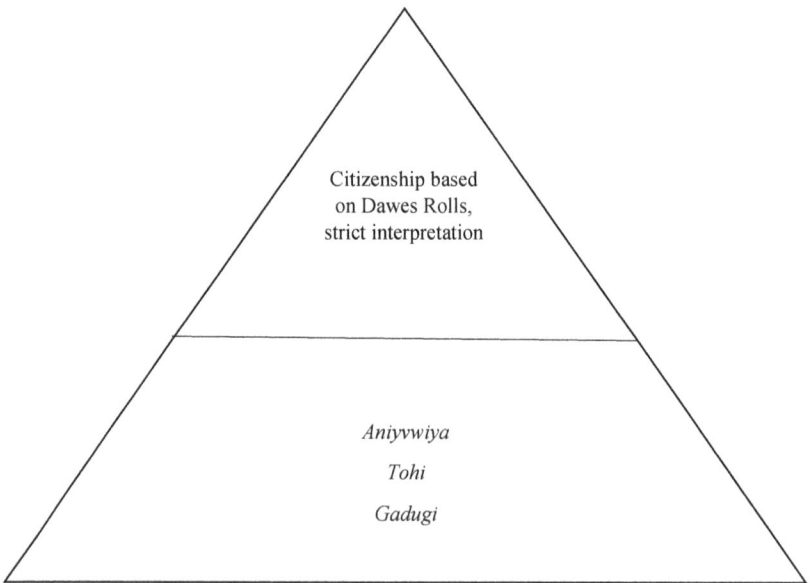

Citizenship based
on Dawes Rolls,
strict interpretation

Aniyvwiya

Tohi

Gadugi

Figure 6. Foundational and Policy Ideas about Cherokee Nation Citizenship, 1975–2017

The treatment of citizenship in the 1975 constitution reflects the same commitment to the foundational idea that citizenship should be exclusive—in this case, as exclusive as possible, given certain constraints. The long history of US interference in Cherokee governance forced a permanent shift away from nineteenth-century citizenship laws. The policy idea of citizenship in the 1970s, therefore, had to be different from what came before. By using the Dawes Rolls as the standard by which to determine citizenship, Cherokee leaders hoped to placate the United States—since the Dawes Rolls were a US project—while remaining dedicated to the principle of exclusive citizenship.

A GROWING NATION

On February 28, 1977, the *Cherokee Advocate* reported on the state of the nation.[20] The newspaper was the result of the merger of two previous papers into one and, like its predecessors in the nineteenth century, run by the Cherokee government. The Council had spent the previous year passing legislation setting procedural rules for meetings, providing compensation for councillors, and establishing the fiscal year. The article also discussed the ongoing registration efforts in the Nation; those who registered under the new rules received a card that displayed their blood quantum. A month prior, the Five Tribes Intertribal Council had decided to self-impose a limit of one-quarter-degree blood quantum. Cherokee Nation leadership, however, was prepared to "take care of all Tribal members regardless of blood degree," as long as individuals possessed at least some.

Later that year, Chief Swimmer announced how monies awarded the Cherokee Nation under the Local Public Works Act would be used to improve the infrastructure of Tahlequah, Oklahoma, the seat of the Cherokee Nation government.[21] Cherokee leaders anticipated an increase in the number of Cherokee citizens and their continued growth as a governmental presence in eastern Oklahoma. True to the corporate model of government Swimmer and others had advocated, the Council did very little by way of legislative acts in those first few years apart from setting down the rules for basic government operations.

The year 1978 was another landmark year in United States federal Indian policy. Congress passed the Indian Child Welfare Act (ICWA), which protected the rights of Indian children, families, and tribes in cases where parents were deemed incompetent to retain custody. The ICWA was a response to decades of United States efforts to "systematically remove Indigenous children from their families and place them into white foster and adoptive homes."[22] ICWA had two goals: to defend against colonial violence and create new institutional structures to rebuild and strengthen the capacity of Indigenous nations to self-govern and sustain and support their citizenry. That same year the United States Supreme Court decided in the case of *Santa Clara Pueblo v. Martinez*, ruling that tribal governments retained as an inherent power the right to decide who could or could not be a tribal citizen.[23] Both events helped strengthen Cherokee Nation sovereignty by bolstering their ability to self-determine authentic tribal belonging.

That year the Council established rules and regulations for conducting elections and created the Tribal Election Committee.[24] The act provided that all enrolled citizens of the Cherokee Nation whose names (or whose ancestor's names) appeared on the Dawes Rolls and who were also over the age of eighteen and registered to vote "shall be entitled to vote in all elections and referendums of the Cherokee Nation." The act reaffirmed that candidates for principal chief and deputy chief must be members by blood of the Cherokee Nation and present a certificate of degree of Indian blood, issued by the Bureau of Indian Affairs. The Tribal Election Committee would have the final say in matters of elections, ballots, and candidate applications.

The Tribal Election Committee members soon realized that using Certificates of Degree of Indian Blood as a metric for registering citizens and establishing election regulations was untenable since some people "had simply purchased membership" from the Bureau of Indian Affairs or had "provided a Dawes Roll number that was not verified through any other documentation."[25] The Tribal Election Committee decided that the election of 1979 would be the last election in which old registration cardholders could vote. This coincided with the Cherokee Nation's ongoing efforts to purge their tribal citizenship rolls—efforts that tended to favor those with Cherokee blood over those without.[26] As the election of 1983 approached, the Tribal Election Committee waived the Certificate of Degree of Indian Blood requirement for original Dawes enrollees, including freedmen and intermarried whites.[27] According to the law as it stood in 1983, Cherokees, freedmen, and whites all ostensibly had the right to vote, while only Cherokees by blood could run as candidates. Yet Reverend Nero and other freedmen were turned away anyway.

The election of 1983 was hotly contested: it featured a race for principal chief in which incumbent Ross Swimmer, alongside deputy chief candidate Wilma Mankiller, faced off against Perry Wheeler and Agnes Cowen (who had been the first woman to sit on the tribal council). respectively. After the polls closed, Wheeler had received 3,300 votes to Swimmer's 2,437, yet after the host of absentee ballots were counted, Swimmer was declared the winner by fewer than 500 votes.[28] Wheeler demanded a recount and took the case before the Judicial Appeals Tribunal, alleging, among other things, that freedmen voters had been disenfranchised because they supported Wheeler and Cowen. Wheeler ultimately lost both the legal case and the election. The race for deputy chief, however, was too close to call and a runoff election was scheduled. Mankiller, a community organizer and activist who had occupied Alcatraz during protests in the late 1960s and early 1970s, defeated Cowen in the runoff to become deputy chief of the Cherokee Nation.[29]

Two years later, President Ronald Reagan appointed Ross Swimmer assistant secretary of the interior for Indian Affairs, an act that, via Article VI of the Cherokee Constitution, promoted Wilma Mankiller to the office of principal chief—the first woman chief of the Cherokee Nation.[30] While Mankiller had received death threats, suffered insults, and had her tires slashed when she ran for deputy chief, she reportedly found the transition to principal chief relatively tranquil.[31] "I certainly love my work," Mankiller said. "I plan to stay on the same path. I've never felt better about the Cherokee Nation."[32] To continue carrying out the work of rebuilding the Cherokee Nation, now nearly 70,000 tribal members strong, Mankiller inherited a nation with an annual budget of $40 million and roughly 700 employees.[33] In 1987, Chief Mankiller won the office outright in her own reelection bid.

Under the Mankiller Administration, the Cherokee Nation continued to shape its election and membership policies. In February 1987, the twelve members of the Council present unanimously passed an act amending the 1978 election law, leaning into policies that privileged Cherokee blood to obtain full access to certain aspects of citizenship, such as voting or running for office. The previous law read: "All enrolled citizens of the Cherokee Nation of Oklahoma whose names appear on the Dawes Commission Roll, or any person 18 years of age or above who has a lineal ancestor on the above mentioned roll and who is registered to vote as provided herein shall be entitled to vote in all elections and referendums of the Cherokee Nation . . ."[34] The amended provision read: "All enrolled citizens of the Cherokee Nation of Oklahoma whose name appear on the Dawes Commission Roll or who have a lineal ancestor whose name appears on that Roll, who are eighteen (18) years of age or older and who possess a certification of Degree of Indian Blood, and are registered to vote as provided herein shall be entitled to vote in all elections and referendum . . ."[35]

National enrollment continued to balloon. In 1989 the Cherokee Nation boasted 96,510 registered tribal citizens.[36] A year later, in 1990, Councilor Muskrat reported to the Council a national enrollment of 106,017.[37] As the Nation increased in size, Chief Mankiller emphasized the need to "state publicly and very firmly" that the Cherokee Nation represents "not only those with a nominal amount of Cherokee blood, but represent[s] all Cherokees."[38] That same year the US Court of Appeals, Tenth Circuit, ruled in the case of *Ross v. Neff* that Oklahoma did not have jurisdiction on Indian land. This ruling followed on the heels of a 1988 decision in *Muskogee (Creek) Nation, a Federally Recognized Indian Tribe, Appellant v. Donald Hodel, Secretary, US Department of Interior*, which held that the Oklahoma Indian Welfare Act of 1936 repealed the 1898 Curtis Act's termination of tribal courts, a decision that was soon applied to the Cherokee Nation courts as well.[39]

In the wake of these loosening federal restrictions, the Council and Chief Mankiller signed an agreement that authorized the Cherokee Nation to "assume responsibility for funds formerly administered by the [Bureau of Indian Affairs]."[40] In 1991 the Cherokee Nation established a new justice department, which included a Cherokee marshal service and a new court with a tribal prosecutor—a job for which the Cherokee Nation hired Chad Smith, who had worked as a tribal planner in the Swimmer Administration, to perform. This growing Cherokee Nation soon came into conflict with the United Keetoowah Band (UKB), which had gained federal recognition as a distinct sovereign government in the 1940s. The Cherokee Nation had imposed a tax on tobacco products sold in Indian smoke shops.[41] The UKB attempted to license its own smoke shops; Cherokee marshals stormed the UKB shops and confiscated tobacco and money. The UKB lost their subsequent court case because their organization did "not have jurisdiction over any 'Indian land.'"[42] Clashes between the two tribes would continue, especially over which organization best represented the keeping of "tradition, culture, language, and the spirit of the Cherokee Indians."[43] Chief Mankiller won her bid for reelection that year by a considerable margin, having become incredibly popular both locally and in the United States at large.

The Council revisited the question of enrolling as a citizen of the Cherokee Nation in 1992. That September, the Council passed the Cherokee Nation Membership Act to establish policies and procedures governing tribal belonging. Section 6 of the act stipulated that "Tribal Membership is derived only through proof of Cherokee blood based on the Final [Dawes] Rolls."[44] The tribal registrar had the authority to issue tribal membership to those who could prove that they or their descendants were listed by blood on the Dawes Rolls. The next year, 1993, the Council amended LA-06-92 to include provisions for newborn children and establish penalties for bartering tribal membership cards or roll numbers.[45] The former provided that newborn children of direct descendance to original Dawes enrollees would be granted temporary citizenship for 240 days, at which point their parents would have to apply for citizenship for the child. The latter provided that anyone who used or allowed another person to use a tribal membership card or roll number for purposes of defrauding the Cherokee Nation could be subject to criminal prosecution: the penalty could be up to a year in prison and up to $5,000 in fines.

The Nation grew and evolved under the Swimmer and Mankiller administrations. While Chief Swimmer oversaw the laying of many building blocks of government, Chief Mankiller worked to solidify the Cherokee Nation's official legal articulation of citizenship and improve the distribution of services. The corporate model of government established in the 1975 constitution, however, did not quite provide the infrastructure to handle the surge in population, services, and governing responsibilities. The judicial branch especially was not built to handle situations like regulating tensions between the different branches of government on a large scale. The situation became a crisis in the late 1990s when the government split in two shortly after the bitterly contested election of 1995.

TOWARD A CONSTITUTIONAL CRISIS

The race for principal chief in 1995 featured a number of candidates vying for Wilma Mankiller's vacated office. That year, Chief Mankiller's handpicked successor, George Bearpaw, faced off against Chad Smith, the tribal prosecutor, and Councilor Joe Byrd. As the votes were tallied, it became clear that no candidate had received the necessary votes to be declared a winner. The Tribal Election Committee called for a runoff election between the top two vote-getters, George Bearpaw (receiving 40 percent of the vote) and Joe Byrd (who garnered 30 percent of the vote).[46] Chad Smith had come in third.

Bearpaw, however, was discovered to have pled guilty to a prior felony conviction—for shooting a man—twenty years earlier.[47] While the charge had been expunged from his record, the Tribal Election Committee determined that Bearpaw was ineligible to run as a candidate for office. Chad Smith argued that his name should replace Bearpaw's on the ballot in the runoff election, but the Judicial Appeals Tribunal disagreed, instead deciding that the election would continue with the existing ballots and that votes for Bearpaw simply would not count. This decision, in effect, handed the victory to Joe Byrd, now unopposed. Chief Mankiller attempted to pardon Bearpaw, the first pardon in modern Cherokee Nation history, but the Tribunal refused to alter their decision.[48] Mankiller, angered by the outcome, refused to attend the inauguration.[49] Chad Smith's further attempts to challenge the election results proved fruitless.

Chief Byrd was the first traditionalist principal chief elected since Lewis Downing in the 1860s and had served on the Council from 1987 to 1995 prior to running for chief. "If you follow Cherokee history," Byrd said at a news conference, "there's always been controversy and tribulation. . . . [Y]ou always have some controversy in getting the people back. I feel like the people are ready to come together and unite."[50] Byrd's administration, however, following the trend of the election of 1995, would prove divisive.[51] In 1997, Council members made repeated requests for contracts and financial records related to public business—records that Chief Byrd's office refused to turn over. Byrd also ignored the Tribunal's subsequent order to produce the records. Tribal marshals went to Byrd's office, warrant in hand, to obtain the records; Byrd responded by firing the fifteen marshals and announced that he did not recognize the high court's authority.[52] The tribal prosecutor retaliated by accusing Chief Byrd of obstructing justice.

In response, on May 2, 1997, Byrd and his supporters on the Council, with only nine members including future principal chief Bill John Baker present, passed Legislative Act 6–97 (later declared void *ab initio*), amending Cherokee Nation law regarding removal from office of justices and declaring an emergency to allow Chief Byrd and his supporters on the Council to dismiss those judicial officers. The Council then impeached the justices of the Judicial Appeals Tribunal.[53] Chad Smith attended the meeting, representing the six absent councillors and announced their intent to boycott "illegal" Council meetings to prevent a quorum. (Ten councillors were necessary for a quorum.)[54] Byrd continued to lay off Cherokee Nation employees by firing the editor of the Nation's newspaper and court clerks.[55]

The marshals, however, "refused to be fired" and continued working in the courthouse building.[56] Chief Byrd stirred up still greater controversy by calling upon the Bureau of Indian Affairs officers to stand between himself and the judicial branch—which had twice tried to officially reinstate the marshals—and to serve as officers of the law in the absence of Cherokee marshals.[57] Byrd, with his own security force, staged a takeover of the courthouse building at 4:00 a.m. on June 20, 1997, to throw out the marshals and judicial officials who had been working there. Shouting matches and arrests followed for the rest of the day, including for Chad Smith, who was thrown to the ground and arrested for attempting to lead a charge to take back the courthouse from Byrd's men around 10:00 a.m.[58]

The next few months were filled with tension, culminating in Cherokee marshals' efforts to move back into the courthouse. The situation turned violent when recently fired Cherokee marshals and impeached justices attempted to physically retake the courthouse from the security force Byrd had hired to protect himself.[59] A brawl ensued and people were thrown from the back porch. Pat Ragsdale, a tribal marshal, was led away bleeding from a head injury; others were also injured in the scuffle.[60] Bureau of Indian Affairs police, deputy sheriffs from two counties, and Oklahoma Highway Patrol officers were all present at the scene.[61] The situation, and the ever-increasing threat of congressional intervention, convinced all parties to eventually come together and discuss their problems. The subsequent dialogue resulted in the establishment of an independent Constitution Convention Commission in 1998, which included representatives from each branch of government and the people generally.[62]

The Cherokee Nation Constitution of 1975 had, in effect, failed to prevent the separate branches of government from colluding with and overpowering one another. Major reforms in the structure of government were needed to prevent the principal chief and a handful of councillors from dissolving the judicial branch. In 1999 the Cherokee people set about debating how to address their constitutional ailments. During the February of 1999 a group of seventy-nine Cherokee Nation citizens assembled for nine days and drafted a new constitution, one more suited to organizing a larger Cherokee Nation responsible for a more diverse constituency, more active branches, and much more money than the 1975 document could support.[63]

THE FOURTH CHEROKEE NATION CONSTITUTION

By 1999 the Cherokee Nation had grown to include over 200,000 enrolled members, and the Nation's budget was $192 million.[64] The seventy-nine individuals that gathered together to draft a new document were keenly aware of those facts when they convened.[65] Charles Gourd called the convention to order on February 26, reminding the delegates and those in attendance that the last time "the Cherokee people came together in a Constitutional Convention was to draft the Constitution of 1839," an act to unify the diasporic Cherokee people after the "forced removal on the infamous Trail of Tears."[66] After invocations in both English and Cherokee, Gourd recounted their shared history and urged them to set aside "individual interests" and "work together as Cherokee people." Chief Byrd then spoke:

> I'd just like to say that the importance of the participation of our citizens in our government has always been something that we have advocated. I feel like there's no service higher than serving as a delegate to a Constitution Convention. . . .
> There is nothing that we cannot accomplish. When the Cherokees work together, in spite of their differences, there is

SELF-DETERMINATION AND THE DAWES ROLLS

nothing that we cannot overcome. And this is the opportunity of a century for all of us to put aside our differences and make sure that we are here to represent all of our tribal members because the world is watching.

I'll leave you with a little quote. "The work that is worthy of reward is a work that endures." Corinthians 13:14.[67]

The convention soon found itself embroiled in the difficult task of debating serious issues. One of the first that arose concerned the legislature and whether to switch from a unicameral to a bicameral legislative body. John Keen moved for the convention to consider bicameralism as a potential check on the abuse of legislative power. Keen, citing *Federalist* No. 51, argued that "a bicameral legislature's dual legislative track structure and form of election as well as its increased size would prevent a small bloc of united Council members from controlling the levers of the Nation's government."[68] Cost, however, worked against the move toward bicameralism, as many delegates argued that money would be more prudently spent delivering better services to Cherokees than in expanding the government apparatus.[69]

The convention did, however, expand the number of seats on the Council. Forty percent of the Nation's 200,000 citizens lived outside of the Cherokee Nation; many delegates, including Julia Coates Foster, argued that these citizens were not being truly represented.[70] She moved to alter the Council so that 20 percent of its members would be reserved for representatives for the Nation's off-reservation residents. David Cornsilk countered that off-reservation Cherokee citizens could already vote and were therefore represented. He added: "[The] Cherokee Nation is a real place, that it is here. That it is within the exterior boundaries of the Cherokee Nation as described in our treaties, and that the focus of the people who live outside the Cherokee Nation should be to strengthen the Nation, the place here."[71] The two sides that formed in this debate reached a compromise by increasing the number of councillors from fifteen to seventeen, with the added two councillors to be elected at-large to represent off-reservation Cherokees.

One of the most heated debates, however, occurred over the issue of whether to create a blood quantum requirement for the office of principal chief. The tension between Cherokees of more or less degree Indian blood manifested itself in this debate, especially once delegates introduced motions to establish a minimum blood quantum for principal chief; the first motion was for candidates to be "citizens by one-sixteenth or greater blood quantum and be bilingual in Cherokee and English."[72] David Cornsilk rejected this idea because of the low blood quanta of Cherokee citizens generally, arguing that "if we put this kind of limitation on ourselves, we are simply saying that we don't trust ourselves to lead our own Nation."[73] Bill John Baker concurred, saying that "we are going to put a time and date on the existence of the Cherokee Nation."[74]

Jonathan Hook disagreed, arguing that "I would like for our Cherokee children, our dark-skinned Cherokee children to be able to look at their Chief and see someone like them. I think that's essential for their self-esteem."[75] Others agreed, one saying that it would be essential for the "integrity of the Cherokee Nation" to institute blood quantum requirements. Yet these arguments eventually lost out to those who declared that blood quantum requirements were an artifact of the US federal government, created for administrative purposes in the age of allotment and that the Cherokee Nation should not bend before every decree of the Bureau of Indian Affairs. The delegates ultimately voted against inserting blood quantum language into the constitution.

As it had in the past, religious belief played a vital role in Cherokee nation building at the convention. While the convention had launched with invocations, some delegates, like Troy Wayne Poteete, were adamant that each session open and close with prayer: "Benjamin Franklin, when they formed the Constitution of the United States, said, if God can keep a sparrow in the tree, he knows all about you and the hairs on your head. How do you think we're going to form a Constitution if we don't go to God in prayer[?] And the way they got through this Constitution then, they had a day of fasting. We've been predominantly a Christian nation since before the removal, and that would probably get us further than all the bickering we could do."[76] Poteete was not alone: Jack Sanders agreed, stating that "we're all brothers and sisters in Christ" and "when we go home, let's get on our knees, everybody, and talk this over."[77] The new preamble ultimately acknowledged that the Cherokee people, "with humility and gratitude," depend upon "the goodness, aid and guidance of the Sovereign Ruler of the Universe."[78] Chief Bill John Baker would later claim that "We are probably the most Christian nation on earth" and that "I don't know that I can separate some of those Christian values from a lot of the Cherokee values."[79] What is clear is that many take the 1999 constitution preamble's reason for ordaining the constitution, to "enrich our culture," to mean also maintaining religious communities, including Christian and traditional Cherokee faiths.[80]

A delegate at the convention, Martha Berry, described in an interview how she believed that the convention changed the political reality in the Cherokee Nation:

One outcome of the convention that I want to share with you is the fresh leadership windfall, which has occurred in the Cherokee Nation as a result of the circumstances prior to the convention, and the crucible of the convention itself. There were many delegates who, like me, lived half their lives as interested but quiet observers. We were ordinary voters, not politicians, not political operatives, not bureaucrats, not even lawyers. Many of us had never even written our council representatives or donated money to campaigns. Through the convention experience, we became reluctant leaders. That process has changed most of our lives for the better and our confidence has grown. For the most part, we are well informed, ethical, intelligent people, very interested in the future of the Cherokee Nation, her structure, and her government. . . . It is a positive result of the convention that no one could have predicted. We may still be without a newly ratified constitution, but we are already enjoying a healthy new crop of leaders at the community level.[81]

While the convention succeeded in addressing the prominent governmental issues at the time, from Berry's perspective, it also served to rejuvenate active citizenship in the Cherokee Nation by giving people a greater sense of agency in their government. Cherokee Nation citizens had successfully applied Jefferson's theory of holding constitutional conventions once a generation and saved their republic from catastrophe. Article XV, Section 9, of the Cherokee Constitution also contained the same provision: that the question of creating a new convention must be submitted to the Cherokee Nation people at least once every twenty years.[82]

The document that the 1999 convention produced was more robust than its immediate predecessor, designed for a government responsible for more money, more citizens, and more power. Article III (the Bill of Rights) now specifically protected the judicial process (rights to council, to trial by jury, and to confront adverse witnesses, among others) and included, for the first time in a Cherokee Nation constitution, explicit protections for the freedom of speech and of the press.[83] In the aftermath of the constitutional crisis, the Tribal Council passed the Cherokee Independent Press Act, which provided protection against undue political influence upon the *Cherokee Phoenix* newspaper to ensure coverage of tribal government affairs without incurring the risk of being fired.[84]

The legislative body retained its unicameral form but now included—in addition to the previous fifteen-member Council—two at-large representatives to represent those Cherokees living outside Cherokee national borders. The seventeen representatives were to be "citizens by blood" of the Cherokee Nation.[85] Article VI, Section 3, also imposed legislative term limits: councillors could serve a maximum of two terms in a row but could return to office after sitting out a term. These terms were staggered to simultaneously prevent collusion and encourage stability.

The executive branch was overhauled to include an office of attorney general and an office of marshal, appointed by the principal chief and confirmed by the Council. The principal chief, similar to the old provision, would be a citizen by blood of the Cherokee Nation. As the convention records indicate, the delegates took great pains to ensure that individuals could not be removed from office as easily as Chief Byrd's Administration had attempted.[86] All individuals cited for removal from office would now stand trial before the Council, "with the accused having been afforded due process and opportunity to be heard," provided that their removal received two-thirds vote of the Council.[87] Article XII further provided that employees of the Cherokee Nation could not be fired for reasons other than cause and only then after being afforded due process, after which they would have the opportunity to appeal the firing. Additionally, the Constitution instituted the recall—the ability of the Cherokee people to recall "any elected official through petition and recall referendum"—as a final popular check on government officials.[88] The judicial branch, however, received the biggest transformation. The Judicial Appeals Tribunal became the Supreme Court of the Cherokee Nation, consisting of five justices, citizens of the Cherokee Nation.[89] Each justice, appointed by the principal chief and confirmed by the Council, would serve a term of ten years. Article VIII also provided for the creation of lower courts, supervised by the Supreme Court. To preserve their independence, the Supreme Court was vested with original jurisdiction over all cases involving the Nation or its officials and appellate jurisdiction over all district court cases.[90] The constitution further provided for an independent Court on the Judiciary: a "seven-member panel vested with powers of suspension, sanction, discipline and recommendation of removal of judges and justices."[91] This special court would preserve the integrity of the judiciary while at the same time prevent the justices from policing themselves.

Regarding citizenship, the 1999 constitution did not depart from the provisions of the 1975 constitution. Citizens of the Cherokee Nation "must be original enrollees or descendants of original enrollees listed on the Dawes Commission Rolls," including the Delaware and Shawnee agreements made in the 1860s, incorporating certain people into the tribe.[92] The constitution established the Cherokee Register, responsible for overseeing the inclusion of Cherokees for citizenship purposes; the Registrar would be responsible for keeping and maintaining citizenship records and other like documentation.

Overall, the 1999 constitution placed more emphasis on the sovereign right of the Cherokee Nation to self-govern and self-determine. Elected in 1999, Chief Smith's Administration—which saw an overall increase in policies reaffirming Cherokee culture, traditional practices, and sovereignty—continued fighting for more governing autonomy before running up against the United States government over issues of sovereignty. That opposition came sooner than many may have anticipated when the Bureau of Indian Affairs initially disapproved of the new constitution, pursuant to Article XV, Section 10, of the 1976 constitution, which stated that all amendments and future constitutions must be approved by the US president. That provision in the old constitution effectively delayed the ratification vote for the 1999 constitution for four years.

RESHAPING THE GOVERNMENT AND AMENDING THE CONSTITUTION

The 1999 election featured yet another runoff as four candidates participated in the race for principal chief and deputy chief. Cherokee Marshal Pat Ragsdale, who had fought against Chief Byrd's Administration both legally and physically over the previous two years, had the support of Wilma Mankiller. Ross Swimmer backed his niece, Meredith Fraley. Chad Smith ran again in protest against Chief Byrd. Finally, Joe Byrd declared his bid for reelection.[93] Since no one received the requisite number of votes, a runoff was held between Joe Byrd and Chad Smith. An outside organization was called in to oversee the entire election process to ensure a fair outcome.

In the runoff, Chad Smith and deputy chief candidate Hastings Shade defeated Chief Byrd and his running mate, Bill John Baker, respectively. Byrd insisted that the trouble had been caused by conspirators who had besmirched his good name and reputation; yet, despite his troubled administration, the close election of 1999 showed that Byrd remained fairly popular among the people.[94] Chief Smith declared that "the adversity of the Constitutional Crisis of 1999 created an opportunity for the people of the Cherokee Nation to develop leadership and gain perspective" on their unique culture and situation.[95] In many ways Chief Smith's Administration would transform the Cherokee Nation, not least of all in the policies regarding tribal citizenship.

When Chief Smith moved into the tribal offices, "locks came off of doors and walls came down. . . . Books [and records] were opened to the general Cherokee public, and a new open-door policy was established."[96] Smith claimed that a disease, a "poverty culture," had taken hold on many people in both the United States and in the Cherokee Nation.[97] This culture, "based on being a victim, blaming others, expecting something for nothing, and transferring responsibility to others," stood in direct opposition to traditional Cherokee beliefs, especially the idea of *gadugi*.[98] In effect, Smith claimed, people in the Cherokee Nation, after decades of bureaucratic imperialism without their own government, had come, as Americans had long before, to see citizenship as a state-ment rather than as a way of life.

Viewing citizenship as a statement means understanding citizenship as a box to check in order to get stuff—to be eligible for government programs or to receive tuition-free education in Oklahoma Universities. Americans had long attempted, and continued to attempt, to become Cherokee Nation citizens so that they might partake in the various mate-rial benefits. Indians had done the same. In 2002 the Council amended the Cherokee Nation Membership Act to prevent tribal members from disenrolling and then reenrolling once it became more profitable for them: "A system of laws that allows the practice of frequent 'switching' of citizenship between or among two or more Indian tribes, simply in order to obtain multiple financial and other benefits, leads to an inequitable distribution of services among citizens of the Cherokee Nation . . ."[99] During that same session, Chief Smith reported in absentia that the Bureau of Indian Affairs had responded favorably to their proposed constitutional amendment—amending the 1975 constitution, the docu-ment produced by the 1999 convention being as yet unratified—that would remove the Bureau of Indian Affairs approval clause from that document in Article XV, Section 10.[100] "This is a wonderful chance," Chief Smith wrote, "to take back a vital right of our sovereignty"[101]—that is, the right to self-govern without asking permission from the federal government. The Council set to work asking for a special election.

That special election came in 2003 when the Cherokee Nation voted on whether to amend the 1975 constitution by striking the provision that required presidential approval. Chief Smith had received assur-ances from the assistant secretary of Indian Affairs that "we have no objection to the referendum as proposed" and that they were prepared to approve the amendment.[102] On March 24, 2003, 65 percent of the Cherokee people voting decided in favor of the amendment.[103] In June of that year, the Cherokee people also voted to adopt their new constitu-tion.[104] During the special election in March, however, freedmen were not permitted to vote, leading to further legal action, led in part by Marilyn Vann.

Vann, a descendent of freedmen, applied for tribal citizenship in 2001 and was denied.[105] After the Cherokee Nation rejected her application, she began her advocacy campaign on behalf of Cherokee freedmen, going on to become president of the Descendants of Freedmen of the Five Civilized Tribes Association. Vann has stated her desire to ensure that freedmen are secure in their citizenship status with access to full citizenship rights as stipulated in the Treaty of 1866.[106] In an August 2017 interview, Vann explained why freedmen desire Cherokee citizenship.[107] She said that, since her ancestors walked the Trail of Tears, labored to build Cherokee cities, and helped "make the tribe," freedmen are an intrinsic part of Cherokee culture, residing not merely *among* Cherokees, but *as* Cherokees.[108] Cherokee Nation citizenship, Vann argued, should be culturally, not racially, based.

Vann's subsequent 2003 legal campaign against the Cherokee Nation not only challenged the legality of not permitting freedmen to vote in the special election but also further delayed the ratification of the 1999 constitution. The Bureau of Indian Affairs decided to review the results of the May 24, 2003, election to remove the presidential approval requirement for any new amendment or constitution, thus also ostensibly preventing the new constitution from taking effect.[109] While Bureau of Indian Affairs officials had told Chief Smith in 2002 that they were favorably disposed to the amendment, they seemingly changed their minds when they disagreed with how the Cherokee Nation had conducted their election. In the meantime, Cherokee citizens lacked clarification about whether the 1999 constitution was operative or not.

Clarification came three years later, in 2006, when the Judicial Appeals Tribunal ruled on June 7 that "the 2003 Constitution had been in effect since its passage by the Cherokee people."[110] Earlier that year, on March 7, 2006, the Tribunal had made another important decision. A lawsuit challenging the 1992 Council Act—which provided that tribal membership would be limited to those with proof of Cherokee blood based upon the Dawes Rolls—won when the Tribunal ruled that "the act violated the Cherokee Nation Constitution."[111] In response, now operating under the new constitution, Cherokee Nation leaders prepared to vote on another amendment to decide the matter once and for all.

In 2007 a Cherokee citizen-led petition was placed on the ballot to add "by blood" language into the Cherokee Constitution itself regarding citizenship.[112] This petition was designed to restrict tribal citizenship.[113] The ballot measure read: "This amendment would take away citizenship of current citizens and deny citizenship to future applicants who are solely descendants of those on either the Dawes Commission Intermarried Whites or Freedmen Rolls."[114] There was historical precedent for the amendment, since the 1839 constitution—a constitution that was in operation until 1907—restricted citizenship to those with Cherokee blood.[115] Chief Smith's Administration proposed that the petition be voted on via special election, separate from the general election that year. Turnout for the special election was low; 8,743 voted. Yet 77 percent (some 6,700) of those who showed up voted "yes."[116] The Cherokee Nation Constitution now read: "Citizenship of the Cherokee Nation shall be limited to those originally enrolled on, or descendants of those enrolled on, the Final Rolls of the Cherokee Nation, commonly referred to as the Dawes Rolls, for those listed as Cherokees *by blood*, Delaware Cherokees . . . and the Shawnee Cherokees . . ."[117] And so the amendment was passed and the letter of the law changed. Many Freedmen, who were not Indian by blood, lost their tribal citizenship status as a result.[118] A total of 2,869 freedmen were affected by the amendment; three hundred of these filed a lawsuit in the Cherokee Nation's district court, challenging the decision.[119]

Reactions to the amendment within the nation were varied. Kirby Brown writes:

Some viewed the amendment's passage in political terms as an exercise of Indigenous sovereignty and self-determination. Others viewed the amendment's articulation of direct lineal descent to an Indian ancestor as an affirmation of family relations and matrilineal and bilateral kinship to existing Cherokee families and communities. Still others read it as a cynical manipulation of Cherokee law that was motivated by political self-interest and was anchored to an unfortunate holdover of racialized understandings of Cherokee identity and belonging dating back to the nineteenth century. In the context of such disparate views, this move to bring the amendment to a referendum hit a nerve that reverberated out of the Nation . . .[120]

Others, like Daniel Heath Justice, were blunter, calling the amendment "ill-conceived and deeply troubling."[121]

The United States responded quickly. Representative Diane Watson (D-CA) introduced a bill in Congress threatening to withhold federal money unless the Cherokee Nation reestablished freedmen's citizenship.[122] The Bureau of Indian Affairs, after the 2007 amendment, renewed their objection to the previous amendment in 2003—when the Cherokee Nation voted to remove presidential oversight of constitutional changes—stating that the Cherokee Nation was in violation of the Treaty of 1866 and could not deny citizenship rights to already existing portions of their own population.[123] In effect, the Bureau of Indian Affairs argued that the Cherokee Nation could not disenroll members previously enrolled due to treaty agreements.

Chief Smith, however, defended the amendments as assertions of tribal sovereignty and self-determination.[124] He indicated that if the Cherokee people wanted to amend their constitution, they should be allowed to as they see fit. "What is at stake here," Smith argued, "is the sovereignty and self-determination of all Indian tribes." The Cherokee people clearly voted in 2007, as they had in 2003, to assert their sovereign ability to act without US approval and to decide who could be considered a legal Cherokee citizen. In 2008, Chief Smith declared that "members of the Congressional Black Caucus asked the U.S. Senate to punish the Cherokee people because we voted that every citizen must have an Indian ancestor on the Dawes Rolls. They abuse the power of the U.S. government in violation of federal courts and are trying to punish us for attempting to protect our sovereignty and retain our cultural identity. . . . Members of the caucus proclaimed disdain for the rule of law by saying that they did not care what the law was and they refused to wait for the courts to decide."[125] The Cherokee Nation, later in 2007, proceeded by general election "to again approve amending the Cherokee Nation Constitution to remove the requirements for federal approval of amendments."[126] Thanks to a tribal court injunction, freedmen who were registered as tribal citizens were permitted to vote in that election.

The legal tug-of-war continued in the courts for several years. In 2009 the Cherokee Nation argued in court that the Five Tribes Act and federal statutes had modified the Treaty of 1866, resulting in a loss of citizenship protections for freedmen.[127] In 2011, Chief Justice Darell R. Matlock of the Cherokee Supreme Court argued that "it stands to reason that if the Cherokee had the right to define citizenship" in 1866, then they would have the "sovereign right" to change it.[128] The situation permeated the Nation, drawing the attention of legal professionals, politicians, and average citizens. James MacKay, writing for the *Guardian*, reported in 2011 that: "The tragedy of the Cherokee supreme court's decision, as [Cherokee citizen] Steve Russell argues in an excoriating editorial, is that it achieves what federal government has always wanted. It makes the Cherokee an ethnic special interest group, no longer deserving of the title of 'nation.'"[129] Cherokee leaders and many others, on the one hand, argued that the Cherokee Nation's right—as Chief Bushyhead claimed over a century earlier—to count and claim its own citizens is a matter of sovereign authority. Many freedmen and Cherokees alike, on the other hand, countered that an obsession with race had delegitimized Cherokee attempts to self-govern in certain arenas.[130] A primary legal question, however, at the heart of the issue was whether the Treaty of 1866 had itself granted citizenship to freedmen or if the freedmen only received tribal citizenship because of the Cherokee constitutional amendment in 1866, as the treaty had mandated.[131] The Cherokee Nation waived its sovereign immunity during this series of court cases, effectively binding itself to the outcome as determined by the federal government.[132]

These and other questions were seemingly put to rest in 2017.[133] In August 2017, US District Judge Thomas F. Hogan remarked that while Native Americans had been marginalized and unjustly removed from their lands, nothing in this history gave the Cherokee the authority to deny previously established citizenship to descendants of their freedmen.[134] Judge Hogan indicated that the Cherokee Nation must interpret their constitution to mean that all Cherokees, all whites and others adopted, and all freedmen are guaranteed citizenship. "The Cherokee Nation," Hogan ruled, "can continue to define itself as it sees fit but must do so equally and evenhandedly with respect to native Cherokees and the descendants of Cherokee freedmen."[135] The Nation, Hogan added, also "concedes that its power to determine tribal membership can be [and is] limited by treaty." The Cherokee Supreme Court in 2017 concurred, ordering the Nation to process freedmen citizenship applications.[136]

The debate, both interpersonal and legal, over the 2007 Cherokee constitutional amendment spanned a decade and included two different principal chief administrations. Bill John Baker, a councilor during and after Chief Byrd's Administration, described his service with Chief Byrd as "a wonderful time. . . . We could talk to him about the needs of the people. He would listen and when he saw a need, we could take care of it."[137] Baker found less satisfaction under Chief Smith, stating that "we couldn't go to him and get the same passion, the same commitment we had to take care of the needs of the people."[138] After twelve years on the Council, Baker decided to run for principal chief in the 2011 election against Smith, who had held the position since 1999.

The 2011 election was another close contest. Held on June 25, Baker and Chief Smith each thought that he had secured victory at one point. Initially, Smith appeared to have won by seven votes. After a recount, Baker appeared to have won by 266 votes. The Cherokee Nation Supreme Court got involved and decided to conduct its own recount. Instead of declaring a winner, the justices declared the election void and a new election was scheduled for that September.[139] A few weeks before that second election, the Cherokee Supreme Court ruled that freedmen were no longer members of the tribe and therefore would not be allowed to vote, a decision that the freedmen quickly had declared null by the United States. Baker alleged that Chief Smith wanted to keep the freedmen from voting since the freedmen supported Baker.[140] When the second election eventually did take place (the deadline was extended by the courts given the freedmen situation), Bill John Baker won by 1,575 votes, winning 54 percent of the vote overall.[141] Chief Smith challenged the outcome, but the Cherokee Supreme Court upheld the final count.[142]

That same year, during a townhall meeting, Muscogee Creek citizen Eli Grayson addressed a group of freedmen who had gathered to discuss the Cherokee Supreme Court ruling that validated the Cherokee decision to exclude freedmen from citizenship.[143] At that meeting the *Phoenix* reported that Grayson encouraged the freedmen to liberate themselves of the argument that "it's about Indian blood" and reminded them, "Your ancestors knew who they were in 1866. They knew they were not American; they knew they were Cherokee."[144] Willadine Johnson, a descendant of freedmen, expressed similar sentiments. Disheartened by the back-and-forth legal proceedings and the uncertainty of citizenship for fellow freedmen descendants, Johnson, too, hearkened back to the

Treaty of 1866 as the document that established once and for all that freedmen were Cherokee citizens and belonged with the Nation.[145]

On the surface, it may seem as though the Freedmen Association, through their desire for political equality, might view citizenship similar to the way that many Americans do. This is, however, not the case, since the freedmen view inclusion in their own ranks much as the Cherokee Nation does. To join the Descendants of Freedmen of the Five Civilized Tribes Association as a full member, individuals must be able to "prove lineage to the 1898–1914 Dawes Freedmen Rolls."[146] The Cherokee Nation has, in the modern era, also used the Dawes Rolls to establish tribal citizenship, albeit excluding the freedmen portion of the Rolls. The Descendants of Freedmen Association does not desire to open up tribal membership to anyone who wants it but rather seeks to maintain the exclusivity of Cherokee Nation citizenship while asserting that freedmen have—since 1866, at least—always been party to it.

THE DEBATE OVER FREEDMEN CITIZENSHIP CONTINUES

While the Cherokee Nation had officially complied with the 2017 US district court ruling concerning freedmen's citizenship, the debate was not over. Freedmen and blood citizenship were featured topics during the 2019 election for principal chief. During a May 16, 2019, televised forum, three candidates for principal chief fielded questions from community members. Dick Lay, David Walkingstick, and Chuck Hoskin Jr. were each asked their position on freedmen's citizenship status.[147] Each candidate offered a different response, suggesting that, at least in public discourse, the 2017 US district court ruling was in dispute.

Councilor Dick Lay answered first, keeping his comments brief. Lay stated that the "issue has been decided, in the federal courts and ours. It's the law. And I will abide by and enforce the law as chief, just like I'm doing now as [councilor]. That's my answer." Lay's terse response and refusal to comment further stood in stark contrast to his opponents. Councilor David Walkingstick expressed a different opinion. While ultimately saying he would uphold the law, Walkingstick reminded viewers that "in 2007 . . . there was a constitutional referendum that went before the Cherokee people, to be voted on, to have a Cherokee

171

by-blood tribe . . . 77 percent of people voted on that."[148] Walkingstick called the issue of freedmen's citizenship a sovereignty issue: Could the Cherokee Nation determine its own citizenship requirements without US interference? The councilman further claimed that the Cherokee Nation displayed weakness in not standing up for what was the will of the people by not challenging the 2017 US court ruling.

Cherokee Nation Secretary of State Chuck Hoskin Jr. distanced himself from both Lay and Walkingstick in his statement. Hoskin openly embraced the inclusion of the freedmen. The secretary reminded viewers of his vote "not to exclude the Freedmen" in the 2007 referendum. Since the 2017 decision, Hoskin reminded his opponents, the Cherokee Nation had complied with the ruling and sought to grant greater protections for freedmen: the general policy under outgoing Chief Bill John Baker had been to embrace and include freedmen. If elected, Hoskin promised to do even more to incorporate freedmen's communities. Hoskin won the election with 57 percent of the vote (7,933 ballots). Lay received 3,856 ballots, or 27 percent. Walkingstick, who was disqualified from the election for unrelated reasons, still garnered 2,006 ballots (14 percent) despite his ineligibility.[149]

That August 2019, during his first state of the nation address, Chief Hoskin declared that the Cherokee Nation was strong because of its strong foundation, built before recorded history; made strong by great suffering, eclipsed by great triumphs.[150] Speaker of the Council and former principal chief Joe Byrd reminded his audience that the Cherokee Nation was about community and that sovereignty was their most treasured possession: "The Trail of Tears was the beginning that made us who we are today," Byrd said, and a citizenry united by history and culture is something worth celebrating.[151] While Chief Hoskin's Administration was optimistic that they had turned a corner in their centuries-long citizenship dispute, the chief and his allies soon found themselves embroiled once more in another controversy involving the freedmen.

The debate over citizenship for freedmen in the Cherokee Nation resurfaced in the February of 2021. Marilyn Vann, president of the Descendants of Freedmen of the Five Civilized Tribes Association, declared her candidacy in the June 5, 2021, general election for an open at-large seat on the Council. Fellow at-large candidate Robin Mayes immediately filed ineligibility complaints against Vann, arguing that, while no doubt qualified in all other particulars, Vann was not Cherokee "by blood" as required in the Cherokee Constitution.[152] Chief Hoskin denounced Mayes' complaint and reiterated his commitment to upholding the law that secured freedmen's citizenship.[153] However, Mayes asserted that the text of the Cherokee Constitution was clear and could not be changed by courts.[154] Around the same time, Cherokee attorney general Sara Hill petitioned the Supreme Court to strike the words "by blood" from the constitution; the Cherokee Supreme Court complied, striking "by blood" from the document, opening up a new series of legal questions.

Hill's request, reportedly an attempt to "bring closure" to the "difficult history" of the Cherokee freedmen, sought to harmonize the wording of the law with the 2017 US district court ruling.[155] Judge Thomas Hogan in that 2017 ruling indicated that the Cherokee Nation mistakenly argued that freedmen's citizenship was bound to the Cherokee Constitution; freedmen's citizenship was instead bound to the "rights of native Cherokees."[156] Hogan based his ruling on the Treaty of 1866, wherein, he argued, "the Cherokee Nation concedes that its power to determine tribal membership can be [and is] limited by treaty." Freedmen, therefore, derived their citizenship not only from the Cherokee Nation Constitution, but also from federal treaty law. While legally Hogan confirmed that freedmen possessed all the rights of Cherokee Nation citizens after that 2017 ruling, the Cherokee Nation Constitution still contained the words "by blood" with respect to citizenship. The Cherokee Supreme Court did as the attorney general requested on February 22, 2021, striking the words "by blood" from the Cherokee Constitution.[157]

Councilor Wes Nofire, backed by other Cherokee councillors, filed a motion to intervene with the Cherokee Supreme Court.[158] They argued that the constitution could not be amended by one branch of government for any reason whatsoever. Indeed, Article XV, Section 1, clearly states that "the People of the Cherokee Nation reserve to themselves the power to propose laws and amendments to this Constitution and to enact or reject the same at the polls independent of the Council, and also reserve power at their own option to approve or reject at the polls any act of the Council." Nofire stated that "Words were stricken illegally from the Constitution, which means we have a broken government."[159] Nofire, who also claimed that ways to fix broken government included removing offending government officials from office, indicated that tribal sovereignty is most clearly threatened when Cherokee Nation legal processes are discarded in favor of political posturing. Others in the Nation also filed motions to intervene, arguing that "a final order by the court nullifying language from the Constitution without a vote of the Cherokee people will do irreparable harm" to the very fabric of the constitution.[160] Although freedmen already possessed legal tribal citizenship after 2017, the attorney general and Cherokee Supreme Court, Nofire and his allies contended, circumvented Cherokee law and the people by changing the wording of their constitution—which still indicated a blood standard for determining citizenship.

Attorney and Cherokee Nation citizen Ralph Keen II offered a different perspective. Keen argued that the Cherokee people were not allowed to vote on changing their constitutional language in this case because the offending words violated federal law.[161] Article XIII of the Cherokee Constitution, containing the oath of office, binds all elected officials to preserve, protect, and defend the constitutions of the Cherokee Nation and the United States, the latter implicitly acknowledged as the supreme law of the land. Since treaty agreements are tantamount to supreme law in the United States (US Constitution, Article VI), the 2007 Cherokee constitutional amendment inserting the "by blood" language into their governing document was technically a dead letter when written. Voting could not occur, therefore, because the Cherokee people could not legally vote to insert the "by blood" terminology in the first place, thanks to the provisions in the Treaty of 1866, which granted freedmen all the rights of native Cherokees.

The Cherokee Nation continues to debate the extent to which racism, the desire to assert tribal sovereignty, and political positioning play in the ongoing debate over tribal freedmen. This situation is continuing to develop. In May 2022, the Council revised Title 26 of the Cherokee Nation Code relative to elections.[162] The old stipulation stated that, to be eligible to run for elective office, each candidate must submit, among other things: "Proof of citizenship and membership by Indian blood consisting of his or her certificate of degree of Indian blood card and a Cherokee Nation citizenship card." This provision now reads: "Proof of Citizenship and a Cherokee Nation Citizenship card." The Cherokee Nation, during Chief Hoskin's administration, has worked to expunge all references to blood restrictions in Cherokee law.

LOOKING AHEAD

Apart from the debates over freedmen citizenship, the Cherokee Nation has found itself engaged in another high-profile citizenship debate— this time with Oklahoma governor and Cherokee Nation citizen Kevin Stitt. Governor Stitt, a member of the Republican Party, was elected governor of Oklahoma in 2019 and is the first tribally enrolled Indigenous person to serve as the governor of a US state. The question here again targets the viability of using the Dawes Rolls as a metric for determining who belongs to the Cherokee Nation. By Cherokee Nation law, Stitt is a Cherokee citizen by virtue of being related to someone listed on the Dawes Rolls.

A number of petitions circulated online aimed at convincing the Cherokee Nation government to revoke Governor Stitt's citizenship status in the Nation.[163] The desire of some to remove Stitt from the tribal rolls came from what some have termed treasonous behavior, namely his attempts to increase Oklahoma's take from casino profits and his opposition to the *McGirt v. Oklahoma* decision, which solidified tribal jurisdiction of Indian-on-Indian crime on tribal lands, virtually all of eastern Oklahoma. Principal Chief Hoskin has claimed that Stitt "has been attacking our sovereignty since he took office," starting by "undermining our gaming compact. . . . When he failed at that, he moved on to McGirt."[164] In their opposition to the governor, some have asserted that Stitt's Cherokee heritage was obtained by fraud—that his ancestor, Francis Dawson, effectively bribed his way onto the Dawes Rolls to take advantage of allotment lands for himself and his family.[165] Opponents alleged that Governor Stitt was not concerned with the well-being of his tribe and, since his actions did not appear to promote the general welfare, he ought to be expelled from the Cherokee Nation. Despite this opposition from the Cherokee Nation, Stitt won reelection handily in November 2022, capturing 55.4 percent of the vote in the heavily Republican Oklahoma.[166]

The Cherokee Nation passed 400,000 enrolled tribal citizens in September 2021: the Cherokee Nation registration department received up to 2,000 citizenship applications weekly after Chief Hoskin announced a

$2,000 COVID stimulus payment to all citizens and those approved as citizens by June 2022.[167] If history is any indication, as the Cherokee Nation continues to grow and prosper, they will face new challenges in determining how to articulate citizenship in their republic. It will be interesting to see whether the Cherokee Nation continues to use the Dawes Rolls as a metric for citizenship in the future or whether they will develop an alternative, a list not as questionably compiled by Congress or perhaps some other innovation entirely.

One further event that occurred in 2023 merits some attention. In late 2022 the United States Supreme Court heard arguments in the case of *Haaland v. Brackeen*—a combination of four cases dealing with challenges to the constitutionality of the Indian Child Welfare Act of 1978. The issue at stake was whether the ICWA was legally enacted; if so, "is it constitutional under either a strict scrutiny standard or rational basis" test, and does it discriminate on the basis of race?[168] The ICWA was challenged by the state of Texas and several individual petitioners—including, most prominently, the Brackeen family—and the law firm Gibson Dunn. On the other side, "the Departments of Interior, Health and Human Services, and (as intervening defendants) the Cherokee Nation, the Oneida Nation, the Quinault Indian Nation, and the Morongo Band of Mission Indians will defend ICWA as an extension of the political status of Indian tribes as sovereigns with a slate of differentiated rights both against and within the US constitutional order."[169] The court ruled in June 2023 that the ICWA is in fact consistent with Congress' constitutional authority. "Congress," Justice Barrett wrote for the 7–2 majority, "possesses plenary power of legislation" regarding tribal nations; this power is not absolute, however, but rather flows from both the Indian Commerce Clause and the Treaty Clause in the US Constitution, the structural relationship between United States and tribal governments, and the "trust relationship between the United States and Indian people" established through precedent.[170]

Justice Neil Gorsuch was even more emphatic. The US Constitution "mediates between competing federal, state, and tribal claims of sovereignty," balancing each against the others.[171] The ICWA resulted from centuries of American attempts to abrogate the Indigenous family by seizing children and stripping them of their cultural heritage. Congress, through its limited and enumerated powers, preserved the appropriate balance between sovereigns by protecting children from loss of tribal identity. The ICWA also preserves a key element of tribal sovereignty: self-determination and the right to count and claim its own citizens.

THE CHEROKEE NATION AND THE DAWES ROLLS AS A METRIC FOR CITIZENSHIP

The search for durable shifts in Cherokee citizenship policies from 1975 to 2023 finds one significant change and potentially two such changes, depending on how durable the 2017 ruling proves. The first shift came in the 1970s when Congress relinquished control of the Cherokee tribal government. Thereafter, the Cherokee Nation reaffirmed its commitment to a form of exclusive hereditary citizenship. By 1992 the Cherokee Nation had codified paths to citizenship: while expanded to include adoptions and other nontraditional familial attachments, citizenship remained driven by Cherokee blood relation to someone listed on the Dawes Rolls.[172] The effort to restrict citizenship to only those on the Cherokee Rolls has failed as of 2017. Federal officials have upheld a definition of Cherokee Nation citizenship that includes individuals listed on both Cherokee and freedmen rolls. Moreover, the United States has asserted that the Cherokee Nation does not have the sovereign right to change their definition of citizenship to exclude currently included peoples.

In this era, the Cherokee Nation has continued to wrestle with and against the United States over the concept of the citizen. As the United States grew, so did its administrative apparatus, which, for a variety of ascriptive reasons, categorized individuals by their race: "For many it [race] had become the master category defining access to citizenship and full rights within it."[173] This became especially, though not exclusively, prominent during the Progressive Era, the time of allotment. One of the legacies of allotment for the Cherokee Nation was that Cherokee people grew up pressured by the federal government to view themselves in terms of blood quanta—or, put another way, one interest group among many competing for access to government programs. While many adopted this mindset, others pushed back against the United States conception of *minority* citizens. The rebuilt Cherokee Nation in the 1970s and 1980s, as a result, faced a difficult challenge: how to preserve the exclusivity of tribal citizenship without losing Cherokees' traditional understanding of active citizenship—citizenship as a way of life, not simply as a means to get things.

This task was made even more difficult by the fact that the United States had deliberately taken Cherokee people and spread them around the country to try to break their communal habits. Others fled drought and poverty in Oklahoma to provide for their families elsewhere. Therefore, when the Cherokee Nation government was reborn, its initial population was small. Cherokee leaders worked hard to facilitate the revival of Cherokee cultural mores for decades, hoping to cultivate a sense of active citizenship—a relational arrangement between a distinct political community. Today the Cherokee Nation boasts over 400,000 citizens.[174] Their efforts in that department have certainly succeeded. Comparatively lenient citizenship policies—the lack of a blood quantum requirement, for example—have helped create the largest tribal nation population in the United States as of this writing. A referendum on another constitutional convention is due to the Cherokee people soon; it remains to be seen how Cherokees will work to articulate their tribal citizenship requirements in the future.[175]

CONCLUSION
CITIZENSHIP AS A WAY OF LIFE

THE SEARCH FOR durable shifts in Cherokee Nation citizenship policies from 1710 to 2023 reveals at least four durable shifts in policy. Table 4 displays the progression of these Cherokee Nation citizenship policies over time. In the eighteenth century, Cherokees knew who belonged by a person's membership in a matrilineal Cherokee clan: if you were born or adopted into a clan, you were Cherokee. This was predominantly a recognition of *blood as culture*. Incidents like Chickawa's adoption—which entailed full membership—and Christian Priber's acceptance into the tribe demonstrate a willingness to accept others, regardless of race, who adopted Cherokee customs and mores as one of their own.

The rise of the Cherokee republic in the 1810s and 1820s led to the first major shift in citizenship policy. Now the offspring of both Cherokee men and women, regardless of clan membership, were legally considered citizens—with the caveat that the individual could not also have Black ancestry. Leaders used their new legal frameworks to open up pathways to citizenship and inheritance to more people while at the same time seeking a means to keep citizenship exclusive. Harriet and Elias Boudinot's children thus became full Cherokee Nation citizens despite Harriet having no clan affiliation. Yet this new legal framework did not abolish traditional mores and practices: citizens were still expected to adhere to certain behaviors, especially when it came to preserving and protecting the land, to wit, Elias Boudinot and others who signed the Treaty of New Echota suffered the consequences of signing away Cherokee lands in the East and subjecting their people to removal. These new laws, along with the old, co-determined legal recognition in the

Table 4. Shifts in Cherokee Legal Citizenship, 1710–2017

Date(s) of Shift	Old Cherokee Policy	New Cherokee Policy	Reason for Shift
1810–1827	Clan membership via birth or adoption.	Cherokee blood or adoption, "excluding African race," or act of the Council.	Restructured Cherokee Nation government, constitution.
1866	Cherokee blood or adoption, "excluding African race," or act of the Council.	Cherokee blood or adoption, or act of the Council, plus freedmen unrelated (strict).	Treaty of 1866.
1887–1907	Cherokee blood or adoption, or act of the Council, plus freedmen unrelated (strict).	Nation dissolved.	Dawes Act, Oklahoma statehood.
1975–1983	Nation dissolved.	Cherokee blood based on lineal descent from Dawes Rolls (strict).	Principal Chiefs Act, new government.
2007–2017	Cherokee blood based on lineal descent from Dawes Rolls (strict).	Lineal descent from Cherokee and freedmen Dawes Rolls.	US court ruling.

Cherokee Nation: combining *blood as culture* and *blood as ancestry* into a unique set of policies.

The next major shift came with the Treaty of 1866, when United States officials forced the Cherokee Nation to adopt freedmen as full and equal citizens. This treaty created a disconnect between Cherokee foundational ideas and citizenship policies—freedmen (as well as Delawares and Shawnees through subsequent agreements) derived their citizenship status first from the treaty and second from the eventual constitutional amendments that Cherokee Nation leaders passed soon thereafter. Many resisted the incorporation of the freedmen especially, having come to support the strict racial hierarchy that Americans observed at the time. Leaders like Joel Mayes and Samuel Houston Mayes articulated cogent defenses of their communal lifestyle against the material considerations of others, like William Jefferson Watts, who favored allotment to better secure their individual property.

Allotment represented the third durable shift in Cherokee Nation citizenship policy. The damage that Congress did to the Cherokee republic through the allotment process cannot be overstated. Reduced to a token of authority, the Cherokee Nation lay dormant for roughly sixty years. The United States in this period worked hard to reduce Cherokee people into tiny pieces in a gigantic bureaucratic machine, identifying individuals based on how much Indian blood they had (or appeared to have) in their veins. The United States effectively worked to turn citizenship into a statement—a box to check in order to receive allotments or to take part in federal programs. Redbird Smith led the spiritual charge against this effort by challenging his people to retain those qualities of their culture that had helped them overcome so many obstacles in the past, like removal—among these, a sense of citizenship as active membership in the community, as a need to work to help one another through the crisis at hand into a better future.

The fourth shift came in the 1970s, after Congress and the president passed legislation enabling tribal nations to reinstitute their national governments. The Cherokees drafted and ratified a constitution that defined citizenship as belonging to those whose ancestors were—or who were themselves—listed on the Dawes Rolls. Old prejudices, coupled with concerted efforts to reestablish a Cherokee Nation grounded in fundamental principles like *gadugi,* led to clashes over access to government services as well as over who counted as a citizen. The Cherokee Nation created an expansive civic education system aimed at not only preserving their cultural memory but also, according to Wilma Mankiller, Joe Byrd, Chad Smith, and Chuck Hoskin Jr., among others, at encouraging people toward active citizenship in their daily lives. In 2017 the US district court in Washington, DC, ruled that the freedmen had been full participants in Cherokee Nation citizenship since the Treaty of 1866 and that the Cherokee Nation had, by treaty, limited its own authority to alter that fact. The Cherokee Nation has many constitutional provisions that encourage active citizenship—like the initiative, the referendum, the recall, and every twenty years deciding upon a constitutional convention—and have shown that these work best when bolstered by a strong culture that sustains a populace.

CITIZENSHIP AS A WAY OF LIFE

The purpose of this book is to challenge Americans to think seriously about citizenship by observing and appreciating how citizenship has developed in another regime. That development in the Cherokee Nation of Oklahoma reveals changes in the law to ensure the continuity of certain foundational ideas. Among these foundational ideas stand *aniyvwiya*, *tohi*, and *gadugi*—which together emphasize a living history, oneness, natural interconnectedness, and the obligations humans have to those beings with whom they are interconnected.[1] These ideas, which do not exhaust the Cherokee cosmovision, point to a desire to keep citizenship exclusive to in turn preserve those ideas. This reciprocal relationship between foundational ideas and policy has endured the last few hundred years of contact with an American regime predicated instead on ideas of individual freedom from obligation, culture, and nature.[2] These two regimes are therefore at loggerheads over their visions of citizenship and, consequently, of what constitutes a good life.

What are Americans, caught in the tempest of a civic crisis, to learn from citizenship in the Cherokee Nation? We cannot join or pretend to be like the Cherokee Nation, although many try.[3] However, neither can we continue to seek out liberal answers for problems caused by American liberalism—like America's disconnection from the past: "Illiteracy about our founding political principles, institutions, and history," civics scholar Paul Carrese points out, is rampant—while ignoring the experiences of neighboring regimes.[4] Let's begin there, with history. As Cherokee Nation councilor Julia Coates suggests: "History is a frame for understanding not only the past, but also the present and future. But history is also one of the strongest vehicles of a people and a nation for developing and imparting senses of personal and collective identities, and fostering investment in shared ideals."[5] Cherokee Nation citizenship policies, and the ideas that have influenced them, reveal the story of how a regime has adapted to changing circumstances, external threats, and internal strife and continues to adhere to a foundational cultural framework not stagnant but living and adaptable. That history does not reveal a utopia; men are not angels.[6] It does reveal an optimism, a drive to sustain sovereignty and a culture that articulates a dynamic vision of the good life—one that people are willing to practice, debate, adapt, and defend.[7]

Citizenship, in that light, places certain demands upon people; it must be a way of life, not simply serve as a stagnant statement. Cherokee Nation leaders have been remarkably consistent over time in their articulation of active citizenship. In 2019, incoming principal chief Chuck Hoskin Jr. called the Cherokee Nation "the most dynamic and progressive government in this country," strong because of their solid foundation, built before recorded history, sustained by great suffering eclipsed by great triumphs.[8] When disasters occur, Hoskin wrote in 2021, "our response can reveal our deepest values. The Cherokee Nation believes in 'gadugi'—working together to better our tribe for the greater good."[9] Hoskin's predecessor, Chief Bill John Baker, made similar claims in his 2011 inaugural address. "We owe it to those who came before us and those who will follow," Baker admonished this audience, to continue giving to one another and fighting for their sovereignty.[10] Baker's predecessor, Chief Smith, was even more poignant in 2001:

Passing on the great Cherokee legacy is one of those important things we can do. We can count a number of Cherokee patriots and elders who did their part by who have gone to be with the Creator. . . . We've learned to focus only on the things that count. Rather than focus on putting ourselves first, we should focus on others. Rather than involve ourselves with petty politics, we should focus on statesmanship. Rather than concerning ourselves with continually buying, we should be focusing on sharing. If the future ever looks gloomy, study our past and look to our children and elders. It is becoming more clear to me daily. We must look to the long haul and prepare.[11]

In 1993, Chief Mankiller offered some advice to college recruiters attempting to woo Cherokee students: "If you're going to go out in the more traditional communities and recruit college students, don't go out and tell them that if they get a college education, that the college education will help them accumulate great personal wealth, or great personal acclaim, or help them get a BMW or whatever. Tell them that they can use their skills to help build their community, and help their family, and help their tribe and you might get their attention."[12] That sense of "interdependence," Mankiller argued, is a core principle of Cherokee political thought: an idea that has transcended political time to form a basis from which Cherokee peoples have grown for centuries.

These themes—interdependence, respect for the past, working in the present, and passing down a stable identity and purpose to the future—permeate nineteenth-century Cherokee arguments as well. The "dignity of antiquity is ours," proclaimed Chief C. J. Harris in 1894, and "lands in common is common interest, and common interest implies equal benefits, whenever the people as a community demand their share of equal rights and benefits in the common property."[13] Land is something not kept for selfish reasons but for the benefit of posterity. Citizenship in the Cherokee Nation, Chief Dennis Bushyhead argued in 1883, "means the right to a home already provided for each and every citizen—[a] right to the soil of the country" and to education, to natural resources, and other materials.[14] Sustaining these rights, however, requires first habituating citizens to *gadugi* and, second, removing imposters who might falsely claim Cherokee Nation citizenship simply to partake in the benefits.[15] "Let the Cherokee people learn that all their interests and hopes lie in union of sentiment and action," Chief William Ross said in 1866.[16] That action should be directed toward sustaining Cherokee political values as one people dedicated to preserving their sovereignty for the future, to train children in "industry, morality and knowledge."[17]

American leaders have, of course, acknowledged the need for active citizenship too.[18] Future president Barrack Obama, in a 2008 campaign speech, recognized that, for over a century, Americans restricted access to a bad system. Then, for better or worse, Americans decided to focus on securing equal access to a bad system instead of fixing the system itself.[19] The system was an administrative bureaucracy that doled out government benefits according to race, gender, and other ascriptive characteristics. As a result, race and ascriptive traits became a fixation for both those in power and those without. America, while it attempted to produce political equality, created a system of racial prejudice that smothered cultures in the name of equality.[20] Obama argued, "In the end, then, what is called for is nothing more, and nothing less, than what all the world's great religions demand—that we do unto others as we would have others do unto us. Let us be our brother's keeper, Scripture tells us. Let us be our sister's keeper. Let us find that common stake we all have in one another, and let our politics reflect that spirit as well."[21] American citizenship must be active, must be lived, to help create a more perfect union. But at the same time that more perfect union will come, not out of envisioning a world where everyone has more money or more power, but out of working toward a world in which people sacrifice for one another because it is an activity worthwhile.

What may Americans learn from the development of citizenship in the Cherokee Nation? We may learn from the culturally grounded efforts of a people to sustain a regime rooted in communal principles that acknowledge and require much from their citizenry: "The Keetoowah way," Tom Holm asserts, "is, frankly, the opposite of the generally accepted Hobbesian idea that human beings by nature (or in spirit) are, and always have been, violent and egocentric."[22] Indigenous nations, "built on affection rather than on anything like Hobbesian fear," writes theologian Andrew Murray, can teach us that American ideals are not settled dogma.[23] The crisis among liberal democracies in the West is the neutrality of the state in relation to ethics and affection, which citizens easily take to mean a rejection of any ethics at all.[24] The American obsession with equality and comfort—and a rejection of history, boundaries, and nature—has led to otherizing regimes like the Cherokee Nation and a refusal to learn from competing visions of the good life because we insist that all ideas are equal and therefore have no intrinsic value apart from private comfort.

As Americans continue to wrestle with dissatisfaction in their own citizenship, observing and understanding how other regimes conceive of the good life may lead us to rethinking how we engage with our own foundational principles and communities. The time is ripe to consider alternative conceptions of the citizen.[25] Some, like Vine Deloria Jr., have argued that future debates between the United States and Indigenous peoples must be rooted in dignity and respect. "Deep down," Deloria wrote, Indigenous complaints "are cries about dignity, complaints about the lack of respect. . . . The land itself must be seen to have a measure of dignity and respect and when it does not receive these accommodations, human beings who live on the land are accordingly incomplete."[26] Americans have spent centuries attempting to transform Indigenous regimes into liberal democracies without pausing to consider what was being lost—and what they have failed to destroy.

ON THE PERPETUATION OF
POLITICAL INSTITUTIONS

In 1838, the problem of attaching citizens to their political institutions perplexed a young Abraham Lincoln. Whereas Americans had once found a source of patriotism in the lives of those who participated in the revolution, by the 1830s they had begun to lose their respect for their own laws. An unmoored individualism had established itself among the Americans, Lincoln warned, and threatened to overturn the established order—an individualism that sought the glory of creation or, alternately, the pathos of destruction. Mob rule was the result. Lynching, murders, vigilantism, and a disrespect for the law followed.

Lincoln's solution to this problem was to cultivate a "civil religion" around America's founding documents, the Declaration of Independence and the Constitution, and the law in general. "The answer is simple," Lincoln proclaimed:

> Let reverence for the laws, be breathed by every American mother, to the lisping babe, that prattles on her lap—let it be taught in schools, seminaries, and in colleges; let it be written in Primers, spelling books, and in Almanacs; let it be preached from the pulpit, proclaimed in legislative halls, and enforced in courts of justice. And, in short, let it become the *political religion* of the nation; and let the old and the young, the rich and the poor, the grave and the gay, of all sexes and tongues, and colors and conditions, sacrifice unceasingly upon its altars.[27]

Six things are then necessary, Lincoln argued, for cultivating a civil religion in the hearts of good citizens. Reverence for the laws ought to be *breathed, taught, written, preached, proclaimed,* and *enforced* to, in effect, habituate Americans toward good citizenship. If Americans took reverence for the rule of law for granted, if they could agree on a system based upon certain principles, this might be enough to fortify against the danger of mob rule—and the danger of suffering a tyrant like Julius Caesar.

The key line in this passage, however, is the last: Let all citizens "sacrifice unceasingly upon its altars." Lincoln did not employ this religious imagery merely to be poetic. To sustain a republican form of government, citizenship must be an activity, not a statement. And active citizenship requires sacrifice. To succeed, Lincoln's plan required Americans to not simply *feel* an attachment to the laws—feelings are fickle—but to *understand* and *choose* to uphold the law for themselves. Good habits thus lead to good choices.

It is deeply ironic that Lincoln gave this speech in 1838, the same year that Americans at the highest levels of government were disregarding treaty laws and forcing thousands of Indigenous peoples away from their homelands. Lincoln did not mention the *institutional* mob that instigated Indian Removal—perhaps he approved of it—but, regardless, a further irony presents itself. Cherokee leaders have adhered to Lincoln's prescription for cultivating republican citizens better than Americans have. To wit, the Cherokee Nation has an expansive cultural preservation program designed to consistently remind its citizens (and guests) of where they've been as a nation, of what they must do to sustain their community today, and of their vision for the future: in effect, to remind citizens that their citizenship is not a statement but a way of life.

NOTES

INTRODUCTION

1. Lindsey Bark, "Teehee Nominated as Cherokee Nation's Delegate to Congress," *Cherokee Phoenix*, August 23, 2019, https://www.cherokeephoenix.org /news/teehee-nominated-as-cherokee-nations-delegate-to-congress/article _d7a18988-adoa-5cf5-843a-05264c798109.html; Kelsey Vlamis, "The US Promised the Cherokee Nation a Seat in Congress in a Treaty That Fueled the Trail of Tears. 188 Years Later, the Cherokee Say Lawmakers May Finally Fulfill That Promise," Business Insider, February 4, 2023, https://www.businessinsider.com /us-188-year-old-treaty-seat-cherokee-nation-delegate-congress-2023-1. As of this writing, Congress still has not seated the delegate.

2. Vine Deloria Jr., *Custer Died for Your Sins: An Indian Manifesto* (Norman: University of Oklahoma Press, 1969); Daniel Heath Justice, *Why Indigenous Literatures Matter* (Waterloo, Ontario: Wilfred Laurier University Press, 2018); Ned Blackhawk, *The Rediscovery of America: Native Peoples and the Unmaking of U.S. History* (New Haven, CT: Yale University Press, 2023).

3. Asma Khalid, "Warren Releases DNA Results, Challenges Trump over Native American Ancestry," NPR, October 15, 2018, https://www.npr.org/2018 /10/15/657468655/warren-releases-dna-results-challenges-trump-over-native -american-ancestry.

4. Chris Cillizza, "Elizabeth Warren Might Have Actually Made Things Worse with Her DNA Gambit," CNN Politics, October 17, 2018, https://www .cnn.com/2018/10/16/politics/elizabeth-warren-donald-trump-pocahontas /index.html.

5. Will Chavez, "Cherokee Nation Responds to Senator Warren's DNA Test," *Cherokee Phoenix*, October 16, 2018, https://www.cherokeephoenix.org/news /cherokee-nation-responds-to-senator-warrens-dna-test/article_d7a84410 -2e21-5fcb-9734-e8219d8cooce.html.

6. Chuck Hoskin Jr., "OPINION: Tribal Citizenship: A Concept Many outside Tribal Governments Do Not Understand," *Cherokee Phoenix*, January 31, 2019, https://www.cherokeephoenix.org/opinion/opinion-tribal-citizenship-a -concept-many-outside-tribal-governments-do-not-understand/article_05853a53 -0673-5fff-bd62-9bf478c387c9.html.

7. There is a robust scholarly conversation over Cherokee *peoplehood* and *nationhood* that, while not specifically within the purview of this book, deserves

mentioning in some detail here. "Peoplehood," Daniel Heath Justice writes, is "the dynamic and active participation in the relational reality of the tribal nation. One does not have the right of affiliation without also sharing the responsibilities of participation in at least some of the relationships that define the community." Indigenous *nationhood*, by contrast, is "an understanding of a common social interdependence within the community, the tribal web of kinship rights *and* responsibilities that link the People, the land, and the cosmos together in an ongoing and dynamic system of mutually affecting relationships. . . . Tribal nationhood is, in this way, distinguished from state-focused nationalism by its central focus on *peoplehood*, the relational system that keeps the people in balance with one another, with other peoples and realities, and with the world." Nationhood is, therefore, "a political extension of the social rights and responsibilities of peoplehood." See Daniel Heath Justice, *Our Fire Survives the Storm: A Cherokee Literary History* (Minneapolis: University of Minnesota Press, 2006), 24–25.

Joshua Nelson is critical of the "tribal nations born of indigenous nationhood" and their tendency toward embodying negative characteristics of modern western nation-states. "In his equation of peoplehood with nationhood, nationalist Daniel Heath Justice" dismisses the connection "between tribal people and ugly versions of the state," Nelson writes. The Cherokee Nation, the product of Cherokee nationhood, possesses many of the qualifications of a nation-state, such as the administration of a police force, "whose officers are trained by federal law enforcement agencies, and are cross-deputized with county and municipal entities; it maintains headquarters; it employs administrative, legislative, judicial, and bureaucratic officials; it operates schools, child welfare offices, and health clinics, among other governmental responsibilities under the rule of law. The Cherokee nation-state now also oversees the business entity Cherokee Nation Industries, an electronics company that manufactures, among other things, wiring harnesses for the Bell Boeing V-22 Osprey combat-troop carrier, under a federal Department of Defense contract." Indigenous regimes, that is to say, are not immune to the dangers of nationalism. See Joshua B. Nelson, *Progressive Traditions: Identity in Cherokee Literature and Culture* (Norman: University of Oklahoma Press, 2014), 14, 21–22.

Kirby Brown defines "nationhood" as "the intersection of politics, peoplehood, imagination, and experience." It is the "*political expression* of the complex matrix of relations through which Native peoples reckon identity, relationality, and belonging." This nationhood is messy, an "often-contested but ultimately generative intersection where Indigenous politics, imagination, peoplehood, and experience meet, mix it up, and sometimes collide." Peoplehood is a component of nationhood, which is a component of tribal government itself. See Kirby Brown, *Stoking the Fire: Nationhood in Cherokee Writing, 1907–1970* (Norman: University of Oklahoma Press, 2018), 6–7. For more on this conversation, see Scott Richard Lyons, *X-Marks: Native Signatures of Assent* (Minneapolis: University of Minnesota Press, 2010).

8. James H. Kettner, *The Development of American Citizenship, 1608–1870* (Chapel Hill: University of North Carolina Press, 1978), 9; John Quincy Adams, *The Social Compact* (Providence, RI: Knowles and Vose, 1842).

9. Kettner, *Development of American Citizenship*, 10.

10. Judith N. Shklar, *American Citizenship: The Quest for Inclusion* (Cambridge, MA: Harvard University Press, 1991), 1; Rogers M. Smith, *Civic Ideals: Conflicting Visions of Citizenship in U.S. History* (New Haven, CT: Yale University Press, 1997).

11. David E. Wilkins and Shelly Hulse Wilkins, *Dismembered: Native Disenrollment and the Battle for Human Rights* (Seattle: University of Washington Press, 2017), 57.

12. Wilkins and Wilkins, *Dismembered*, 57, emphasis in the original.

13. Wilkins and Wilkins, 58. The authors draw these definitions from the *Oxford English Dictionary*.

14. Hoskin, "OPINION: Tribal Citizenship."

15. The Dawes Act of 1887 and the Dawes Commission are covered more thoroughly in Chapter 4.

16. Constitution of the Cherokee Nation (1999), Article IV, Section 1.

17. Brice Obermeyer, *Delaware Tribe in a Cherokee Nation* (Lincoln: University of Nebraska Press, 2009).

18. Asma Khalid, "Warren Apologizes to Cherokee Nation for DNA Test," NPR, February 1, 2019, https://www.npr.org/2019/02/01/690806434/warren -apologizes-to-cherokee-nation-for-dna-test; Maggie Astor, "Why Many Native Americans Are Angry with Elizabeth Warren," *New York Times*, October 17, 2018, https://www.nytimes.com/2018/10/17/us/politics/elizabeth-warren-dna -test.html.

19. Khalid, "Warren Apologizes."

20. Jeffrey K. Tulis and Nicole Mellow, *Legacies of Losing in American Politics* (Chicago: University of Chicago Press, 2018), 29–67.

21. Smith, *Civic Ideals*; Kettner, *Development of American Citizenship*.

22. David Myer Temin, "Custer's Sins: Vine Deloria Jr. and the Settler-Colonial Politics of Civic Inclusion," *Political Theory* 46, no. 3 (June 2018): 357–79, https://doi.org/10.1177/0090591717712151.

23. There is, of course, a rich and much older literature on Cherokee Nation history from the likes of Daniel Littlefield, William McLaughlin, Theda Perdue, Angie Debo, Grant Foreman, Emmet Starr, and many others. I reference the seminal works of these scholars extensively throughout this manuscript.

24. Brown, *Stoking the Fire*; Kirby Brown, "Citizenship, Land, and Law: Constitutional Criticism and John Milton Oskison's *Black Jack Davy*," *Studies in American Indian Literatures* 23, no. 4, Special Issue: Constitutional Criticism (Winter 2011): 77–115, https://doi.org/10.5250/studamerindilite.23.4.0077; Nelson, *Progressive Traditions*; Justice, *Why Indigenous Literatures Matter*; Justice, *Our Fire Survives the Storm*; Jace Weaver, *That the People Might Live: Native American Literatures and Native American Community* (New York: Oxford University Press, 1997).

25. Christopher B. Teuton and Hastings Shade, *Cherokee Earth Dwellers: Stories and Teachings of the Natural World* (Seattle: University of Washington Press,

2023); Christopher B. Teuton, *Cherokee Stories of the Turtle Island Liars' Club* (Chapel Hill: University of North Carolina Press, 2012).

26. Tiya Miles, *Ties That Bind: The Story of an Afro-Cherokee Family in Slavery and Freedom* (Oakland: University of California Press, 2015); Tiya Miles, "'Circular Reasoning': Recentering Cherokee Women in the Antiremoval Campaigns," *American Quarterly* 61, no. 2 (June 2009): 221–43; Julie Reed, *Serving the Nation: Cherokee Sovereignty and Social Welfare, 1800–1907* (Norman: University of Oklahoma Press, 2016); Andrew Denson, *Demanding the Cherokee Nation: Indian Autonomy and American Culture, 1830–1900* (Lincoln: University of Nebraska Press, 2004); Rose Stremlau, *Sustaining the Cherokee Family: Kinship and the Allotment of an Indigenous Nation* (Chapel Hill: University of North Carolina Press, 2011).

27. Kennan Ferguson, "Why Does Political Science Hate American Indians?," *Perspectives on Politics* 14, no. 4 (December 2016): 1029–38, https://doi.org/10.1017/S1537592716002905.

28. Ferguson, "Why Does Political Science," 1029.

29. Ferguson, 1033–35.

30. Lauren M. MacLean, "Marginalizing Politics: The Conceptual and Epistemological Barriers to American Indians," *Perspectives on Politics* 14, no. 4 (December 2016): 1044–45, https://doi.org/10.1017/S1537592716002930.

31. David E. Wilkins, "Absence Does Not Make the Indigenous Heart Grow Fonder," *Perspectives on Politics* 14, no. 4 (December 2016): 1049, https://doi.org/10.1017/S1537592716002954.

32. Franke Wilmer, "Indigenizing Political Science or Decolonizing Political Scientists?," *Perspectives on Politics* 14, no. 4 (December 2016): 1050, https://doi.org/10.1017/S1537592716002966.

33. Wilmer, "Indigenizing Political Science," 1050.

34. Wilmer, 1051; Linda Tuhiwai Smith, *Decolonizing Methodologies: Research and Indigenous Peoples* (London: Zed Books, 1999).

35. Paul Frymer, "Why Aren't Political Scientists Interested in Native American Politics?," *Perspectives on Politics* 14, no. 4 (December 2016): 1042–43, https://doi.org/10.1017/S1537592716002929. See also David E. Wilkins and K. Tsianina Lomawaima, *Uneven Ground: American Indian Sovereignty and Federal Law* (Norman: University of Oklahoma Press, 2001); Kevin Bruyneel, *The Third Space of Sovereignty: The Post-Colonial Politics of U.S.-Indigenous Relations* (Minneapolis: University of Minnesota Press, 2007); David Myer Temin, *Remapping Sovereignty: Decolonization and Self-Determination in North American Indigenous Political Thought* (Chicago: University of Chicago Press, 2023); and Samuel Piccolo, "Indigenous Sovereignty, Common Law, and Natural Law," *American Journal of Political Science* (January 2023): 1–13, https://doi.org/10.1111/ajps.12762. This is to say nothing of the rich political science research being conducted with Indigenous peoples globally. See Katherine Becerra Valdivia's *Indigenous Collective Rights in Latin America: The Role of Coalitions, Constitutions, and Party Systems* (Lanham, MD: Lexington Books, 2022) for an excellent recent example.

36. Frymer, "Why Aren't Political Scientists," 1042.

37. Rennard Strickland, *Fire and the Spirits: Cherokee Law from Clan to Court* (Norman: University of Oklahoma Press, 1975); Vine Deloria Jr. and David E. Wilkins, *Tribes, Treaties, and Constitutional Tribulations* (Austin: University of Texas Press, 1999); Kevin Bruyneel, "Challenging American Boundaries: Indigenous Peoples and the 'Gift' of US Citizenship," *Studies in American Political Development* 18 (Spring 2004): 30–43; David E. Wilkins, *Native American Political Development: 1500s to 1933* (New York: Oxford University Press, 2009); Paul Frymer, "'A Rush, A Push, and the Land Is Ours': Territorial Expansion, Land Policy, and U.S. State Formation," *Perspectives on Policy* 12, no. 1 (March 2014): 119–44; Aaron Kushner, "Cherokee Political Thought and the Development of Tribal Citizenship," *Studies in American Political Development* 35, no. 1 (2021): 1–15, https://doi.org/10.1017/S0898588X20000176; J. Matthew Martin, *The Cherokee Supreme Court: 1823–1835* (Durham, NC: Carolina Academic Press, 2021).

38. For more on scholarly debates over decolonization, see Eve Tuck and K. Wayne Yang, "Decolonization Is Not a Metaphor," *Decolonization: Indigeneity, Education & Society* 1, no. 1 (2012): 1–40; Tapji Garba and Sara-Maria Sorentino, "Slavery Is a Metaphor: A Critical Commentary on Eve Tuck and K. Wayne Yang's 'Decolonization Is Not a Metaphor,'" *Antipode* 52, no. 1 (March 2020): 764–82, https://doi.org/10.1111/anti.12615; Curley et al., "Decolonisation Is a Political Project: Overcoming Impasses between Indigenous Sovereignty and Abolition," *Antipode* 54, no. 4 (July 2022): 1043–62, https://doi.org/10.1111/anti.12830.

39. See Aaron Kushner and Stephen Clouse, "Citizenship and the Good Life: Cherokee and American Regimes in Conflict." *Political Science Reviewer* 47, no. 3 (2023): 1–34.

40. Karen Orren and Stephen Skowronek, *The Search for American Political Development* (Cambridge, UK: Cambridge University Press, 2004), 6, 123.

41. James W. Ceaser, "Foundational Concepts and American Political Development," in *Nature and History in American Political Development*, ed. James W. Ceaser (Cambridge, MA: Harvard University Press, 2006), 5. Ideas favor and privilege certain institutions. Foundational ideas find their empirical referents in institutional designs. Actors working within the confines of institutional rules are therefore necessarily limited in what they can and cannot do. Policymaking needs may drive the rise of rules, leadership structures, and committee systems, yet these referent points derive their form from the ideas upon which they were grounded. In other words, policies are institutions in the way that they provide incentives for shaping behavior. See Jay K. Dow, *Electing the House: The Adoption and Performance of the US Single-Member District Electoral System* (Lawrence: University Press of Kansas, 2017), 8; Karen Orren and Stephen Skowronek, "Have We Abandoned a 'Constitutional Perspective' on American Political Development?," *Review of Politics* 73, no. 2 (March 2011): 295–99, https://doi.org/10.1017/S0034670511000088; and Peverill Squire, *The Evolution of American Legislatures: Colonies, Territories, and States, 1619–2009* (Ann Arbor: University of Michigan Press, 2012).

42. Nancy L. Rosenblum, "Replacing Foundations with Staging: Second Story Concepts and American Political Development," in *Nature and History in*

American Political Development, ed. James W. Ceaser (Cambridge, MA: Harvard University Press, 2006), 116.

43. Kushner, "Cherokee Political Thought."

44. Kushner, 2.

45. Kushner, 2.

46. Suzanne Mettler and Richard M. Valelly, "Introduction: The Distinctiveness and Necessity of American Political Development," in *Oxford Handbook of American Political Development*, eds. Suzanne Mettler and Richard M. Valelly (New York: Oxford University Press, 2016), 4.

47. Wilkins and Wilkins, *Dismembered*, 11.

48. Crosslin Fields Smith, *Original Teachings Designed to Stand as One: Early Keetoowah Teachings and Traditions* (Ranchos de Taos, NM: Dog Soldier Press, 2021. 57–65).

49. Constitution of the Cherokee Nation (1827), Article III, Section 4.

50. Yule Kim, "The Cherokee Freedmen Dispute: Legal Background, Analysis, and Proposed Legislation," U.S. Congressional Research Service, order code RL34321, updated August 7, 2008, https://www.everycrsreport.com/files/20080807_RL34321_a3af70824a5ac2377f3625be371d61b58b32ff48.pdf, 7 (emphasis added).

51. Felix S. Cohen, *Handbook of Federal Indian Law with Reference Tables* (Washington, DC: U.S. Government Printing Office, 1945).

52. David E. Wilkins, "A Most Grievous Display of Behavior: Self-Decimation in Indian Country," *Michigan State Law Review* 2 (June 2013): 328.

53. *Baltimore Sun*, July 29, 1984, cited in Circe Sturm, *Blood Politics: Race, Culture, and Identity in the Cherokee Nation of Oklahoma* (Berkeley: University of California Press, 2002), 179. The Cherokee Nation is much more lenient than many other tribal nations, including the United Keetoowah Band and the Eastern Band of Cherokee Indians, in their views on blood as designating citizenship. While other nations implement a minimum blood quantum policy (e.g., a citizen must have a certain fraction of Indian blood to enroll), the Cherokee Nation has often favored policies that allow those with a very small degree of Indian blood to enroll.

54. "Tribal Council Meeting—2/22/2021," Cherokee Nation Official Newsroom, February 22, 2021, video file, at 9:50, https://www.youtube.com/watch?v=wrn8qXFo_Lk.

55. Will Chavez, "UPDATE: Freedmen Descendants Have Citizenship Restored and May Vote Sept. 24," *Cherokee Phoenix*, September 21, 2011, https://www.cherokeephoenix.org/news/update-freedmen-descendants-have-citizenship-restored-and-may-vote-sept-24/article_70491727-8093-5f0e-8566-59b34ecbe6cf.html; Marilyn Vann, "Cherokee Freedmen Overjoyed by Federal Court Ruling Granting Citizenship," interview by Allison Herrera, PRI, August 31, 2017, audio, 4:40, https://www.pri.org/stories/2017-08-31/cherokee-freedmen-overjoyed-federal-court-ruling-granting-tribal-citizenship.

56. Nelson, *Progressive Traditions*, 165–83.

57. Chad Hunter, "Cherokee Nation Attorney General Asks Supreme Court to Strike Constitution's 'by Blood' Reference," *Cherokee Phoenix*, February 19, 2021, https://www.cherokeephoenix.org/news/cherokee-nation-attorney-general -asks-supreme-court-to-strike-constitution-s-by-blood-reference/article _96ba59d4-72e4-11eb-8164-8fd4e0083f67.html. This Cherokee Nation court decision and its complexity are covered more fully in chapter 5.

58. Cherokee Nation Legislative Act 14–22: An Act Revising and Restating Title 26 ("Elections") of the Cherokee Nation Code Annotated.

59. Miles, *Ties That Bind*, 125–28.

60. Teuton, *Turtle Island Liars' Club*, 12.

61. Denson, *Demanding the Cherokee Nation*, 201–3.

62. Justice, *Why Indigenous Literatures Matter*, 194, 193.

63. Sturm, *Blood Politics*, 178–86.

64. Wilma Mankiller and Michael Wallis, *Mankiller: A Chief and Her People* (New York: St. Martin's, 1993); Crosslin Fields Smith, *Stand as One: Spiritual Teachings of Keetoowah* (Ranchos de Taos, NM: Dog Soldier Press, 2018; Heidi M. Altman and Thomas N. Belt, "Tohi: The Cherokee Concept of Well-Being," in *Under the Rattlesnake: Cherokee Health and Resiliency*, ed. Lisa J. Lefler (Tuscaloosa: University of Alabama Press, 2009), 9–22; Teuton and Shade, *Cherokee Earth Dwellers*; Emmet Starr, *History of the Cherokee Indians and Their Legends and Folklore* (Oklahoma City: Genealogical Publishing, 1921).

65. Tom Holm, "Untitled Review," in Crosslin Fields Smith, *Stand as One: Spiritual Teachings of Keetoowah; Awakening to the Original Truths* (Ranchos de Taos, NM: Dog Soldier Press, 2018), 71.

66. Reed, *Serving the Nation*, 3–4; Teuton and Shade, *Cherokee Earth Dwellers*, 22; Stremlau, *Sustaining the Cherokee Family*, 244.

67. Durbin Feeling, GWY-ᏉᎪᏆᏍ ᎫᏍᏛᏆᏬᏉᎫ (*Cherokee-English Dictionary*) (Tahlequah, OK: Cherokee Nation of Oklahoma, 1975), 93; Chadwick Corntassel Smith, *Leadership Lessons from the Cherokee Nation* (New York: McGraw-Hill, 2013).

68. Chadwick Corntassel Smith, Foreword to Mark Edwin Miller, *Claiming Tribal Identity: The Five Tribes and the Politics of Federal Acknowledgement* (Norman: University of Oklahoma Press, 2013), x.

69. Gregory D. Smithers, "Why Do So Many Americans Think They Have Cherokee Blood?," Slate, October 1, 2015, https://slate.com/news-and-politics /2015/10/cherokee-blood-why-do-so-many-americans-believe-they-have -cherokee-ancestry.html; Scott Jaschik, "Fake Cherokee?," Inside Higher Ed, July 6, 2015, https://www.insidehighered.com/news/2015/07/06/scholar-who -has-made-name-cherokee-accused-not-having-native-american-roots. For a fuller discussion of this phenomenon, see also see Philip J. Deloria, *Playing Indian* (New Haven, CT: Yale University Press, 1998).

70. Alexis de Tocqueville, *Democracy in America*, eds. and trans. Harvey C. Mansfield and Delba Winthrop (Chicago: University of Chicago Press, 2000), II.3.13, 577–78.

71. Tocqueville, *Democracy in America*, II.3.19, 599.

72. Tocqueville, II.3.19, 603.

73. Sam Yellowhorse Kesler, "The Race-Shifting of 'Pretendians,'" NPR, February 23, 2022, https://www.npr.org/2022/02/23/1082622851/native-american -communities-concerned-about-self-identification-wannabes.

74. Teuton, *Turtle Island Liars' Club*, 114–15.

75. Deloria, *Custer Died for Your Sins*, 188, 193.

76. Patrick Deneen, *Why Liberalism Failed* (New Haven, CT: Yale University Press, 2018), xiii–xiv.

77. Deneen, *Why Liberalism Failed*, xiv.

78. Justice, *Why Indigenous Literatures Matter*, 15.

79. Holm, "Untitled Review," 84–85.

80. Smith, *Original Teachings*; Smith, *Stand as One*; Teuton and Shade, *Cherokee Earth Dwellers*; Teuton, *Turtle Island Liars' Club*.

81. Alan Bloom, *The Closing of the American Mind: How Higher Education Has Failed Democracy and Impoverished the Souls of Today's Students* (New York: Simon & Schuster, 1987), 82–88.

82. Michael Paul Rogin, *Fathers & Children: Andrew Jackson and the Subjugation of the American Indian* (New Brunswick, NJ: Transaction, 1991), 8.

83. Smith, *Leadership Lessons*, 93.

84. Smith, 482.

85. Deloria, "Self-Determination and the Concept of Sovereignty," 22, quoted in Wilkins, "A Most Grievous Display," 329.

CHAPTER 1

1. The name of the Indian trader is disputed in the record. A sworn affidavit accepted by the Cherokee Supreme Court presents the name as "Tom Dent," while the judgment docket refers to the same individual as "Saml Bend." I here follow J. Matthew Martin's usage, identifying the man as "Sam Dent." Both documents drawn from the appendices in J. Matthew Martin, *The Cherokee Supreme Court: 1823–1835* (Durham, NC: Carolina Academic Press, 2021), 196–97. See also Theda Perdue, "Clan and Court: Another Look at the Early Cherokee Republic," *American Indian Quarterly* 24, no. 4 (2000): 562–69; William G. McLaughlin, *Cherokee Renascence in the New Republic* (Princeton, NJ: Princeton University Press, 1986), 347; and Tiya Miles, *Ties That Bind: The Story of an Afro-Cherokee Family in Slavery and Freedom* (Oakland: University of California Press, 2015), 56–57.

2. Judgment Docket, *supra* note 31, at Friday, October 18, 1833, in Martin, *Cherokee Supreme Court*, 196–97; Perdue, "Clan and Court," 562–63. For more on the Deer Clan, see Chistopher B. Teuton and Hastings Shade, *Cherokee Earth Dwellers: Stories and Teachings of the Natural World* (Seattle: University of Washington Press), 31.

3. Perdue, "Clan and Court," 562.

4. Judgment Docket, *supra* note 31, at Friday, October 18, 1833.

5. Judgment Docket, *supra* note 31, at Friday, October 18, 1833.
6. Judgment Docket, *supra* note 31, at Friday, October 18, 1833.
7. Crosslin Fields Smith, *Original Teachings Designed to Stand as One: Early Keetoowah Teachings and Traditions* (Ranchos de Taos, NM: Dog Soldier Press, 2021), 58.
8. Charles R. Hicks, "From Charles R. Hicks, Feb. 1, 1826," in John Ross, *The Papers of Chief John Ross*, Vol. 1, *1807–1839*, ed. Gary E. Moulton (Norman: University of Oklahoma Press, 1985), 111–113, at 112; Emmet Starr, *Early History of the Cherokees: Embracing Aboriginal Customs, Religion, Laws, Folk Lore, and Civilization* (Baltimore: Clearfield, 1917), 35–37; Grace Steele Woodward, *The Cherokees* (Norman: University of Oklahoma Press, 1963), 17.
9. John Phillip Reid, *A Law of Blood: The Primitive Law of the Cherokee Nation* (DeKalb: Northern Illinois University Press, 2006); Aaron Kushner and Stephen Clouse, "Citizenship and the Good Life," *Political Science Reviewer* 47, no. 3 (2023): 1–34.
10. Charles Hudson, *The Southeastern Indians* (Knoxville: University of Tennessee Press, 1976), 148–56; James Mooney, "Myths of the Cherokee," Smithsonian Institution, part 1, paper no. 1 (Washington, DC: Government Printing Office, 1900), 242–49; William G. McLoughlin, *Cherokee Renascence in the New Republic* (Princeton, NJ: Princeton University Press, 1986); Starr, *Early History of the Cherokees*; Strickland, *Fire and the Spirits*; Adair, *History of the American Indians*; Albert James Pickett, *The Annotated Pickett's History of Alabama and Incidentally of Georgia and Mississippi, from the Earliest Period*, ed. James P. Pate (Montgomery, AL: New South Books, 2018).
11. Nelson, *Progressive Traditions*.
12. Smith, *Original Teachings*, 57–66.
13. R. Halliburton Jr., *Red over Black: : Black Slavery among the Cherokee Indians* (Westport, CT: Greenwood Press, 1977), 139; Robert Conley Jr., *Cherokee Nation: A History* (Albuquerque: University of New Mexico Press, 2005), 7; Justice, *Our Fire Survives the Storm*, 42; Mankiller and Wallis, *Mankiller*, 16–17.
DhBӨ◌Ө may also be translated as "The Pure People": DBӨ (*ayvwi*) meaning person—the pluralized form being DhBӨ (*aniyvwi*) and the suffix ◌Ө (*ya*) being an indication of purity or *realness*. See Feeling, GWУ-ƃЈℐ ᎫSꝯⱵ◌ᎧVᎫ (*Cherokee-English Dictionary*), 310.
14. Cherokees were forbidden to couple with members of both their own clan and of their fathers' clans as these relationships were considered incestuous and would therefore corrupt the world. See McLoughlin, *Cherokee Renascence*, 11; Circe Sturm, *Blood Politics: Race, Culture, and Identity in the Cherokee Nation of Oklahoma* (Berkeley: University of California Press, 2002), 30–31; Reid, *Law of Blood*, 43–45; Teuton and Shade, *Cherokee Earth Dwellers*, 31; and Smith, *Original Teachings*, 57–66.
15. Reid, *Law of Blood*, 39.
16. Hudson, *Southeastern Indians*, 191; Raymond Fogelson writes that "the Cherokee theory of procreation holds . . . that the female contributes blood and flesh to the fetus, while the father provides the skeleton through the agency

of sperm . . ." Thus, Cherokee relatives believed that they shared actual blood, not in a metaphorical sense, but in an actual, tangible way. A mother's blood was powerful, be that menstrual or birthing blood. See Raymond Fogelson, "On the 'Petticoat Government' of the Eighteenth-Century Cherokee," *Personality and Cultural Construction of Society: Papers in Honor of Melford E. Spiro*, eds. David K. Jordan and Marc J. Swartz (Tuscaloosa: University of Alabama Press, 1990), 173–74.

17. Reid, *Law of Blood*, 39–40.

18. Miles, *Ties That Bind*; Theda Perdue, *Cherokee Women* (Lincoln: University of Nebraska Press, 1998).

19. Reid, *Law of Blood*, 117–19.

20. Smith, *Original Teachings*, 59.

21. Reed, *Serving the Nation*, 6.

22. Reed, 6; Stremlau, *Sustaining the Cherokee Family*, 22; Gregory D. Smithers, *The Cherokee Diaspora: An Indigenous History of Migration, Resettlement, and Identity* (New Haven, CT: Yale University Press), 2015, 6; Starr, *Early History of the Cherokees*, 2–4.

23. Adair, *History of the American Indians*, 17.

24. Smith, *Original Teachings*, 58.

25. Reed, *Serving the Nation*, 5.

26. Reed, 6–7; Starr, *Early History of the Cherokees*.

27. Henry Timberlake, *The Memoirs of Lieut. Henry Timberlake: Who Accompanied the Three Cherokee Indians to England in the Year 1762* (London: J. Ridley, 1765), 69.

28. Heidi M. Altman and Thomas N. Belt, "Tohi: The Cherokee Concept of Well-Being." in *Under the Rattlesnake: Cherokee Health and Resiliency*, ed. Lisa J. Lefler. (Tuscaloosa: University of Alabama Press, 2009), 13–14.

The treatment of the Cherokee cosmovision and religion in this book does not even begin to scratch the surface; for our purposes here, I focus on those foundational ideas, those core principles, most closely and ultimately related to citizenship—in other words, those concepts associated with the trail that runs between Cherokee peoplehood, Cherokee nationhood, and Cherokee government. There is a rich and expansive literature, old and new, on Cherokee belief systems that I draw from. Among these are Jack F. Kilpatrick and Anna G. Kilpatrick, *Friends of Thunder: Folktales of the Oklahoma Cherokees* (Norman: University of Oklahoma Press, 1964); Mankiller and Wallis, *Mankiller*; Justice, *Our Fire Survives the Storm*; Weaver, *That the People Might Live*; Smith, *Original Teachings*; Smith, *Stand as One*; Teuton and Shade, *Cherokee Earth Dwellers*; Teuton, *Turtle Island Liars' Club*; Smith, *Leadership Lessons*; Hudson, *Southeastern Indians*; Justice, *Our Fire Survives the Storm*; Reed, *Serving the Nation*; and Stremlau, *Sustaining the Cherokee Family*.

29. Altman and Belt, "Tohi," 14.

30. Teuton and Shade, *Cherokee Earth Dwellers*, 21.

31. Teuton and Shade, 21; Altman and Belt, "Tohi," 14–15.

32. Teuton and Shade, *Cherokee Earth Dwellers*, 21.

NOTES TO CHAPTER 1

33. Smith, *Stand As One*, xv.

34. Altman and Belt, "Tohi," 14.

35. Murray L. Wax and Rosalie H. Wax, "Religion among the American Indians," *Annals of the American Academy of Political and Social Science* 436 (1978): 28; Mankiller and Wallis, *Mankiller*, 20.

36. Teuton and Shade, *Cherokee Earth Dwellers*, 35.

37. Eva Marie Garroutte, *Real Indians: Identity and the Survival of Native America* (Berkeley: University of California Press, 2003), 137, quoted in Nelson, *Progressive Traditions*, 56. Emphasis in original.

38. Teuton and Shade, *Cherokee Earth Dwellers*, 11.

39. Clint Carroll, *Roots of Our Renewal: Ethnobotany and Cherokee Environmental Governance* (Minneapolis: University of Minnesota Press, 2015), ix.

40. Teuton, *Turtle Island Liars' Club*, 7.

41. Teuton, 7–8; Smith, *Stand as One*, 22, 30–33; Smith, *Original Teachings*.

42. Mooney, "Myths," 242–49; Hudson, *Southeastern Indians*, 148–56; Smithers, *Cherokee Diaspora*, 13–16; Smith, *Original Teachings*, 11–13; Brown, *Stoking the Fire*, 170; Nelson, *Progressive Traditions*, 77, 108; Teuton and Shade, *Cherokee Earth Dwellers*, 124–27; Stremlau, *Sustaining the Cherokee Family*, 21–22, 242–43; McLoughlin, *Cherokee Renascence*, 176; Perdue, *Cherokee Women*, 17–28; Johnson, *Voices of Cherokee Women*, 5–6; Marilou Awiakta, *Selu: Seeking the Corn-Mother's Wisdom* (Golden, CO: Fulcrum Publishing, 1993), 16–23; Sturm, *Blood Politics*, 34–35; Justice, *Our Fire Survives the Storm*, 28.

43. Mooney, "Myths," 242–49.

44. Mooney, 242–44.

45. Mooney, 244.

46. Mooney, 244.

47. Mooney, 244–45.

48. Teuton and Shade, *Cherokee Earth Dwellers*, 124.

49. Smith, *Original Teachings*, 11.

50. Kilpatrick and Kilpatrick, *Friends of Thunder*, 129–34.

51. Stremlau, *Sustaining the Cherokee Family*, 243.

52. Nelson, *Progressive Traditions*, 108.

53. Carolyn Ross Johnston, ed., *Voices of Cherokee Women* (Winston-Salem, NC: John F. Blair, 2013), 5; Brown, *Stoking the Fire*, 170.

54. Johnston, *Voices of Cherokee Women*, 5.

55. Johnston, 6.

56. Femaleness was associated with menstruation, childbirth, motherhood, blood, the sun, clan, corn, and agriculture. Masculinity was associated with warfare, hunting, animals, water, and fatherhood. Women who fought in battle or who hunted were considered a mixture of two categories, male and female, and thus especially powerful, since they shed blood not only through menstruation and childbirth but also in battle. See Perdue, *Cherokee Women*; Norma Tucker, "Nancy Ward: Ghighau of the Cherokees," *Georgia Historical Quarterly* 53, no. 2 (June 1969): 192–200; and Awiakta, *Selu*.

57. Justice, *Our Fire Survives the Storm*, 28.

58. Hudson, *Southeastern Indians*, 156; Teuton and Shade, *Cherokee Earth Dwellers*.

59. Perdue, *Cherokee Women*, 17.

60. Perdue, 17–18.

61. Perdue, 25.

62. Perdue, 25.

63. Stremlau, *Sustaining the Cherokee Family*, 21.

64. Justice, *Our Fire Survives the Storm*, 28.

65. Hudson, *Southeastern Indians*, 155; Stremlau, *Sustaining the Cherokee Family*, 242.

66. Stremlau, 22.

67. Mooney, "Myths," 2.

68. Mooney, 242–44.

69. Teuton and Shade, *Cherokee Earth Dwellers*, 124–27.

70. Justice, *Our Fire Survives the Storm*, 25.

71. Teuton, *Turtle Island Liars' Club*, 2–4; Smith, *Original Teachings*; Smith, *Stand as One*; Teuton and Shade, *Cherokee Earth Dwellers*.

72. Smith, "ᏏᏴᏍᎩ ᏗᏐᏓᎶᏗ," 320–22, quoted in Teuton and Shade, *Cherokee Earth Dwellers*, 141.

73. Nelson, *Progressive Traditions*, 80.

74. Reid, *Law of Blood*, 6–7.

75. Pickett, *Annotated Pickett's History of Alabama*, 115; Adair, *History of the American Indians*, 227. The reader will note that the exact number of Cherokee towns in the eighteenth century is disputed in the historical record. The upper town residents were also called Overhill Cherokees because of the need for others to travel over the mountains to reach them; the middle and lower towns lay east of the Appalachians. For a brief overview, see Gerald F. Schroedl, "Overhill Cherokees," *Tennessee Encyclopedia*, October 8, 2017, http://tennesseeencyclopedia.net/entries/overhill-cherokees/.

76. Wilbur R. Jacobs, ed., *Indians of the Southern Colonial Frontier: The Edmond Atkin Report and Plan of 1755* (Columbia: University of South Carolina Press, 1954), 48–54.

77. Jacobs, *Indians of the Southern Colonial Frontier*, 49.

78. For an excellent discussion of this, see Justice, *Our Fire Survives the Storm*.

79. Strickland, *Fire and the Spirits*, 24.

80. Strickland, 24.

81. Strickland, 224.

82. McLoughlin, *Cherokee Renascence*, 278.

83. McLoughlin, 395.

84. McLoughlin, 11.

85. Reed, *Serving the Nation*, 8. Cherokees did not define "incest" the way that Americans today do; for Cherokees, incest meant coupling with anyone from your own clan—or coupling with anyone from your father's clan.

86. Smithers, *Cherokee Diaspora*, 118–19.

87. McLoughlin, *Cherokee Renascence*, 12.

88. Reed, *Serving the Nation*, 8; Strickland, *Fire and the Spirits*, 26–30.

89. Strickland, *Fire and the Spirits*, 11.

90. Altman and Belt, "Tohi."

91. John Haywood, *The Natural and Aboriginal History of Tennessee* (Nashville: George Wilson, 1823), 243, cited in Strickland, *Fire and the Spirits*, 11.

92. Strickland, *Fire and the Spirits*, 11.

93. Smith, *Original Teachings*, 47–56.

94. Hudson, *Southeastern Indians*, 367–70.

95. Perdue, *Cherokee Women*, 25.

96. Johnston, *Cherokee Women*, 8–21.

97. Mankiller and Wallis, *Mankiller*, 29.

98. Altman and Belt, "Tohi"; Smith, *Stand as One*; Teuton and Shade, *Cherokee Earth Dwellers*.

99. Altman and Belt, "Tohi"; Smith, *Original Teachings*; Teuton and Shade, *Cherokee Earth Dwellers*; Holm, "Untitled Review"; Nelson, *Progressive Traditions*; Reed, *Serving the Nation*; Kilpatrick and Kilpatrick, *Friends of Thunder*; Stremlau, *Sustaining the Cherokee Family*; Mankiller and Wallace, *Mankiller*; Justice, *Our Fire Survives the Storm*; Smith, *Leadership Lessons*.

100. Adair, *History of the American Indians*, 15, 18.

101. Adair himself authored a two-hundred-page argument in defense of the idea that Indigenous Americans were descendants of the Jewish people, due to what he stylized as the similarities in their modes of living and worshipping.

102. Thomas G. West, *The Political Theory of the American Founding* (Cambridge, UK: Cambridge University Press, 2017), 117.

103. Earl Boyd Pierce and Rennard Strickland, *The Cherokee People* (Phoenix: Indian Tribal Series, 1973), 7.

104. Woodward, *Cherokees*, 22–25; Miles, *Ties That Bind*, 28.

105. *Final Report of the de Soto Expedition*, 76th Cong., 1st Sess. (1939), H. Doc. 71; Stanley Hoig, *The Cherokees and Their Chiefs in the Wake of Empire* (Fayetteville: University of Arkansas Press, 1998), 7–8; Stanley Hoig, *Beyond the Frontier: Exploring the Indian Country* (Norman: University of Oklahoma Press, 1998).

106. Strickland, *Fire and the Spirits*, 40.

107. Strickland, 41.

108. Strickland, 41. Some point to 1690 as the year of the first official marriage between a white settler and a Cherokee woman. See Starr, *History of the Cherokee*, 24.

109. Starr, *History of the Cherokee*, 23; Adair, *History*, 15; Perdue, *Cherokee Women*, 159. According to Perdue, the Moravians sought United States approval, which was granted, to set up a mission school in the Cherokee Nation in 1799.

110. Smith, *Stand As One*; Smith, *Original Teachings*; Nelson, *Progressive Traditions*.

111. Adair, *History of the American Indians*, 240.

112. Adair, 240; Starr, *History of the Cherokee*, 247; Pickett, *Annotated Pickett's History of Alabama*, 217; Knox Mellon Jr., "Christian Priber's 'Kingdom of Paradise,'" *Georgia Historical Quarterly* 57, no. 3 (Fall 1973): 320.

113. Mellon, "'Kingdom of Paradise,'" 319, quoted from "James Oglethorpe to the Trustees of the Georgia Colony, Frederica," April 22, 1743, Colonial Office Series 5, Vol. 655 (Pt. II) (Extracts). Public Record Office, London.

114. The main historical account of Priber's deeds is related by James Adair in his *History of the American Indians*, 240–43.

115. Adair, *History of the American Indians*, 240.

116. Samuel Williams, *Early Travels in the Tennessee Country* (Johnson City, TN: Watauga Press, 1928), 154, cited in Mellon, "'Kingdom of Paradise,'" 322.

117. Williams, *Early Travels*, 156–57; Mellon, "'Kingdom of Paradise,'" 324.

118. Williams, *Early Travels*, 157.

119. Adair, *History*, 240; Pickett, *Annotated Pickett's History of Alabama*, 217–18; Gaston L. Litton, "Principal Chiefs of the Cherokee Nation," *Chronicles of Oklahoma* 15, no. 3 (September 1937): 253–70, at 258.

120. Mellon, "'Kingdom of Paradise,'" 324–25.

121. Mellon, 326.

122. Adair, *History of the American Indians*, 243.

123. Starr, *History of the Cherokee*, 24.

124. William G. McLoughlin, *Champions of the Cherokees: Evan and John B. Jones* (Princeton, NJ: Princeton University Press, 1990), 65, 76; Thurman Wilkins, *Cherokee Tragedy: The Ridge Family and the Decimation of a People* (Norman, OK: University of Oklahoma Press, 1986), 8.

125. McLoughlin, *Champions*, 76.

126. Starr, *Early History of the Cherokees*, 18–26.

127. McLoughlin, *Champions*, 75; Perdue, *Cherokee Women*, 159; Miles, *Ties That Bind*, 91, 98–99.

128. Perdue, *Cherokee Women*, 159.

129. Perdue, 168.

130. Catharine Brown, *Cherokee Sister: The Collected Writings of Catharine Brown, 1818–1823*, ed. Theresa Strouth Gaul (Lincoln: University of Nebraska Press, 2014); Nelson, *Progressive Traditions*, 82–109.

131. Nelson, 70; William G. McLoughlin, *Cherokees and Missionaries, 1789–1839* (New Haven, CT: Yale University Press, 1994), 27, 147.

132. Joyce B. Philips and Paul Garry Philips, eds., *The Brainerd Journal: A Mission to the Cherokees, 1817–1823* (Lincoln: University of Nebraska Press, 1998), 50–51.

133. Philips and Philips, *Brainard Journal*, 51.

134. Philips and Philips, n.72, 462, See also McLoughlin, *Cherokee Renascence*, 358–59.

135. Romans 3:23.

136. Starr, *History of the Cherokees*, 247.

137. Smith, *Stand as One*, 6–8, 46.

138. Nelson, *Progressive Traditions*, 71.

139. Teuton and Shade, *Cherokee Earth Dwellers*, 226–30.

140. Perdue, *Cherokee Women*, 164.

141. Claudio Saunt, *Unworthy Republic: The Dispossession of Native Americans and the Road to Indian Territory* (New York: W. W. Norton, 2020), 13.

142. Halliburton, *Red over Black.*

143. Almon W. Lauber, *Indian Slavery in Colonial Times within the Present Limits of the United States* (New York: Longmans, Green, 1913), 49, 63, 136, 170.

144. Halliburton, *Red over Black,* 4–6.

145. Mooney, "Myths."

146. Miles, *Ties That Bind.*

147. Halliburton, *Red over Black,* 6–7.

148. Miles, *Ties That Bind,* 32–36.

149. David H. Corkran, *The Cherokee Frontier: Conflict and Survival, 1740–1762* (Norman: University of Oklahoma Press, 1962).

150. Patricia Nelson Limerick, *The Legacy of Conquest: The Unbroken Past of the American West* (New York: W. W. Norton, 1987); Patrick N. Minges, *Slavery in the Cherokee Nation: The Keetoowah Society and the Defining of a People, 1855–1867* (New York: Routledge, 2003).

151. Miles, *Ties That Bind,* 32–36.

152. Claudio Saunt, "The Paradox of Freedom: Tribal Sovereignty and Emancipation during the Reconstruction of Indian Territory," *Journal of Southern History* 70, no. 1 (February 2004): 63–94, https://doi.org/10.2307/27648312.

153. Miles, *Ties That Bind.*

154. Theda Perdue, *Slavery and the Evolution of Cherokee Society, 1540–1866* (Knoxville: University of Tennessee Press, 1979), 36; Halliburton, *Red over Black*; Minges, *Slavery in the Cherokee Nation.*

155. Kenneth W. Porter, *The Negro on the American Frontier* (New York: Arno Press, 1971).

156. Perdue, *Slavery,* 50.

157. Alan Taylor, *American Revolutions: A Continental History, 1750–1804* (New York: W. W. Norton, 2016); Blackhawk, *The Rediscovery of America.*

158. Perdue, *Slavery,* 30.

159. Reid, *Law of Blood,* 258.

160. Taylor, *American Revolutions,* 61.

161. Adair, *History of the American Indians,* 251.

162. Saunt, *Unworthy Republic.*

163. Taylor, *American Revolutions,* 252.

164. Taylor, 253. Taylor states that John Stuart urged patience and restraint, which militant Cherokees like Dragging Canoe disapproved of. Emmet Starr conversely suggests that Stuart urged the Cherokees to attack, feeding the flames of war chiefs like Dragging Canoe, who wanted to push the colonists back. Starr, *History of the Cherokees,* 31. See also Brent Alan Cox, *Heart of the Eagle: Dragging Canoe and the Emergence of the Chickamauga Confederacy* (Milan, TN: Chenanee Publishers, 1999), 105–7.

165. Justice, *Our Fire Survives the Storm,* 35–37.

166. Nadia Dean, "A Demand of Blood: The Cherokee War of 1776: The Cherokee War of 1776," *National Museum of the American Indian* 14, no. 4 (Winter 2013): 36–40; Pat Alderman, *Nancy Ward, Cherokee Chieftainess: Dragging Canoe, Cherokee-Chickamauga War Chief* (Johnson City, TN: Overmountain Press, 1990),

38. The exact orator of this speech is disputed; while commonly attributed to Dragging Canoe, it may also have been delivered by Tecumseh of the Shawnee, who may have been close with Dragging Canoe. The lack of definitive evidence may also suggest that this speech is apocryphal, representing a common sentiment rather than a real historical event.

167. Woodward, *Cherokees*, 89.

168. Carole Barrett and Harvey Markowitz, eds., *American Indian Biographies*, revised edition (Pasadena, CA: Salem Press, 2005), 161.

169. Starr, *History of the Cherokees*, 32. A "beloved woman" was a woman who had bled as men did, in battle, and who therefore was specially regarded by fellow Cherokees for their great deeds. Beloved women could also free captives. Nancy Ward earned this title by fighting against the Creeks in the mid-eighteenth century. See Ben Harris McClary, "Nancy Ward: The Last Beloved Woman of the Cherokees," *Tennessee Historical Quarterly* 21, no. 4 (December 1962): 352–64.

170. Taylor, *American Revolutions*, 253.

171. Justice, *Our Fire Survives the Storm*, 40.

172. McClary, "Nancy Ward," 352–61.

173. Justice, *Our Fire Survives the Storm*, 40.

174. Theda Perdue, *The Cherokee Removal: A Brief History with Documents*, 3rd edition (Boston: Bedford/St. Martin's Press, 2016).

175. Starr, *History of the Cherokees*, 33.

176. Starr, 33; Albert Bender, "Dragging Canoe's War: A War Chief's Ingenious Defense of the Cherokee Homeland," *Military History* 28 (2012): 68–75.

177. Starr, *History of the Cherokees*, 35.

178. Corn Tassel, "Let Us Examine the Facts," in *Native American Testimony*, ed. Peter Nabokov (New York: Penguin Books, 1991), 123.

179. Wilkins, *Cherokee Tragedy*, 17.

180. Wilkins, 35; Bender, "Dragging Canoe's War," 75.

181. Wilkins, *Cherokee Tragedy*, 17.

182. Wilkins, 19.

183. Wilkins, 19.

184. Justice, *Our Fire Survives the Storm*, 36; Bender, "Dragging Canoe's War," 75.

185. Justice, *Our Fire Survives the Storm*, 35; E. Raymond Evans, "Notable Persons in Cherokee History: Dragging Canoe," *Journal of Cherokee Studies* 2, no. 2 (1977): 187.

186. In 1782, seeking a new life away from the eastern strife, "a group of Cherokees petitioned the governor of Louisiana for permission to settle on lands west of the Mississippi." The governor assented and many emigrated to the territory we now call Arkansas and there lived separately there. These Cherokees steadily grew in their new lands, eventually organizing their government "along democratic lines" in 1824, when they delegated executive power among three chiefs. Within five years, these would remove to Indian Territory, headquartering themselves at Tehlontiskee on Deep Creek, and there were joined by

the great mass of Cherokees removed from the east a decade later. See Litton, "Principal Chiefs," 253–54.

187. Ronald N. Saltz, *American Indian Policy in the Jacksonian Era* (Lincoln: University of Nebraska Press, 1975), 1–3.

188. Thomas Valentine Parker, *The Cherokee Indians: With Special Reference to Their Relations with the United States Government* (New York: Grafton Press, 1907), 8–10.

189. Smith, *Civic Ideals*, 131.

190. Andrew Denson, *Demanding the Cherokee Nation: Indian Autonomy and American Culture, 1830–1900* (Lincoln: University of Nebraska Press, 2004).

191. Parker, *Cherokee Indians*, 2.

192. George Washington, "Third Annual Message to Congress, October 25, 1791," in *George Washington: Writings*, ed. John Rhodehamel (New York, NY: Library of America, 1997), 786–93, at 788.

193. Washington, *George Washington: Writings*, 788.

194. In his fifth message to Congress, Washington spoke on the need for commerce, "but it ought to be conducted without fraud, without extortion, with constant and plentiful supplies, with a ready market for the commodities of the Indians and a stated price for what they give in payment and receive in exchange." Teaching Indigenous peoples the benefits of civilization could only work in the absence of immorality in the marketplace. See George Washington, "Fifth Annual Message to Congress, December 3, 1793," in Washington, *George Washington: Writings*, 846–50, at 849.

195. Tocqueville, *Democracy in America*, I.2.10, 317.

196. Tocqueville, 318, 319; Denson, *Demanding the Cherokee Nation*, 18–20.

197. Denson, *Demanding the Cherokee Nation*, 15–18.

198. Thomas Jefferson, "To the Cherokee Nation, 4 May, 1808."

199. Jefferson, "To the Cherokee Nation." See also Thomas Jefferson, "Letter to William Henry Harrison, February 27, 1803," in Francis Paul Prucha, ed., *Documents of United States Indian Policy* (Lincoln: University of Nebraska Press, 1975), 22–23.

200. Theda Perdue, "Rising from the Ashes: The Cherokee Phoenix as an Ethnohistorical Source," *Ethnohistory* 24, no. 3 (Summer 1977): 213, https://doi.org/10.2307/481695.

201. Strickland, *Fire and the Spirits*, 95.

202. *Laws of the Cherokee Nation* (New York: Legal Classics Library, 1995), 3.

203. Strickland, *Fire and the Spirits*, 96. Strickland argues that these laws were not simply copied from state laws but were created to serve the unique needs of a society at once matrilineal of tradition and that held land in common.

204. Strickland, 97.

205. *Cherokee Phoenix*, "Cherokee Laws" March 13, 1828, 1, column 1a.

206. *Laws of the Cherokee Nation*, 4. On April 10, 1810, Principal Chief Black Fox signed "an act of oblivion," a law intended to halt the practice of clan revenge.

207. Strickland, *Fire and the Spirits*, 77.

208. McLoughlin, *Renascence*, 60.
209. McLoughlin, 119.
210. McLoughlin, 120.
211. Strickland, *Fire and the Spirits*, 77.
212. McLoughlin, *Champions*, 9.
213. McLoughlin, 9–11.
214. McLoughlin, 12.
215. Starr, *History of the Cherokee*, 225.
216. Rogin, *Fathers & Children*.
217. *Laws of the Cherokee Nation*, 4.
218. *Laws of the Cherokee Nation*, 5.
219. Cherokee Women, "Petition, May 2, 1817," in Perdue, *Cherokee Removal*, 124–125, at 124.
220. Perdue, 125.
221. The Treaty of 1817 was signed by a mixture of chiefs, thirty-one of the sixty-seven chiefs in the east and by thirteen from the west. Treaty commissioners considered all Cherokees, those east and west, as a single people and thus had no issues counting the thirteen from the west to reach a majority, signifying, in their minds, full approval. The staunch nationalists John Ross, Major Ridge, George Lowrey, and Pathkiller did not sign the treaty and were opposed to the agreement. See McLoughlin, *Cherokee Renascence*, 230–31.
222. "Creation of a Bureau of Indian Affairs in the War Department, March 11, 1824," in Prucha, *Documents*, 37–38.
223. Saltz, *Indian Policy*, 3.
224. Reid, *Law of Blood*.
225. Starr, *Early History of the Cherokee*, 37.
226. Starr, 42.
227. McLoughlin, *Champions*, 39. McLoughlin writes that the syllabary was finished in 1821, three years earlier than Starr indicates.
228. Althea Bass, *Cherokee Messenger* (Norman: University of Oklahoma Press, 1936).
229. *Laws of the Cherokee Nation*, 11–12.
230. *Laws of the Cherokee Nation*, 4, 10, 57.
231. *Laws of the Cherokee Nation*, 37–38; Miles, *Ties That Bind*.
232. Perdue, *Cherokee Removal*, 58; McLoughlin, *Cherokee Renascence*; Minges, *Slavery in the Cherokee Nation*.
233. Perdue, *Cherokee Removal*, 58.
234. Francis Paul Prucha, *Indian Policy in the United States: Historical Essays* (Lincoln: University of Nebraska Press, 1981).
235. Woodward, *Cherokees*.

CHAPTER 2
1. Miles, *Ties That Bind*, 22–23.
2. Nelson, *Progressive Traditions*, 157–59.

3. Theda Perdue, ed., *Cherokee Editor: The Writings of Elias Boudinot* (Knox-ville: University of Tennessee Press, 1983), 7–9; Miles, *Ties That Bind*, 22.

4. Perdue, *Cherokee Editor,* 9–10.

5. Cherokee Nation, *Laws of the Cherokee Nation* (New York: Legal Classics Library, 1995), 57.

6. Grant Foreman, *Indian Removal* (Norman: University of Oklahoma Press, 1934), 20.

7. Theda Perdue, "Traditionalism in the Cherokee Nation: Resistance to the Constitution of 1827," *Georgia Historical Quarterly* 66, no. 2 (Summer 1982): 159–70; McLoughlin, *Cherokee Renascence*, 388–410; Nelson, *Progressive Traditions*, 146; Miles, *Ties That Bind*, 123–24.

8. Martin, *Cherokee Supreme Court*, 62.

9. Constitution of the Cherokee Nation (1827), Article I, Section 1; McLough-lin, *Cherokee Renascence*, 390–94.

10. Miles, *Ties That Bind*, 228–30.

11. St. Thomas Aquinas, *On Being and Essence*, trans. Armand Maurer (Toronto, Canada: Pontifical Institute of Mediaeval Studies, 1968), 29.

12. John Ross, "Annual Message" in John Ross, *The Papers of Chief John Ross,* vol. 1, *1807–1839*, ed. Gary E. Moulton (Norman: University of Oklahoma Press, 1985), 140–44, at 140.

13. McLoughlin, *Cherokee Renascence*, 450.

14. Gary E. Moulton, "Editor's Introduction," in Ross, *Papers of Chief John Ross*, vol. 1, 3–11; Smithers, *Cherokee Diaspora*, 22–23.

15. Constitution of the Cherokee Nation (1827), Article I, Section 2. The lands they referred to in 1827 were those in modern-day Tennessee, North Carolina, Alabama, and Georgia.

16. *Laws of the Cherokee*, 5–6.

17. Constitution of the Cherokee Nation (1827), Article I, Section 2.

18. Article VI, Section 9, also reiterated the right to a trial by jury. This right was so important to their vision of a civilized nation, since traditional practice permitted clan members to mete out justice as they deemed appropriate, that they said it twice. See Strickland, *Fire and the Spirits*.

19. *Laws of the Cherokee Nation*, 4. On April 10, 1810, Principal Chief Black Fox signed "an act of oblivion," a law intended to halt the practice of clan revenge.

20. McLoughlin, *Cherokee Renascence*, 399.

21. Perdue, *Cherokee Editor,* 3–38.

22. Ross, "Annual Message," in Ross, *Papers of Chief John Ross*, vol. 1, 140–44, at 141.

23. Elias Boudinot, "To the Public," in Perdue, *Cherokee Editor,* 91–95, at 92. The *Cherokee Phoenix* printed the public correspondence of the nation as well as the laws themselves in both English and ᎠᎳ.

24. John Ridge, "Letter to Albert Gallatin," in Perdue, *Cherokee Removal,* 34–41, at 41; Kelly Wisecup, "Practicing Sovereignty: Colonial Temporalities, Cherokee Justice, and the 'Socrates' Writings of John Ridge," *Native American*

and Indigenous Studies 4, no. 1 (Spring 2017): 30–60, https://doi.org/10.1353 /nai.2017.a661471.

25. Nelson, *Progressive Traditions*, 66–71.

26. McLoughlin, *Cherokee Renascence*, 390.

27. Strickland, *Fire and the Spirits*, 183.

28. Constitution of the Cherokee Nation, Article VI, Section 1.

29. Perdue, "Traditionalism," 167.

30. In an acknowledgment of traditionalist concerns, Article III, Section 4, states that "the descendants of Cherokee men by all free women, except the African race, whose parents may have been living together as man and wife, according to the customs and laws of this Nation, shall be [full citizens]." Any form of cohabitation as man and wife, not merely a Christian marriage, was therefore considered valid.

31. Kettner, *Development of American Citizenship*.

32. Teuton and Shade, *Cherokee Earth Dwellers*, 44–45.

33. Johnston, *Voices of Cherokee Women*, 68–74.

34. Johnston, 69.

35. Sturm, *Blood Politics*, 51.

36. Tiya Miles, "Recentering Cherokee Women," 221–43.

37. Tiya Miles, *Ties That Bind*; Aaron Kushner, "The Imposition of Freedom: Tribal Citizenship and the Case of the Cherokee Freedmen," in *American Citizenship and Constitutionalism in Principle and Practice*, eds. Steven Pittz and Joseph Postell (Norman: University of Oklahoma Press, 2022), 83–108.

38. Miles, *Ties That Bind*, 1, 26–27, 63.

39. Miles, 126; emphasis in original.

40. Saunt, "Paradox of Freedom"; Halliburton, *Red over Black*.

41. Daniel Henderson, *Cherokee Census 1835* (Superintendent for Five Civilized Tribes, 1835), 30, cited in Perdue, *Traditionalism*, 168.

42. McLoughlin, *Cherokee Renascence*; Miles, *Ties That Bind*.

43. Perdue, *Cherokee Removal*, 20.

44. Perdue, 20; Foreman, *Indian Removal*, 15.

45. Stremlau, *Sustaining the Cherokee Family*, 24, 29.

46. Ridge, "Letter to Albert Gallatin," 40.

47. *Laws of the Cherokee Nation*, 4, 10, 57.

48. *Laws of the Cherokee Nation*, 37–38.

49. *Laws of the Cherokee Nation*, 11–12.

50. Starr, *Early History of the Cherokees*, 60–66; Nelson, *Progressive Traditions*, 80–81.

51. Constitution of the Cherokee (1827), Article VI, Section 10.

52. Altman and Belt, "Tohi," 13–14; Teuton and Shade, *Cherokee Earth Dwellers*, 21.

53. McLoughlin, *Champions*, 74–77.

54. Yael Tamir, *Liberal Nationalism* (Princeton, NJ: Princeton University Press, 1995).

55. Keith Banting and Will Kymlicka, "Introduction," in *The Strains of Commitment: The Political Sources of Solidarity in Diverse Societies*, eds. Keith Banting and Will Kymlicka. (Oxford, UK: Oxford University Press, 2017), 3–6, quoted in Eric P. Cheng, *Hanging Together: Role-Based Constitutional Fellowship and the Problem with Difference and Disagreement* (Cambridge, UK: Cambridge University Press, 2022), 64.

56. The Treaty of 1866, more officially called the Treaty of Washington, has many names, but is most commonly referred to as the Treaty of 1866.

57. Justice, *Why Indigenous Literatures Matter*, 187–91.

58. Denson, *Demanding the Cherokee Nation*, 38–42.

59. *Cherokee Phoenix*, May 14, 1828, 2, Column 5b.

60. *Register of Debates*, Senate 21st Congress, 1st Session, 326. See US Constitution, Article IV, Section 4.

61. *Register of Debates*, 327.

62. *Register of Debates*, 326.

63. Saltz, *American Indian Policy*, 1–2; McLoughlin, *Cherokee Renascence*, 277–79; Denson, *Demanding the Cherokee Nation*, 16–18.

64. Theda Perdue and Michael D. Green, *Cherokee Nation and the Trail of Tears* (New York: Penguin Books, 2007), 20–31.

65. Saltz, *Indian Policy*, 1–3.

66. Saltz, 3; Perdue, *Cherokee Removal*, 13–14.

67. *Register of Debates*, Senate 21st Congress, 1st Session, 327.

68. *Cherokee Phoenix*, May 14, 1828, 2, Column 5b.

69. *Cherokee Phoenix*, May 14, 1828, 2, Column 5b.

70. The Old Settler Cherokees, who had moved west of their own volition earlier, passed a similar law banning clan revenge, but not until 1824.

71. *Cherokee Phoenix*, April 24, 1828, 2, Column 1–4.

72. *Cherokee Phoenix*, April 24, 1828, 2, Column 1–4.

73. *Cherokee Phoenix*, April 24, 1828, 2, Column 1–4.

74. William Hicks and John Ross, "To Hugh Montgomery, April 16th, 1828," in Ross, *Papers of Chief John Ross*, vol. 1, 136–37.

75. *Cherokee Phoenix*, April 24, 1828, 2, Column 1–4.

76. *Laws of the Cherokee Nation*, 131–32.

77. *Laws of the Cherokee Nation*, 136.

78. Wilson Lumpkin, *The Removal of the Cherokee Indians from Georgia* (New York: Dodd, Mead, 1907).

79. Denson, *Demanding the Cherokee Nation*, 22–27.

80. Perdue, *Cherokee Removal*, 73.

81. Foreman, *Indian Removal*, 231–33.

82. Deloria and Wilkins, *Tribes, Treaties, & Constitutional Tribulations*, 53.

83. Saltz, *American Indian Policy*, 19–30.

84. Deloria and Wilkins, *Tribes, Treaties, & Constitutional Tribulations*, 53.

85. *Cherokee Nation v. Georgia*, 30 U.S. 5 Pet. 1 1 (1831).

86. Perdue, *Cherokee Removal*, 79.

87. Perdue, 80; Deloria and Wilkins, *Tribes, Treaties, & Constitutional Tribulations*, 53.

88. Worcester was eventually pardoned in 1933 by Governor Wilson Lumpkin.

89. Perdue, *Cherokee Editor*, 26.

90. *Laws of the Cherokee Nation*, 149–79. Due to dissatisfaction with the United States delayed action in fulfilling the obligations of the Treaty of 1817, a group of Cherokees, led by The Bowl, left Arkansas and emigrated to Texas. These Texas Cherokees remained there until they dispersed in 1839 and reunited with the main group in Indian Territory. See Litton, "Principal Chiefs," 256; Denson, *Demanding the Cherokee Nation*, 41–43.

91. Foreman, *Indian Removal*, 234. Additionally, Foreman reports that some who had emigrated west of their own accord had returned, spreading word of the sadness of that country compared to their own, making it even more challenging to convince Cherokees to remove and solidifying their resolve to remain.

92. Bethany Schneider, "Boudinot's Change: Boudinot, Emerson, and Ross on Cherokee Removal," *ELH* 75, no. 1 (Spring 2008): 151–77.

93. Perdue, *Cherokee Editor*, 10–11, 25–26.

94. Elias Boudinot, "Letters and Other Papers Relating to Cherokee Affairs: Being a Reply to Sundry Publications Authorized by John Ross," in Perdue, *Cherokee Removal*, 151–54, at 151.

95. Boudinot, "Letters and Other Papers," 154.

96. Perdue, *Cherokee Removal*, 137–38.

97. Moulton, "Editor's Introduction," 7–8.

98. Major Ridge, James Foster, Long Shere et al., "To Messrs. John Ross and others, Cherokee Delegation, now in Washington City," in Perdue, *Cherokee Editor*, 196–99, at 197.

99. Daniel F. Littlefield Jr., *The Cherokee Freedmen: From Emancipation to American Citizenship* (Westport, CT: Greenwood Press, 1978).

100. Tiya Miles, "Pain of 'Trail of Tears' Shared by Blacks as well as Native Americans," CNN, February 25, 2012, https://www.cnn.com/2012/02/25/us/pain-of-trail-of-tears-shared-by-blacks-as-well-as-native-americans/index.html.

101. Littlefield, *Cherokee Freedmen*.

102. George Hicks, "Letter from the Trail of Tears, January 13, 1839," in Perdue, *Cherokee Removal*, 164–65, at 164.

103. Patrick N. Minges, ed., *Black Indian Slave Narratives* (Winston-Salem, NC: John F. Blair, Publisher, 2004), 34.

104. Minges, *Black Indian Slave Narratives*, 34.

105. Litton, "Principal Chiefs," 258.

106. John Finger, *The Eastern Band of the Cherokees, 1819–1900* (Knoxville: University of Tennessee Press, 1984), 6.

107. Finger, *Eastern Band of Cherokees*, 29.

108. Finger, 41–42; Litton, "Principal Chiefs," 258–59.

The Eastern Band of the Cherokees' home in North Carolina is officially called the Qualla Boundary, formally established in 1876, outside of federal and state jurisdiction. These lands, 57,000 acres, were purchased by William Holland Thomas for the Cherokees in the 1840s and 1850s. The United States recognized the right of the tribe to own and control the lands in 1866. In 1868, Congress formally recognized the Cherokees in North Carolina as distinct from the Cherokee Nation in Indian Territory in order to transact business more easily with the federal government and North Carolina. In 1886 the Supreme Court of the United States (in *Eastern Band of the Cherokee Indians v. United States and Cherokee Nation, Commonly Called Cherokee Nation West*) ruled that the Eastern Band of Cherokees had dissolved their connection with the Cherokee Nation when they refused to remove with them and were therefore not able to share in per capita payments for land acquisitions, nor could they claim the rights and privileges of citizens of the Cherokee Nation. See Finger, *Eastern Band of the Cherokees*, 101–25.

109. John Brown, John Looney, and John Rodgers, "Letter to Ross and George Lowrey," in Ross, *Papers of Chief John Ross*, vol. 1, 714–15, at 714.

110. Foreman, *Indian Removal*, 249.

111. Gary E. Moulton, *John Ross: Cherokee Chief* (Athens: University of Georgia Press, 1978), 113.

112. Moulton, *John Ross*, 114.

113. Denson, *Demanding the Cherokee Nation*, 42.

114. John Ross, "To Matthew Arbuckle, June 22nd, 1839," in Ross, *Papers of Chief John Ross*, vol. 1, 717; Moulton, *John Ross*, 109.

115. Moulton, 115.

116. *Laws of the Cherokee Nation*, 16.

117. *Laws of the Cherokee Nation*, 16.

118. Starr, *Early History of the Cherokees*, 51.

119. Moulton, *John Ross*, 115–16.

120. E. Moore and John Watie, "Letter to Stand Watie, March 31, 1840," in Edward Everett Dale and Gaston Litton, *Cherokee Cavaliers: Forty Years of Cherokee History as Told in the Correspondence of the Ridge-Watie-Boudinot Family* (Norman: University of Oklahoma Press, 1995), 18–19.

121. Denson, *Demanding the Cherokee Nation*.

122. Dale and Litton, *Cherokee Cavaliers*, 25n61.

123. Littlefield, *Cherokee Freedmen*, 3–6.

124. Constitution of the Cherokee Nation (1839), Article IV, Section 1.

125. Constitution of the Cherokee Nation (1839), Article III, Section 5.

126. Miles, *Ties That Bind*, 124–28.

127. Starr, *Early History of the Cherokees*, 62–63, 65.

128. *Laws of the Cherokee Nation*, 19. Act passed on September 19, 1839.

129. *Laws of the Cherokee Nation*, 32.

130. Thus secularizing legal marriage in the Cherokee Nation by permitting judges to marry two individuals—although in many cases judges were also ministers themselves, like the Reverend Jesse Bushyhead. See Dan B. Wimberly,

Cherokee in Controversy: The Life of Jesse Bushyhead (Macon, GA: Mercer University Press, 2017).

131. *Laws of the Cherokee Nation*, 44.

132. *Laws of the Cherokee Nation*, 106. "An Act relative to the right of Citizenship."

133. *Laws of the Cherokee Nation*, 91.

134. *Compact Between the Several Tribes of Indians*, done in General Council at Tahlequah, Cherokee Nation, July 3rd, 1843, Article I, Sections 2–3.

135. These individuals included one John W. West in 1848, John Clark in 1848, George Johnston in 1849, and Coleman Robertson in 1850. *Laws of the Cherokee Nation*, 169, 173, 200, 217.

136. *Laws of the Cherokee Nation*, 70: "An Act against the Sale of Land, &c."

137. Strickland, *Fire and the Spirits*, 29.

138. Wilkins and Wilkins, *Dismembered*, 27.

139. Wilkins and Wilkins, 28.

140. Wilkins and Wilkins, 28.

141. Littlefield, *Cherokee Freedmen*, 7–10.

142. Daniel F. Littlefield Jr., "Utopian Dreams of the Cherokee Fullbloods: 1890–1934," *Journal of the West* 10, no. 3 (Fall 1971): 404–27.

143. For an excellent discussion of the nuances contained within the labels *progressive* and *traditionalist* in the Cherokee Nation in the nineteenth and twentieth centuries, see Nelson, *Progressive Traditions*.

144. Minges, *Slavery in the Cherokee Nation*; Bruyneel, *The Third Space of Sovereignty*, 29–30.

145. Denson, *Demanding the Cherokee Nation*, 53–63.

146. Henry M. Rector to John Ross, January 29, 1861, 38th Congress, 1st Session, House Executive Document 1, part 3, 345, quoted in Littlefield Jr., *Cherokee Freedmen*, 10.

147. Minges, *Slavery in the Cherokee Nation*; Littlefield, *Cherokee Freedmen*.

148. Minges, *Slave Narratives*, 73.

149. Minges, *Slavery in the Cherokee Nation*.

150. McLoughlin, *Champions*, 233.

151. McLoughlin, 230–32; Wimberly, *Cherokee in Controversy*, 143. By the time he joined the Baptist Church, Jesse Bushyhead owned at least one slave.

152. For more on the debate over Cherokee abolitionism, see Minges, *Slavery in the Cherokee Nation*; Halliburton, *Red over Black*, 11; Perdue, *Slavery*, 90–95; McLoughlin, *Champions*, 230–37; and James W. Parins, *John Rollin Ridge: His Life and Works* (Lincoln: University of Nebraska Press, 1991).

153. Perdue, *Slavery*, 91–95.

154. Perdue, 91; McLoughlin, *Champions*, 232–35; Parins, *John Rollin Ridge*, 176–77.

155. Halliburton, *Red over Black*, 93–104.

156. Quoted in Parins, *John Rollin Ridge*, 177.

157. Sturm, *Blood Politics*; Miles, *Ties That Bind*.

158. McLoughlin, *Champions*, 231.

159. Bruyneel, *Third Space of Sovereignty*, 30.
160. Bruyneel, 31–32.
161. Shelby Foote, *The Civil War: A Narrative: Red River to Appomattox* (New York: Vintage, 1974).
162. Foote, *Civil War*, 1022.
163. Dale and Litton, *Cherokee Cavaliers*, 229–31; Annie Heloise Abel, *The American Indian under Reconstruction* (Cleveland: Arthur H. Clark, 1925); M. Thomas Bailey, *Reconstruction in Indian Territory: A Story of Avarice, Discrimination, and Opportunism* (Port Washington, NY: Kennikat Press, 1972).
164. Littlefield, *Cherokee Freedmen*, 28.
165. Strickland, *Fire and the Spirits*.
166. Miles, *Ties That Bind*, 125.
167. *Laws of the Cherokee Nation*, 91.

CHAPTER 3

1. William Jefferson Watts and Henry Edwards Huntington, *Cherokee Citizenship and a Brief History of Internal Affairs in the Cherokee Nation* (Muldrow, Indian Territory: Register Print, 1895), 10.
2. Watts and Huntington, *Cherokee Citizenship*, 2.
3. Watts and Huntington, 2.
4. On December 7, 1871, the National Council repealed the 1870 act, "making it the duty of the Chief Justice to take and hear testimony in all cases presented to him" and report to the National Council his decision regarding citizenship. See Watts and Huntington, *Cherokee Citizenship*, 3.
5. Watts and Huntington, 3.
6. Smithers, *Cherokee Diaspora*, 174.
7. Miles, *Ties That Bind*, 191–96.
8. Miles, 192–93.
9. "Treaty with the Cherokee, 1866," Article 27, Tribal Treaties Database, https://treaties.okstate.edu/treaties/treaty-with-the-cherokee-1866.-(0942) (accessed July 14, 2022); Watts, *Cherokee Citizenship*.
10. Moulton, *John Ross*, 185; Denson, *Demanding the Cherokee Nation*, 53–54.
11. Moulton, *John Ross*, 187.
12. Cooley's report of the Fort Smith Council, October 30, 1865, U.S., House, "Report of the Commissioner of Indian Affairs, 1865," Executive Document 1, 519–20, cited in Moulton, *John Ross*, 186–87; see also Denson, *Demanding the Cherokee Nation*, 66–68.
13. Halliburton, *Red over Black*, 133.
14. Perdue, *Slavery*, 141.
15. "J. W. Washbourne to J. A. Scales, June 1, 1866," in Dale and Litton, *Cherokee Cavaliers*, 243–45, at 244.
16. Moulton, *John Ross*, 187–88.
17. Moulton, 194; Perdue, *Slavery*, 141.
18. McLoughlin, *Champions*, 424.

19. McLoughlin, 424–25; *Congressional Globe*, 38th Congress, 2nd Session, 1021–24 (February 23, 1865).

20. *Congressional Globe*, 38th Congress, 2nd Session, 1024 (February 23, 1865).

21. Halliburton, *Red over Black*, 134.

22. Halliburton, 134; Moulton, *John Ross*, 185–87.

23. Circe Sturm, *Blood Politics*, 74.

24. Miles, *Ties That Bind*, 187–88;

25. Moulton, *John Ross*, 194.

26. McLoughlin, *Champions*, 426; Treaty of 1866, Article 11.

27. Littlefield, *Cherokee Freedmen*, 28.

28. Elias Cornelius Boudinot, "To Stand Watie," in Dale and Litton, *Cherokee Cavaliers*, 247.

29. Denson, *Demanding the Cherokee Nation*, 100–102.

30. Mollie Ross, *The Life and Times of William P. Ross* (Fort Smith, AR: Weldon and Williams Printers, 1893), 2.

31. Smithers, *Cherokee Diaspora*, 173.

32. Ross, *Life and Times*, 3.

33. Ross, 3–4.

34. Ross, 4.

35. Ross, 5.

36. Reed, *Serving the Nation*, 92; Bruyneel, *The Third Space of Sovereignty*, 47–64.

37. Bushyhead, "First Annual Message."

38. Denson, *Demanding the Cherokee Nation*, 127–32.

39. Halliburton, *Red over Black*, 134.

40. Miles, *Ties That Bind*, 188, 192, 195; Bruyneel, *Third Space of Sovereignty*, 57, 63–64.

41. Bailey, *Reconstruction in Indian Territory*.

42. "Agreement with the Delawares" (1867), in *Laws of the Cherokee Nation*, 340.

43. "Agreement with the Delawares," 344.

44. "Agreement between Shawnees and Cherokees" (1869), in *Laws of the Cherokee Nation*, 345–48.

45. Miles, *Ties That Bind*, 191–203.

46. Littlefield, *Cherokee Freedmen*, 11.

47. Littlefield, 12.

48. The Cherokee Nation, following Lincoln's example, emancipated their slaves during the war, in 1863—the only tribal nation to do so. However, also like Lincoln, the Cherokee Nation lacked the physical ability to enforce emancipation until the war was concluded.

49. W. E. B. Du Bois, *The Souls of Black Folk* (Mineola, NY: Dover Publications, 1994), 59.

50. Linda W. Reese, "Cherokee Freedwomen in Indian Territory, 1863–1890," *Western Historical Quarterly* 33, no. 3 (Autumn 2002): 283, https://doi.org/10.2307/4144838.

51. Miles, *Ties That Bind*, 191–93.

52. Ross, *Life and Times*, 73.
53. Minges, *Slave Narratives*.
54. Reese, "Cherokee Freedwomen."
55. Minges, *Slave Narratives*, 70. It had previously been illegal to educate Blacks in the Cherokee Nation, so freedmen were predominantly illiterate. "An Act Prohibiting the Teaching of Negroes to Read and Write," passed October 22, 1841, in *Laws of the Cherokees*, 55–56,
56. Reese, "Cherokee Freedwomen," 287.
57. Minges, *Slave Narratives*, 40–44.
58. Minges, 48–53.
59. Littlefield, *Cherokee Freedmen*, 28.
60. Minges, *Slave Narratives*, 44–45.
61. Minges, 39.
62. Minges, 22.
63. Reese, "Cherokee Freedwomen," 284.
64. Reese, 275, 296.
65. Bailey, *Reconstruction in Indian Territory*.
66. Bailey, 182; Circe Sturm, "Blood Politics, Racial Classification, and Cherokee National Identity: The Trials and Tribulations of the Cherokee Freedmen," *American Indian Quarterly* 22, nos. 1–2 (Winter–Spring 1998): 230–58.
67. Minges, *Slave Narratives*, 78–83.
68. Minges, 74–77.
69. Minges, 55. Moses Lonian was interviewed in July 1937; his story and others are recounted in Patrick Minges' *Slave Narratives*, 55–62.
70. Minges, 58.
71. Minges, 62.
72. Minges, 62.
73. Miles, *Ties That Bind*, 193.
74. Littlefield, *Cherokee Freedmen*, 178–79.
75. Littlefield, 180.
76. Littlefield, 181.
77. Lydia M. Edwards, "Protecting Black Tribal Members: Is the Thirteenth Amendment the Linchpin to Securing Equal Rights within Indian Country?," *Berkeley Journal of African-American Law & Policy* 8 (2006): 122–54; Saunt, "Paradox of Freedom"; Circe Sturm, "Blood Politics," 230–58.
78. Minges, *Slave Narratives*.
79. Sturm, *Blood Politics*, 75.
80. Ross, *Life and Times*, 56.
81. John Bartlett Meserve, "Chief Lewis Downing and Chief Charles Thompson (Oochalata)," *Chronicles of Oklahoma* 16, no. 3 (September 1938): 318; Denson, *Demanding the Cherokee Nation*, 101–2.
82. Meserve, "Chief Lewis Downing," 320; Denson, *Demanding the Cherokee Nation*, 221–22.
83. Littlefield, *Cherokee Freedmen*, 35.
84. Littlefield, 35.

85. Denson, *Demanding the Cherokee Nation*, 101–2.

86. Debo, *And Still the Waters Run*, 14.

87. Lewis Downing, "Letter from Lewis Downing, Principal Chief of the Cherokee Nation, Inclosing Petitions of numbers of various tribes against a proposed territorial government over them," U.S. House of Representatives, 41st Congress, 2nd Session, Miscellaneous Document No. 76.

88. Ross, *Life and Times*, 21.

89. Ross, *Life and Times*.

90. Watts and Huntington, *Cherokee Citizenship*, 2.

91. Watts and Huntington, 4.

92. Watts and Huntington, 9–10.

93. Watts and Huntington, 7.

94. Watts and Huntington, 13.

95. Watts and Huntington, 16.

96. Watts and Huntington, 16.

97. Watts and Huntington, 16.

98. Ross, *Life and Times*, 120.

99. Denson, *Demanding the Cherokee Nation*, 221–30.

100. George, *Progress and Poverty*, 242.

101. Denson, *Demanding the Cherokee Nation*, 229.

102. George, *Progress and Poverty*, 242–44.

103. Denson, *Demanding the Cherokee Nation*, 224–25.

104. Debo, *Still the Waters Run*, 21.

105. *Seventeenth Annual Report of the Board of Indian Commissioners for the Year 1885* (Washington, D.C.: U.S. Government Printing Office, 1886), 90–91. Emphasis added.

106. George, *Progress and Poverty*.

107. Ross, *Life and Times*, 158.

108. Stremlau, *Sustaining the Cherokee Family*.

109. Joel B. Mayes, "First Annual Message (Second Term) of Hon. Joel B. Mayes, Principal Chief of the Cherokee Nation Delivered at Tahlequah, I.T., November 4, 1891," at 12, Indigenous Histories and Cultures of North America, https://www.indigenoushistoriesandcultures.amdigital.co.uk/Documents/Detail/first-annual-message-second-term-of-hon.-joel-b.-mayes-principal-chief-of-the-cherokee-nation-delivered-at-tahlequah-i.t.-november-4-1891/7019983?item=7019987 (accessed April 16, 2024).

110. Mayes, "First Annual Message," 13–14.

111. Stremlau, *Sustaining the Cherokee Family*, 92.

112. Stremlau, 93–94.

113. Mayes, "First Annual Message," 12.

114. Mayes, 3.

115. John Ross, "To the Senate and House of Representatives," in John Ross, *The Papers of Chief John Ross*, vol. 1, *1807–1839*, ed. Gary E. Moulton (Norman: University of Oklahoma Press, 1985), 458–61.

116. Debo, *Still the Waters Run*, 12.

117. Debo, 13.

118. Denson, *Demanding the Cherokee Nation*.

119. Smithers, *Cherokee Diaspora*, 228.

120. Bushyhead, "First Annual Message."

121. Bushyhead.

122. Bushyhead.

123. Bailey, *Reconstruction in Indian Territory*, 182.

124. Sturm, *Blood Politics*, 235.

125. Conley, *Cherokee Nation*, 193.

126. Joel B. Mayes, "Third Annual Message of Hon. J. B. Mayes: Principal Chief of the Cherokee Nation," privately published, https://search-alexanderstreet -com.ezproxy1.lib.asu.edu/view/work/bibliographic_entity|bibliographic _details|4410263 (accessed April 15, 2024).

127. Mayes, "Third Annual Message."

128. Littlefield, *Cherokee Freedmen*, 238.

129. Debo, *Still the Waters Run*, 23; Conley, *Cherokee Nation*, 194.

130. Debo, *Still the Waters Run*, 24.

131. Debo, 25.

132. Debo, 26.

133. Stremlau, *Sustaining the Cherokee Family*; Reed, *Serving the Nation*.

134. Denson, *Demanding the Cherokee Nation*, 214–15.

135. Conley, *Cherokee Nation*, 196.

136. Watts and Huntington, *Cherokee Citizenship*, 128.

137. Watts and Huntington, 129.

138. Ibid.; Denson, *Demanding the Cherokee Nation*, 215.

139. Nelson, *Progressive Traditions*, 50, 60.

140. Starr, *History of the Cherokee*, 479.

141. Smithers, *Cherokee Diaspora*, 232.

142. Nelson, *Progressive Traditions*, 60, 115–16.

143. Smithers, *Cherokee Diaspora*, 233.

144. Quoted in Starr, *History of the Cherokee*, 481–82.

145. Starr, *History of the Cherokee*, 480; Nelson, *Progressive Traditions*, 115–18.

146. Starr, *History of the Cherokee*, 480–81; Denson, *Demanding the Cherokee Nation*, 241.

147. Debo, *Still the Waters Run*, 33.

148. Sturm, *Blood Politics*.

149. Samuel Houston Mayes, "Third Annual Message of S. H. Mayes, Principal Chief of the Cherokee Nation, Delivered at Tahlequah, I.T., November 3, 1897."

150. Mayes, "Third Annual Message."

151. Debo, *Still the Waters Run*, 34.

152. Debo, 34.

153. Star, *History of the Cherokee*, 480.

154. Debo, *Still the Waters Run*, 47. Daniel Littlefield, however, reports different numbers: a total enrollment of 41,798—4,919 of whom were freedmen. See Littlefield, *Cherokee Freedmen*, 238.

155. Some names were added by an act of Congress in 1914. See Debo, *Still the Waters Run*, 47.

156. Theodore Roosevelt, "First Annual Message to Congress," December 3, 1901.

157. Nelson, *Progressive Traditions*, 212–13; see also Littlefield, *Cherokee Freedmen*; and Miles, *Ties That Bind*.

158. Miles, 198–200.

159. Bruce N. Duthu, *American Indians and the Law* (New York: Penguin, 2008), xvi.

160. Pierce and Strickland, *Cherokee People*, 46.

161. Morris L. Wardell, *A Political History of the Cherokee Nation, 1838–1907* (Norman, OK: University of Oklahoma Press, 1938), 349. A large number of scholars wrote in the 1930s and 1940s about the seeming demise of Indigenous governments after allotment, rushing to capture what was once deemed a dying way of life in their scholarship. See also Marion L. Sharkey, *Cherokee Nation* (New York: Alfred A. Knopf, 1946).

162. Miles, *Ties That Bind*.

163. Denson, *Demanding the Cherokee Nation*.

CHAPTER 4

1. Mankiller and Wallis, *Mankiller*, 4–5.

2. Smith, *Leadership Lessons*, 213. According to Principal Chief Chad Smith, Congress, during the allotment era, exerted over the Cherokee Nation a "bureaucratic imperialism" that kept the latter government in a dormant state, unable to effect meaningful change.

3. Dawes Rolls, 1898–1914, Roll No. 25671, Card 8200.

4. Dawes Rolls, 1898–1914, Roll No. 32704, Card 10924.

5. Graham Lee Brewer, "The Cherokee Nation Once Fought to Disenroll Gov. Kevin Stitt's Ancestors," *High Country News*, February 24, 2020, https://www.hcn.org/articles/indigenous-affairs-the-cherokee-nation-once-fought-to-disenroll-gov-kevin-stitts-ancestors.

6. Brewer, "Cherokee Nation Once Fought."

7. Brewer.

8. Brown, *Stoking the Fire*, xii.

9. Brown, xii; Sturm, *Blood Politics*; Nelson, *Progressive Traditions*.

10. Brown, *Stoking the Fire*, xvi, emphasis in original.

11. Justice, *Why Indigenous Literatures Matter*, 193–94.

12. D. S. Otis, *The Dawes Act and the Allotment of Indian Lands*, ed. Francis P. Prucha (Norman: University of Oklahoma Press, 1973), 3, quoted in Wilkins and Wilkins, *Dismembered*, 33.

13. David A. Chang, *The Color of the Land: Race, Nation, and the Politics of Land-ownership in Oklahoma, 1832–1929* (Chapel Hill: University of North Carolina Press, 2010), 75–76. 75–76. As Chang notes, different Americans had differing goals for allotment: there were many who wished to partake in the land itself, but also others, like Henry Dawes, who had no intention of acquiring land personally.

14. Angie Debo, *And Still the Waters Run: The Betrayal of the Five Civilized Tribes* (Princeton, NJ: Princeton University Press, 1940), 37.

15. Tom Holm, "Indian Lobbyists: Cherokee Opposition to the Allotment of Tribal Lands," *American Indian Quarterly* 5, no. 2 (May 1979): 116, https://doi .org/10.2307/1183752.

16. Holm, "Indian Lobbyists," 45.

17. Dawes Commission, *Report*, 1902, 31–4, quoted in Debo, *And Still the Waters Run*, 46.

18. Holm, "Indian Lobbyists"; Chang, *Color of the Land*.

19. Debo, *And Still the Waters Run*, 46.

20. Debo, 47.

21. Debo, 47.

22. Stremlau, *Sustaining the Cherokee Family*, 116–17.

23. Stremlau, 135; Holm, "Indian Lobbyists," 129–30.

24. Stremlau, *Sustaining the Cherokee Family*, 137.

25. Debo, *And Still the Waters Run*, 50.

26. Debo, 50.

27. Debo, 50.

28. Justice, *Why Indigenous Literatures Matter*, 193–95; Denson, *Demanding the Cherokee Nation*, 243–51.

29. Stremlau, *Sustaining the Cherokee Family*, 148; Kushner, "Development."

30. Sturm, *Blood Politics*.

31. Stremlau, *Sustaining the Cherokee Family*, 148.

32. Rennard Strickland, "Address: To Do the Right Thing: Reaffirming Cherokee Traditions of Justice under Law," *American Indian Law Review* 17, no. 1 (1992): 340, https://doi.org/10.2307/20068729.

33. Strickland, "Address: To Do the Right Thing," 343.

34. Amy M. Ware, *The Cherokee Kid: Will Rogers, Tribal Identity, and the Making of an American Icon* (Lawrence: University Press of Kansas, 2015).

35. Justice, *Why Indigenous Literatures Matter*; Brown, *Stoking the Fire*, 10; Chang, *The Color of the Land*, 2–3.

36. Stremlau, *Sustaining the Cherokee Family*, 210.

37. Denson, *Demanding the Cherokee Nation*, 241–42.

38. Richard Mize, "Sequoyah Convention," *Encyclopedia of Oklahoma History and Culture*, https://www.okhistory.org/publications/enc/entry.php?entry =SE021 (accessed August 30, 2022).

39. Mize; Chang, *Color of the Land*, 85–86, 95.

40. Mize, "Sequoyah Convention"; Debo, *And Still the Waters Run*, 163.

41. Debo, 163.

42. This SCOTUS opinion was a consolidation of four cases: *Cherokee Nation v. United States*; *Red Bird v. United States*; *Fife v. United States*; and *Persons Claiming Rights in the Cherokee Nation by Intermarriage v. United States*. See Wilkins and Wilkins, *Dismembered*, 31.

43. Wilkins and Wilkins, *Dismembered*, 31.

44. Wilkins and Wilkins, 31.

45. Wilkins and Wilkins, 32.

46. Stacy L. Leeds, "Defeat or Mixed Blessing—Tribal Sovereignty and the State of Sequoyah," *Tulsa Law Review* 43, no. 1 (Fall 2007): 5–16.

47. Leeds, "Defeat or Mixed Blessing," 15.

48. Leeds, 15.

49. Debo, *And Still the Waters Run*, 159.

50. Littlefield, "Utopian Dreams," 405.

51. Denson, *Demanding the Cherokee Nation*, 241–42.

52. Debo, *And Still the Waters Run*.

53. Michael G. Cunniff, "The New State of Oklahoma," *World's Work* 12, no. 2 (June 1906): 7618–19.

54. Cunniff, "New State of Oklahoma," 7618–19; Sean Beienburg and Aaron Kushner, "Conservative Progressivism? Michael Cunniff, Federalism, and the Founding of Arizona," *American Political Thought* 12, no. 4 (Fall 2023): 571, https://doi.org/10.1086/727045. For more on Progressive thought surrounding allotment and the expansion of the American empire, see Paul Frymer, *Building an American Empire: The Era of Territorial and Political Expansion* (Princeton, NJ: Princeton University Press, 2017), 263–75.

55. John M. Oskison, "New Indian Leadership," *American Indian Magazine* 5 (Summer 1917): 93–100; see also Kirby Brown, "Citizenship, Land, and Law," 77–115.

56. Kiara M. Vigil, *Indigenous Intellectuals: Sovereignty, Citizenship, and the American Imagination, 1880–1930* (New York: Cambridge University Press, 2015), 130–31.

57. Oskison, "New Indian Leadership," 97.

58. Littlefield, "Utopian Dreams," 407.

59. Angie Debo, *A History of the Indians* (Norman: University of Oklahoma Press, 1970), 263.

60. Littlefield, "Utopian Dreams," 407. Littlefield details the extended interactions between Cherokees and Mexico, including attempts by prominent Cherokees to move to Mexico in the 1840s and 1860s after the Civil War.

61. Litton, "Principal Chiefs," 256.

62. John Ross, "To Joaquin Maria del Castillo y Lanzas, March 22, 1835," in John Ross, *The Papers of Chief John Ross*, vol. 1, *1807–1839*, ed. Gary E. Moulton (Norman: University of Oklahoma Press, 1985), 334–36.

63. Littlefield, "Utopian Dreams," 411.

64. *Cherokee Advocate*, October 30, 1897, 2, column 1.

65. *Cherokee Advocate*, April 16, 1898, 2, column 1; Littlefield, "Utopian Dreams," 414.

66. Henry E. Fritz, *The Movement for Indian Assimilation, 1860–1890* (Philadelphia: University of Pennsylvania Press, 1963), 213.

67. Debo, *And Still the Waters Run*, x.

68. Littlefield, "Utopian Dreams," 421.

69. *Daily Oklahoman*, February 26, 1922, Section B, 2, columns 5–7, quoted in Littlefield, "Utopian Dreams," 424.

70. Littlefield, 426.

71. Smith, *Leadership Lessons*, 214.

72. DeWitt Clinton Duncan, "The Outrage of Allotment," in *Native American Testimony*, ed. Peter Nabokov (New York: Penguin, 1991), 267.

73. Starr, *History of the Cherokee*, 263.

74. Nelson, *Progressive Traditions*, 50–55; see also Brown, *Stoking the Fire*, 10, 214–15.

75. Starr, *History of the Cherokee*, 482.

76. Starr, 483.

77. Starr, 505.

78. Denson, *Demanding the Cherokee Nation*, 247.

79. Sam Smith, "To Mr. Levi Gritts, December 9th, 1920," in Starr, *History of the Cherokee*, 484–86.

80. Mankiller and Wallace, *Mankiller*, 171.

81. Mankiller and Wallace, 139.

82. Mankiller and Wallace, 171.

83. Stremlau, *Sustaining the Cherokee Family*, 189–190; Mankiller and Wallace, *Mankiller*, 172. For an account of some of the atrocities suffered by the Osage people during this period in Oklahoma history, see David Grann, *Killers of the Flower Moon: The Osage Murders and the Birth of the FBI* (New York: Vintage, 2017).

84. Duthu, *American Indians and the Law*, xvi; Prucha, *Documents*, 218.

85. *Congressional Record*, 68th Congress, 1st Session, 9674.

86. Mankiller and Wallace, *Mankiller*, 174.

87. The Institute for Government Research later became known as the Brookings Institution; Prucha, *Documents*, 219.

88. Debo, *And Still the Waters Run*, 356.

89. Graham D. Taylor, *The New Deal and American Indian Tribalism: The Administration of the Indian Reorganization Act, 1934–45* (Lincoln: University of Nebraska Press, 1980), 6–7.

90. Littlefield, "Utopian Dreams," 423.

91. Ruth Muskrat Bronson, "Life on the Checkerboard," *Native American Testimony*, ed. Peter Nabokov (New York: Penguin, 1991), 262–63.

92. Chang, *Color of the Land*, 84–105.

93. Deloria, *Custer Died for Your Sins*, 48.

94. Taylor, *New Deal and American Indian Tribalism*, 15.

95. Taylor, 17.

96. Taylor, 19.

97. Prucha, *Documents*, 225.

98. 73rd Congress, 48 Stat. 984, 25 USC 461 et seq.

99. Deloria, *Custer Died for Your Sins*, 48.

100. Sturm, *Blood Politics*, 86.

101. Prucha, *Documents*, 230.

102. Albert L. Wahrhaftig, "In the Aftermath of Civilization: The Persistence of the Cherokee Indians in Oklahoma," PhD diss., Department of Anthropology, University of Chicago, 1975; Sturm, *Blood Politics*, 90; Prucha, *Documents*, 231.

103. Brown, *Stoking the Fire*, xii–xiii.

104. Wilma Mankiller reports that this convention was so controversial that the Keetoowah Society expelled Milam while complaining that the convention and the executive committee were too dominated by white lawyers and white sympathizers. See Mankiller and Wallace, *Mankiller*, 179.

105. Daniel M. Cobb, "Devils in Disguise: The Carnegie Project, the Cherokee Nation, and the 1960s," *American Indian Quarterly* 31, no. 3 (Summer 2007): 465–90.

106. Josh Clough, "United Keetoowah Band," *Encyclopedia of Oklahoma History and Culture*, Oklahoma Historical Society, https://www.okhistory.org/publications/enc/entry.php?entry=UN006 (accessed September 2, 2022); see also Nelson, *Progressive Traditions*, 130–31; Smith, *Original Teachings*; Teuton, *Turtle Island Liars' Club*, 40–41.

107. Richard Allen, "The Cherokees: One People, Separated by Politics and Spirituality," *Cherokee Phoenix*, August 10, 2006, https://www.cherokeephoenix.org/opinion/the-cherokees-one-people-separated-by-politics-and-spirituality/article_7fd6571c-c2d9-5053-8a3a-940c1b435ab1.html; Obermeyer, *Delaware Tribe*, 225.

108. Constitution and By-Laws of the United Keetoowah Band of Cherokee Indians Oklahoma, Article IV, Section 1.

109. Robert Conley Jr., *A Cherokee Encyclopedia* (Albuquerque: University of New Mexico Press, 2007), 249. The tension between the Cherokee Nation and the UKB continues today. According to Joshua Nelson, "the UKB has attempted to establish its legitimate governance on a platform of superior cultural authenticity disingenuous historical claims to an uninterrupted history of Keetoowah leadership steeped in traditionalism and bloodedness from the time before European contact," while the Cherokee Nation has opposed Keetoowah sovereignty, "anxious over Keetoowah claims to land within its borders and the confusion that would result from an *imperium in imperio*, or a state within a state." See Nelson, *Progressive Traditions*, 131.

110. Sturm, *Blood Politics*, 96.

111. Sturm, 91.

112. Sturm, 91; Wahrhaftig, "In the Aftermath of Civilization," 57.

113. Donald L. Fixico, *Termination and Relocation: Federal Indian Policy, 1945–1960*. Albuquerque: University of New Mexico Press, 1986, ix.

114. Fixico, *Termination and Relocation*, ix.
115. Mankiller and Wallace, *Mankiller*, xx; Duthu, *American Indians and the Law*, xvii.
116. Duthu, *American Indians and the Law*, xvi; Prucha, *Documents*, 233.
117. Deloria, *Custer Died for Your Sins*, 55.
118. Deloria, 61.
119. Mankiller and Wallace, *Mankiller*, 68.
120. Smith, *Leadership Lessons*, 8.
121. Mankiller and Wallace, *Mankiller*, 68–71.
122. Cobb, "Devils in Disguise," 466.
123. Cobb, 467. The Indian Claims Commission (ICC) ruled in favor of the tribes' Outlet claim in 1961. See Denson, *Demanding the Cherokee Nation*, 249; Sturm, "Blood Politics," 238.
124. Denson, *Demanding the Cherokee Nation*, 249; Sturm, "Blood Politics," 238; Conley, *Cherokee Nation*, 215.
125. Denson, *Demanding the Cherokee Nation*, 249.
126. Teuton and Shade, *Cherokee Earth Dwellers*, 10. The Center's Cherokee National Museum opened in 1975. See also Conley, *Cherokee Encyclopedia*, 53, 58.
127. Conley, *Cherokee Nation*; Conley, *Cherokee Encyclopedia*.
128. Denson, *Demanding the Cherokee Nation*, 249.
129. Cobb, "Devils in Disguise," 470.
130. Conley, *Cherokee Encyclopedia*, 134, 169–70; Cobb, "Devils in Disguise," 480.
131. Mankiller and Wallace, *Mankiller*, 181.
132. Cobb, "Devils in Disguise," 468.
133. Albert L. Wahrhaftig and Jane Lukens-Wahrhaftig, "New Militants or Resurrected State? The Five County Northeastern Oklahoma Cherokee Organization," in *The Cherokee Indian Nation: A Troubled History* (Knoxville: University of Tennessee Press, 1979), 230.
134. Albert L. Wahrhaftig, "Making Do with the Dark Meat: A Report on the Cherokee Indians in Oklahoma," in *American Indian Economic Development*, ed. Sam Stanley (Berlin, NY: De Gruyter Mouton, 2011), 409–10; see also Carroll, *Roots of Our Renewal*.
135. Conley, *Cherokee Nation*, 214.
136. Carroll, *Roots of Our Renewal*.
137. Cobb, "Devils in Disguise," 475; Doris Kearns Goodwin, *Lyndon Johnson and the American Dream* (New York: St. Martin's Griffin, 1976), 188–90.
138. Cobb, "Devils in Disguise," 473.
139. Cobb, 475.
140. Cobb, 477–78.
141. A. G. Hopkins, *American Empire: A Global History* (NJ: Princeton University Press, 2018), 668.
142. Hopkins, *American Empire*, 668–69.
143. Denson, *Demanding the Cherokee Nation*, 250.

144. Richard Nixon, "Special Message to the Congress on Indian Affairs," July 8, 1970, American Presidency Project, https://www.presidency.ucsb.edu /documents/special-message-the-congress-indian-affairs.

145. Principal Chiefs Act of 1970, Public Law 91–495, 91st Congress, 2nd Session (October 22, 1970).

146. Cobb, "Devils in Disguise," 482.

147. Eric D. Lemont, "Overcoming the Politics of Reform: The Story of the Cherokee Nation of Oklahoma Constitution Convention," in *American Indian Constitutional Reform and the Rebuilding of Native Nations*, ed. Eric D. Lemont (Austin: University of Texas Press, 2006), 291.

148. Conley, *Cherokee Nation*, 219.

149. Mankiller and Wallace, *Mankiller*, 182.

150. Conley, *Cherokee Nation*, 220.

151. Lemont, "Overcoming the Politics of Reform," 291.

152. Ware, *Cherokee Kid*; Cobb, "Devils in Disguise"; Denson, *Demanding the Cherokee Nation*.

153. Brown, *Stoking the Fire*, 211–19, especially 214.

154. Stremlau, *Sustaining the Cherokee Family*, 244.

155. *McGirt v. Oklahoma*, 591 U.S. (2020).

156. Brown, *Stoking the Fire*, 219.

157. Conley, *Cherokee Encyclopedia*, 249; Georgia Rae Leeds, *United Keetoowah Band of Cherokee Indians in Oklahoma* (New York: Peter Lang, 2000).

158. Leeds, *United Keetoowah Band*, 14–21; Denson, *Demanding the Cherokee Nation*, 248.

159. Smith, *Stand as One*, xiii.

160. Sturm, *Blood Politics*, 96.

161. Tocqueville, *Democracy in American*, 333, 387; Beienburg and Kushner, "Conservative Progressivism?," 571.

162. Wilkins and Wilkins, *Dismembered*, 59.

163. Wilkins and Wilkins, 58.

CHAPTER 5

1. Dawes Rolls, Roll No. 1267, Card No. 500.

2. Sturm, *Blood Politics*, 178–79.

3. *Tahlequah Daily Press*, June 21, 1984, quoted in Sturm, *Blood Politics*, 181.

4. Sturm, 183.

5. *Oklahoma Eagle*, July 5, 1984, quoted in Sturm, *Blood Politics*, 183.

6. Constitution of the Cherokee Nation (1975), Article III, Section 1.

7. Mankiller and Wallace, *Mankiller*, 219, quoted in Kushner, "Development," 1.

8. *Nero v. Cherokee Nation of Oklahoma*, No. 86-1271, 892 F.2d 1457 (1989). The Cherokee Nation, the court ruled, among other things, could not be sued because it possessed sovereign immunity.

9. Justice, *Why Indigenous Literatures Matter*, 15; Miles, *Ties That Bind*, xviii–xix.

10. The Cherokee Nation Constitutions of 1827 and 1839 each restricted citizenship in the Nation to those with Cherokee blood, excepting Black persons.

11. R. Perry Wheeler, "Minutes of Regular Meeting, December 4, 1976," Cherokee Nation Council, Tahlequah, OK.

12. Ross Swimmer quoted in Lemont, "Overcoming the Politics of Reform," 292.

13. Constitution of the Cherokee Nation (1975), Article V, Section 1.

14. Lemont, "Overcoming the Politics of Reform," 300.

15. Lemont, "Story of the Cherokee Nation of Oklahoma Constitutional Convention," 1–34.

16. Constitution of the Cherokee Nation (1975), Article VII, Section 1.

17. Cobb, "Devils in Disguise"; Denson, *Demanding the Cherokee Nation,* 246–51.

18. Ross O. Swimmer, "Firsthand Accounts," in *American Indian Constitutional Reform and the Rebuilding of Native Nations,* eds. Eric D. Lemont (Austin: University of Texas Press, 2006), 181.

19. Interview with David Goodwin, 1984, quoted in Sturm, *Blood Politics,* 184.

20. Cherokee Nation, "Report on State of the Nation," *Cherokee Advocate* (Tahlequah, OK), vol. 1, no. 1, February 28, 1977, ProQuest.

21. Ross O. Swimmer, "Letter to the Cherokees," *Cherokee Advocate* (Tahlequah, OK), vol. 1, no. 11, December 31, 1977, ProQuest.

22. David Myer Temin, "Indigenous Sovereignty Against Family Separation," Starting Points Journal, December 1, 2022, https://startingpointsjournal .com/indigenous-sovereignty-against-family-separation/. Temin writes that "in some cases, child welfare agents literally stole Native children from their own front yards and their parents and/or extended family had no recourse to get them back. The numbers were staggering at the time of ICWA's passage, with an estimated 25% to 35% of Native children separated from their families and, of those, 90% placed in non-Indian homes."

23. Wilkins, "Most Grievous Display," 328.

24. Cherokee Nation Legislative Act 01-78.

25. Sturm, *Blood Politics,* 180.

26. Wilkins and Wilkins, *Dismembered.*

27. Sturm, *Blood Politics,* 181.

28. Sturm, 183.

29. Mankiller and Wallace, *Mankiller,* 242–43.

30. Conley, *Cherokee Encyclopedia,* 144; Mankiller and Wallace, *Mankiller,* 245. Swimmer was the first elected chief to head the BIA.

31. Mankiller and Wallace, 244–45.

32. Cherokee Nation, "Mankiller Sworn-in as Chief," *Cherokee Advocate* (Tahlequah, OK), vol. 9, no. 12, December 31, 1985, ProQuest.

33. "Mankiller Sworn-in as Chief."

34. Cherokee Nation LA-1-78.

35. Cherokee Nation LA-5-87.

36. Cherokee Nation Regular Tribal Council Meeting Minutes, June 10, 1989—Counselor Jeff Muskrat reporting from the Registration Committee.

37. Cherokee Nation Regular Tribal Council Meeting Minutes, June 9, 1990—Counselor Jeff Muskrat reporting from the Registration Committee.

38. Cherokee Nation Regular Tribal Council Meeting Minutes, June 9, 1990.

39. Conley, *Cherokee Nation*, 224–25.

40. Conley, 224.

41. Conley, 224.

42. Conley, 224.

43. Richard Allen, "The Cherokees: One People, Separated by Politics and Spirituality," *Cherokee Phoenix*, August 10, 2006, https://www.cherokeephoenix.org/opinion/the-cherokees-one-people-separated-by-politics-and-spirituality/article_7fd6571c-c2d9-5053-8a3a-940c1b435ab1.html. The quote referenced was from a reprinted letter by the Keetoowah Society Chief William Smith to the public in 1991; Leeds, *United Keetoowah Band*.

44. Cherokee Nation LA-06-92, passed September 12, 1992, by a unanimous vote (14 voting "yes," including Joe Byrd, with one absence).

45. Cherokee Nation LA-02-93, passed July 12, 1993.

46. Doug Ferguson, "Byrd Sworn in as Cherokees' Principal Chief Campaign Tumult Still Not Resolved," *Oklahoman*, August 15, 1995, https://www.oklahoman.com/story/news/1995/08/15/byrd-sworn-in-as-cherokees-principal-chief-campaign-tumult-still-not-resolved/62382271007/.

47. Ferguson, "Byrd Sworn In."

48. Conley, *Cherokee Encyclopedia*, 46–47.

49. Lois Romano, "A Nation Divided," *Washington Post*, July 17, 1997, https://www.washingtonpost.com/archive/lifestyle/1997/07/17/a-nation-divided/209aae32-9fc5-459f-8897-00328a9e7b64/.

50. Ferguson, "Byrd Sworn In."

51. Nelson, *Progressive Traditions*, 40–41.

52. Lois Romano, "Nation Divided."

53. Romano; see also Justice, *Our Fire Survives the Storm*, 21–22.

54. Special Tribal Council Meeting Minutes, May 2, 1997.

55. Smith, *Leadership Lessons*, 179.

56. Anne Farris, "Controversy over Tribal Funds Splits Cherokee Nation into Warring Camps," *Washington Post*, July 5, 1997, https://www.washingtonpost.com/archive/politics/1997/07/05/controversy-over-tribal-funds-splits-cherokee-nation-into-warring-camps/c7da03f3-e3ed-4703-a45e-01166dc9491d/.

57. Charles T. Jones, "Cherokee Chief Removes Marshals from Courthouse," *Oklahoman*, June 21, 1997, https://www.oklahoman.com/story/news/1997/06/21/cherokee-chief-removes-marshals-from-courthouse/62310620007/.

58. Smith, *Leadership Lessons*, 179.

59. Lemont, "Overcoming the Politics of Reform," 288.

60. Staff, "3 Cherokee Injured in Tribal Courthouse Protest," *Orlando Sentinel*, August 13, 1997, https://www.orlandosentinel.com/news/os-xpm-1997-08-14-9708140246-story.html.

61. Conley, *Cherokee Encyclopedia*, 47.

62. Lemont, "Overcoming the Politics of Reform," 293–94.

63. Lemont, "Story of the Cherokee Nation Constitutional Convention," 1–2.

64. Lemont, 19.

65. Marla J. Cullison, *1999 Cherokee Nation Constitution Convention*, vol. I (Muskogee, OK: Courtemanche Reporting Service, 1999).

66. Cullison, *1999 Cherokee Nation Constitution Convention*, 1.

67. Cullison, 2–3.

68. Lemont, "Story of the Cherokee Nation Constitutional Convention," 21.

69. Lemont, 22.

70. Lemont, 24–25.

71. Lemont, 25.

72. Lemont, 26.

73. Lemont, 26; Cherokee Constitution Convention Transcripts, *supra note* 61, at 11.

74. Lemont, "Story of the Cherokee Nation Constitutional Convention," 26.

75. Lemont, 27.

76. Cullison, *1999 Cherokee Nation Constitution Convention*, vol. I, 111.

77. Cullison, 111.

78. Constitution of the Cherokee Nation (1999), Preamble. The 1976 Constitution had a similar but slightly different formulation.

79. Keith, *From One Fire*, 51; see also Teuton and Shade, *Cherokee Earth Dwellers*, 226–30.

80. Keith, *From One Fire*; Smith, *Leadership Lessons*; Mankiller and Wallace, *Mankiller*. According to the Cherokee Nation government website: "Today the majority of Cherokees practice some denomination of Christianity, with Baptist and Methodist the most common. However, a significant number of Cherokees still observe and practice older traditions, meeting at stomp grounds in local communities to hold stomp dances and other ceremonies." See Cherokee Nation, "Culture Frequently Asked Questions," https://www.cherokee.org/about-the-nation/frequently-asked-questions/culture/?page=2&pageSize=7 (accessed September 30, 2022).

81. Martha Berry, "Firsthand Account," in *American Indian Constitutional Reform and the Rebuilding of Native Nations*, ed. Eric D. Lemon (Austin: University of Texas Press, 2006), 332.

82. In 2019, the Tribal Council's rules committee debated putting forward the question of another constitutional convention; the discussion was tabled. See D. Sean Rowley, "Heated Discussion Takes Place in Rules Committee Meeting," *Cherokee Phoenix*, March 1, 2019, https://www.cherokeephoenix.org/news/heated-discussion-takes-place-in-rules-committee-meeting/article_833a9ad4-e2ff-5edf-b994-667c5862bbe8.html.

83. Constitution of the Cherokee Nation (1999), Article III, Section 4.

84. Staff Reports, "History of the *Cherokee Phoenix*," *Cherokee Phoenix*, January 13, 2015, https://www.cherokeephoenix.org/archives/history-of-the-cherokee-phoenix/article_30c25bf9-bc26-5628-9687-75e1be8581ba.html.

85. Constitution of the Cherokee Nation (1999), Article VI, Section 3. This has recently been amended to remove all instances of the word "blood."

86. Lemont, "Story of the Cherokee Nation Constitutional Convention," 19–21.

87. Constitution of the Cherokee Nation (1999), Article XI, Section 1–3.

88. Constitution of the Cherokee Nation (1999), Article XI, Section 4.

89. Constitution of the Cherokee Nation (1999), Article VIII, Section 1.

90. Lemont, "Story of the Cherokee Nation Constitutional Convention," 22.

91. Lemont, 23; Constitution of the Cherokee Nation (1999), Article VIII, Section 5.

92. Constitution of the Cherokee Nation (1999), Article IV, Section 1.

93. Conley, *Cherokee Nation*, 240.

94. Conley, *Cherokee Encyclopedia*, 46–47.

95. Smith, *Leadership Lessons*, 12.

96. Conley, *Cherokee Nation*, 240.

97. Smith, *Leadership Lessons*, 12.

98. Smith, 12.

99. Cherokee Nation Legislative Act 16-02, passed May 13, 2002 (signed May 21), with 10 councillors in favor, 1 opposed, and 4 absent or abstaining.

100. Cherokee Nation Tribal Council Meeting—Regular Session Minutes, May 13, 2002.

101. Cherokee Nation Tribal Council Meeting, May 13, 2002.

102. *Cherokee Nation v. Raymond Nash et al. and Marilyn Vann et al. and Ryan Zinke, Secretary of the Interior, and the US Department of the Interior*, 13-01313: 267 F. Supp. 3d 86 (D.D.C. 2017), 24.

103. Cherokee Nation, "Cherokee Nation Election Results," 2003, Cherokee Nation Director of Communications, Tahlequah, OK.

104. *Cherokee Nation v. Nash*, 24–25; Denson, *Demanding the Cherokee Nation*, 251.

105. Christina A. Li, "Blood Quantum and the Freedmen Controversy: The Implications for Indigenous Sovereignty," Harvard Political Review, September 17, 2021, https://harvardpolitics.com/blood-quantum/.

106. Will Chavez, "UPDATE: Freedmen Descendants Have Citizenship Restored and May Vote Sept. 24," *Cherokee Phoenix*, September 21, 2011, https://www.cherokeephoenix.org/news/update-freedmen-descendants-have-citizenship-restored-and-may-vote-sept-24/article_70491727-8093-5f0e-8566-59b34ecbe6cf.html.

107. Marilyn Vann, "Cherokee Freedmen Overjoyed by Federal Court Ruling Granting Citizenship," interview by Allison Herrera, PRI, August 31, 2017, audio, 4:40, https://www.pri.org/stories/2017-08-31/cherokee-freedmen-overjoyed-federal-court-ruling-granting-tribal-citizenship.

108. Vann, "Cherokee Freedmen Overjoyed."

109. Lemont, "Story of the Cherokee Nation Constitutional Convention," 32.

110. *Cherokee Nation v. Nash*, 25.

111. *Cherokee Nation v. Nash*, 24–25.

112. Council of the Cherokee Nation, Special Council Meeting, January 10, 2007: Resolution No. 01–07, "A Resolution Confirming the Dates of the Special Election as Transmitted by the Cherokee Nation Election Commission."

113. Miles, *Ties That Bind*, xviii–xix; Nelson, *Progressive Traditions*, 41; Justice, *Why Indigenous Literatures Matter*, 15.

114. *Cherokee Nation v. Nash*, 25; Brown, *Stoking the Fire*, 117.

115. Kushner, "Development."

116. Cherokee Nation, 2007 Special Election Results (updated May 21, 2019), https://election.cherokee.org/media/j4wbrqh3/cnspecialelectionresults.xls.

117. Constitution of the Cherokee Nation (1999), Article IV, Section 1, emphasis added.

118. Miles, *Ties That Bind*, xviii–xix.

119. *Cherokee Nation v. Nash*, 25.

120. Brown, *Stoking the Fire*, 118.

121. Justice, *Why Indigenous Literatures Matter*, 15.

122. A Bill to Sever United States Government Relations with the Cherokee Nation of Oklahoma, HR 2824, 100th Congress, 1st Session, *Congressional Record* 153, no. 147, daily ed. (October 1, 2007): H 11053; Miles, *Ties That Bind*, xix.

123. Teddye Snell, "BIA Disputes Tribe's Removal of Feds from Constitutional Process," *Tahlequah Daily Press*, May 23, 2007, http://www.tahlequahdailypress .com/news/local_news/bia-disputes-tribe-s-removal-of-feds-from-constituti onal-process/article_11eed474-a578-5364-a999-0a429331fe9e.html.

124. "Cherokee Nation Reacts to BIA Rejection of Constitution," Indianz .com, May 23, 2007, https://www.indianz.com/News/2007/05/23/cherokee _nation_10.asp.

125. Smith, *Leadership Lessons*, 259.

126. *Cherokee Nation v. Nash*, 25.

127. *Cherokee Nation v. Nash*, 25.

128. Kushner, "Development," 13; *Cherokee Nation Registrar v. Raymond Nash et al.*, SC-2011-02 (Supreme Court of the Cherokee Nation, 2011).

129. James MacKay, "The Cherokee Nation Must Be Free to Expel Black Freedmen," *Guardian*, September 17, 2011, https://www.theguardian.com /commentisfree/2011/sep/17/cherokee-nation-black-freedmen.

130. Miles, *Ties That Bind*, xix; Nelson, *Progressive Traditions*, 40–41.

131. Chief Bill John Baker filed motions in 2013 and 2014 to, in effect, secure a ruling in favor of the idea that the Cherokees' own constitutional amendment in 1866 had granted freedmen citizenship, not the Treaty of 1866 itself. See *Cherokee Nation v. Nash*, 27.

132. Chad Hunter, "Cherokee Attorney Offers Take on 'by Blood' Removal," *Cherokee Phoenix*, April 12, 2021, https://www.cherokeephoenix.org/news /cherokee-attorney-offers-take-on-by-blood-removal/article_d8e20434-9b92 -11eb-adb1-fb0d81409aba.html.

133. Justice, *Why Indigenous Literatures Matter*, 15.

134. *Cherokee Nation v. Nash.*

135. *Cherokee Nation v. Nash*, 53.

136. Travis Snell, "Supreme Court Orders Processing of Freedmen Citizenship Applications," *Cherokee Phoenix*, September 2, 2017, https://www.cherokee phoenix.org/news/supreme-court-orders-processing-of-freedmen-citizenship -applications/article_c0408a05-8a9e-5e2b-a78b-3e55ca381fe6.html.

137. Keith, *From One Fire*, 11.

138. Keith, 12.

139. Keith, 63–66.

140. Keith, 67.

141. Nelson, *Progressive Traditions*, 41.

142. Keith, *From One Fire*, 68–69.

143. Will Chavez, "Freedmen Vow to Continue Fighting Cherokee Nation for Their Rights," *Cherokee Phoenix*, August 30, 2011, https://www.cherokeephoenix .org/news/freedmen-vow-to-continue-fighting-cherokee-nation-for-their-rights /article_57ac3536-58e6-592f-93b6-13afeb708fcf.html.

144. Chavez, "Freedmen Vow to Continue Fighting."

145. Will Chavez, "Freedmen Descendant Says Issue Is Still a Struggle," *Cherokee Phoenix*, September 23, 2011, https://www.cherokeephoenix.org/news /freedmen-descendant-says-issue-is-still-a-struggle/article_0e2f7052-bd0b -5910-a101-4e9f8bc2bfa3.html.

146. "Membership and Official Supporter Application," Descendants of Freedmen of the Five Civilized Tribes Association, http://websites.godaddy.com /blob/b94b4dc8-e0df-448a-a658-31349283b956/downloads/Descendants%20 Membership%20Application%20revised%20%208%2025%202014%20-%20revi sion%201%20(1).pdf?cb52130b&fbclid=IwAR3AgSQP2BQrNbIuVAZ5ZHC50 igmbct2PAFIfWMhC39aQeLQCrFYchgRNbY (accessed January 20, 2019).

147. Chuck Hoskin Jr., Dick Lay, and David Walkingstick, "Cherokee Nation's Principal Chief Forum," interview by Royal Aills, RSU Public TV, May 16, 2019, video file, at 22:30; no longer online.

148. Hoskin, Lay, and Walkingstick, "Cherokee Nation's Principal Chief Forum."

149. D. Sean Rowley, "UPDATED: Hoskin Wins Cherokee Nation Principal Chief Race," *Cherokee Phoenix*, June 2, 2019, https://www.cherokeephoenix .org/news/updated-hoskin-wins-cherokee-nation-principal-chief-race/article _88f62f72-9a59-5f8e-9711-d1c06612903b.html.

150. State of the Nation Address, *Cherokee Nation*, August 31, 2019, video file, https://www.youtube.com/watch?v=6zzOoHCsMfM at 1:00:41. Hoskin's full remarks at 1:00:41–1:12:30.

151. State of the Nation Address, *Cherokee Nation*, full remarks at 23:22–30:25. Conley reports that, despite Joe Byrd's troubled administration as principal chief, he remains very popular in the Cherokee Nation. See Conley, *Cherokee Encyclopedia*, 46–47. In 2021, Chief Hoskin appointed Byrd special envoy for international affairs and language preservation. See Staff Reports, "Byrd

Named Cherokee Nation's International Affairs Special Envoy," *Cherokee Phoenix*, August 16, 2021, https://www.cherokeephoenix.org/news/byrd-named -cherokee-nation-s-international-affairs-special-envoy/article_40eea920-fecf -11eb-b237-270d4df15df9.html.

152. Chad Hunter, "Court Tosses Complaint Filed over Freedmen's Eligibility," *Cherokee Phoenix*, February 9, 2021, https://www.cherokeephoenix.org/news /court-tosses-complaint-filed-over-freedmens-eligibility/article_7e9302f9-e737 -50c8-8066-fd02c607ca97.html. In 2017, the Election Commission decided to bar Cherokee Nation citizen Randy White from running for the District 11 seat on the Tribal Council because he was not a "Cherokee by blood" but instead belonged to the class of Shawnee Cherokees. These debates have not been restricted to freedmen. See Jami Murphy, "Supreme Court Upholds Ruling against White's Candidacy," *Cherokee Phoenix*, March 27, 2017, https://www.cherokeephoenix.org/news /supreme-court-upholds-ruling-against-whites-candidacy/article_62598f7d -74d2-58f0-b72a-943b90bc542d.html.

153. Michael Overall, "Cherokee Chief Backs Right of Freedmen Descendants to Run for Tribal Office," *Tulsa World*, February 4, 2021, https://tulsaworld .com/news/local/cherokee-chief-backs-right-of-freedmen-descendants-to-run -for-tribal-office/article_d00d913e-6654-11eb-b474-0770a9d19568.html?utm _medium=social&utm_source=email&utm_campaign=user-share.

154. Chad Hunter, "Election Complaint Filed over Freedmen Descendant's Eligibility," *Cherokee Phoenix*, February 2, 2021, https://www.cherokeephoenix .org/news/election-complaint-filed-over-freedmen-descendants-eligibility /article_3589c336-b676-5906-bb9b-d55292529663.html.

155. Chad Hunter, "Cherokee Nation Attorney General Asks Supreme Court to Strike Constitution's 'by Blood' Reference," *Cherokee Phoenix*, February 19, 2021, https://www.cherokeephoenix.org/news/cherokee-nation-attorney-general-asks -supreme-court-to-strike-constitution-s-by-blood-reference/article_96ba59d4 -72e4-11eb-8164-8fd4e0083f67.html.

156. Will Chavez, "Federal Court Rules in Cherokee Freedmen Case," *Cherokee Phoenix*, August 31, 2017, https://www.cherokeephoenix.org/news/federal -court-rules-in-cherokee-freedmen-case/article_9356691a-8a8c-5daa-98ef -775f143c7f49.html.

157. Admin, "Cherokee Nation Supreme Court Issues Decision That 'by Blood' Reference be Stricken from Cherokee Nation Constitution," ᎤᏃ ᏥᏳ ᎤᏤᎷ (*Cherokee One Feather*), February 22, 2021, https://theonefeather.com /2021/02/22/cherokee-nation-supreme-court-issues-decision-that-by-blood -reference-be-stricken-from-cherokee-nation-constitution/; Cherokee Nation Supreme Court in re: Effect of *Cherokee Nation v. Nash* and *Vann v. Zinke*, District Court for the District of Columbia, Case No. 13–01313 (TFH) and Petition for Writ of Mandamus Requiring Cherokee Nation Registrar to Begin Processing Citizenship Applications, Case No. SC-17-07, https://www.cherokeecourts.org /Portals/cherokeecourts/Documents/Supreme%20Court/Order%20and%20 Opinions/SC-17-07%2037-Final%20Order%202-22-21.pdf?ver=2021-02-26 -135726-990.

158. Lindsey Chastain, "Cherokee Nation Supreme Court Issues Decisions That 'by Blood' Reference Be Stricken from Cherokee Nation Constitution," *Skiatook Journal*, March 2, 2021, https://tulsaworld.com/community/skiatook /news/cherokee-nation-supreme-court-issues-decision-that-by-blood-reference -be-stricken-from-cherokee-nation/article_cf73b1b4-7797-11eb-8b60 -93c3f7273d87.html.

159. Chastain, "Cherokee Nation Supreme Court Issues Decisions."

160. Hunter, "Cherokee Nation Attorney General Asks Supreme Court."

161. Hunter, "Cherokee Attorney Offers Take."

162. Cherokee Nation Legislative Act 14-22: An Act Revising and Restating Title 26 ("Elections") of the Cherokee Nation Code Annotated.

163. Walela Knight, "Stitt's Removal of Cherokee Citizenship," MoveOn, https://sign.moveon.org/petitions/stitt-s-removal-of-cherokee-citizenship (accessed July 7, 2022); Louis Quinton, "Remove the Cherokee Citizenship of Kevin Stitt Governor of Oklahoma," Change.org, started December 21, 2021, https://www.change.org/p/cherokee-nation-remove-the-cherokee-citizenship -of-kevin-stitt-governor-of-oklahoma (accessed July 7, 2022).

164. Chad Hunter, "Chief Says Stitt Continues Campaign against Tribal Sovereignty," *Cherokee Phoenix*, May 19, 2022, https://www.cherokeephoenix.org /council/chief-says-stitt-continues-campaign-against-tribal-sovereignty/article _50f6385e-d789-11ec-8851-078eba2b0324.html.

165. Graham Lee Brewer, "The Cherokee Nation Once Fought to Disenroll Gov. Kevin Stitt's Ancestors," *High Country News*, February 24, 2020, https:// www.hcn.org/articles/indigenous-affairs-the-cherokee-nation-once-fought-to -disenroll-gov-kevin-stitts-ancestors.

166. D. Sean Rowley, "Stitt Keeps Governor's Seat after Thwarting Challenge by Hofmeister," *Cherokee Phoenix*, November 10, 2022, https://www.cherokeephoenix .org/news/stitt-keeps-governor-s-seat-after-thwarting-challenge-by-hofmeister /article_bd66386c-6146-11ed-834a-bbafcde30b72.html.

167. Associated Press, "Cherokee Nation Announces It Now Has 400,000 Tribal Citizens," *U.S. News & World Report*, September 29, 2021, https://www .usnews.com/news/best-states/oklahoma/articles/2021-09-29/cherokee -nation-announces-it-now-has-400-000-tribal-citizens.

168. Barbara L. Jones, "*Haaland v. Brackeen, Cherokee Nation v. Brackeen, Texas v. Haaland*, and *Brackeen v. Haaland*," *American Bar Association*, December 7, 2022, https://www.americanbar.org/groups/public_education/publications /preview_home/haaland-v-brackeen-cherokee-nation/.

169. David Myer Temin, "Indigenous Sovereignty against Family Separation," Starting Points Journal, December 1, 2022, https://startingpointsjournal .com/indigenous-sovereignty-against-family-separation/.

170. *Haaland v. Brackeen*, 599 U.S. (2023), 10, 12.

171. Gorsuch's concurring opinion: *Haaland v. Brackeen*, 2.

172. Legislative Act 6-92—An Act Relating to the Process of Enrolling as a Member of the Cherokee Nation.

173. Smith, *Civic Ideals*, 424.

174. Adam Barnes, "Changing America: Cherokee Nation Membership Surges to 400,000 Strong," *The Hill*, September 30, 2021, https://thehill .com/changing-america/enrichment/arts-culture/574649-cherokee-nation -membership-surges-to-400000-strong/.

175. D. Sean Rowley, "Heated Discussion Takes Place in Rules Committee Meeting," *Cherokee Phoenix*, March 1, 2019, https://www.cherokeephoenix .org/news/heated-discussion-takes-place-in-rules-committee-meeting/article _833a9ad4-e2ff-5edf-b994-667c5862bbe8.html. The Council briefly discussed another constitutional convention referendum in 2019.

CONCLUSION

1. Altman and Belt, "Tohi"; Smith, *Original Teachings*; Teuton and Shade, *Cherokee Earth Dwellers*; Holm, "Untitled Review"; Nelson, *Progressive Traditions*; Reed, *Serving the Nation*; Kilpatrick and Kilpatrick, *Friends of Thunder*; Stremlau, *Sustaining the Cherokee Family*.

2. Deloria, *Custer Died for Your Sins*; Deneen, *Why Liberalism Failed*; Rogin, *Fathers and Children*; Justice, *Why Indigenous Literatures Matter*; Kushner and Clouse, "Citizenship and the Good Life."

3. Circe Sturm, *Becoming Indian: The Struggle over Cherokee Identity in the Twenty-First Century* (Santa Fe, NM: School for Advanced Research Press, 2011); Deloria, *Playing Indian*.

4. Carrese, "Montesquieu's Call to Civic Education," 10.

5. Julia Coates, "Foreword," vi.

6. Wilkins and Wilkins, *Dismembered*; Miles, *Ties That Bind*; Littlefield, "Utopian Dreams."

7. Teuton and Shade, *Cherokee Earth Dwellers*; Teuton, *Turtle Island Liars' Club*; Smith, *Stand as One*; Smith, *Original Teachings*; Mankiller and Wallace, *Mankiller*; Smith, *Leadership Lessons*.

8. Chuck Hoskin Jr., "State of the Nation Address," Cherokee National Newsroom, August 31, 2019, video file, at 1:02:26, https://www.youtube.com/watch ?v=6zzOoHCsMfM&list=PL1A5EA5EF4FE47D24&index=7.

9. Chuck Hoskin Jr., "OPINION: Winter Storms Show How Much Cherokee Nation Means to Communities, Families," March 6, 2021, https://www .cherokeephoenix.org/opinion/opinion-winter-storms-show-how-much-cherokee -nation-means-to-communities-families/article_3a0b3dd8-7dcb-11eb-9249 -5fde048f220d.html.

10. Bill John Baker, "First Inaugural Address," in Keith, *From One Fire*, 214–19, at 218.

11. Smith, *Leadership Lessons*, 207–8.

12. Wilma Mankiller, "Rebuilding the Cherokee Nation," April 2, 1993, https://awpc.cattcenter.iastate.edu/2017/03/21/rebuilding-the-cherokee -nation-april-2-1993/.

13. C. J. Harris, "Third Annual Message of C. J. Harris, Principal Chief," Tahlequah, C.N., 1894.

14. Dennis W. Bushyhead, "First Annual Message."

15. Bushyhead, "First Annual Message"; Stremlau, *Sustaining the Cherokee Family*.

16. Ross, *Life and Times*, 2.

17. Ross, 5.

18. West, *Political Theory*.

19. Or, put another way, inclusion over decolonization.

20. Deneen, *Why Liberalism Failed*; Deloria, *Custer Died for Your Sins*.

21. Barack Obama, "A More Perfect Union," in *American Soul: The Contested Legacy of the Declaration of Independence*, ed. Justin Buckley Dyer (New York: Roman & Littlefield, 2012), 146.

22. Smith, *Stand as One*, 71.

23. Murray, *Thinking About Political Things*, 151.

24. Murray, 149–53; Deneen, *Why Liberalism Failed*.

25. Collins, *Aristotle and the Rediscovery of Citizenship*.

26. Deloria, "Foreword," xviii–xix.

27. Lincoln, *Selected Speeches and Writings*, 17–18.

Bibliography

Abel, Annie Heloise. *The American Indian under Reconstruction*. Cleveland: Arthur H. Clark, 1925.

Adams, John Quincy. *The Social Compact*. Providence, RI: Knowles and Vose, 1842.

Aquinas, St. Thomas. *On Being and Essence*. Translated by Armand Maurer. Toronto, Canada: Pontifical Institute of Mediaeval Studies, 1968.

Adair, James. *Adair's History of the American Indians, Edited under the Auspices of the National Society of the Colonial Dames of America, in Tennessee, by Samuel Cole Williams*. New York: Promontory Press, 1930.

Alderman, Pat. *Nancy Ward, Cherokee Chieftainess: Dragging Canoe, Cherokee-Chickamauga War Chief*. Johnson City, TN: Overmountain Press, 1990.

Altman, Heidi M., and Thomas N. Belt. "Tohi: The Cherokee Concept of Well-Being." In *Under the Rattlesnake: Cherokee Health and Resiliency*, 9–22. Edited by Lisa J. Lefler. Tuscaloosa: University of Alabama Press, 2009.

Awiakta, Marilou. *Selu: Seeking the Corn-Mother's Wisdom*. Golden, CO: Fulcrum Publishing, 1993.

Bailey, M. Thomas. *Reconstruction in Indian Territory: A Story of Avarice, Discrimination, and Opportunism*. Port Washington, NY: Kennikat Press, 1972.

Banting, Keith, and Will Kymlicka. "Introduction." In *The Strains of Commitment: The Political Sources of Solidarity in Diverse Societies*. Edited by Keith Banting and Will Kymlicka. Oxford, UK: Oxford University Press, 2017.

Barrett, Carole, and Harvey Markowitz, eds. *American Indian Biographies*, revised edition. Pasadena, CA: Salem Press, 2005.

Bass, Althea. *Cherokee Messenger*. Norman: University of Oklahoma Press, 1936.

Beienburg, Sean, and Aaron Kushner. "Conservative Progressivism? Michael Cunniff, Federalism, and the Founding of Arizona." *American Political Thought* 12, no. 4 (Fall 2023): 552–80. https://doi.org/10.1086/727045.

Bender, Albert. "Dragging Canoe's War: A War Chief's Ingenious Defense of the Cherokee Homeland." *Military History* 28 (2012): 68–75.

Berry, Martha. "Firsthand Account." In *American Indian Constitutional Reform and the Rebuilding of Native Nations*, 332. Edited by Eric D. Lemont. Austin: University of Texas Press, 2006.

Blackhawk, Ned. *The Rediscovery of America: Native Peoples and the Unmaking of U.S. History*. New Haven, CT: Yale University Press, 2023.

Bloom, Alan. *The Closing of the American Mind: How Higher Education Has Failed Democracy and Impoverished the Souls of Today's Students.* New York: Simon & Schuster, 1987.

Bronson, Ruth Muskrat. "Life on the Checkerboard." In *Native American Testimony,* 262–63. Edited by Peter Nabokov. New York: Penguin, 1991.

Brown, Catharine. *Cherokee Sister: The Collected Writings of Catharine Brown, 1818–1823.* Edited by Theresa Strouth Gaul. Lincoln: University of Nebraska Press, 2014.

Brown, John P. *Old Frontiers: The Story of the Cherokee Indians from Earliest Times to the Date of Their Removal to the West, 1838.* Kingsport, TN: Southern Publishers, 1938.

Brown, Kirby. "Citizenship, Land, and Law: Constitutional Criticism and John Milton Oskison's *Black Jack Davy.*" *Studies in American Indian Literatures* 23, no. 4, Special Issue: Constitutional Criticism (Winter 2011): 77–115. https://doi.org/10.5250/studamerindilite.23.4.0077.

———. *Stoking the Fire: Nationhood in Cherokee Writing, 1907–1970.* Norman: University of Oklahoma Press, 2018.

Bruyneel, Kevin. "Challenging American Boundaries: Indigenous Peoples and the 'Gift' of US Citizenship." *Studies in American Political Development* 18 (Spring 2004): 30–43.

———. *The Third Space of Sovereignty: The Post-Colonial Politics of U.S.-Indigenous Relations.* Minneapolis: University of Minnesota Press, 2007.

Burkhart, Brian. *Indigenizing Philosophy Through the Land: A Trickster Methodology for Decolonizing Environmental Ethics and Indigenous Futures.* Ann Arbor: Michigan State University Press, 2019.

Carpenter, Kristen A., and Angela R. Riley. "Privatizing the Reservation?" *Stanford Law Review* 71 (April 2019): 791–878.

Carrese, Paul. "Montesquieu's Call to Civic Education: Roots and Remedies for America's Civic Crisis." In *American Citizenship and Constitutionalism in Principle and Practice,* 10–37. Edited by Steven F. Pittz and Joseph Postell. Norman: University of Oklahoma Press, 2022.

Carroll, Clint. *Roots of Our Renewal: Ethnobotany and Cherokee Environmental Governance.* Minneapolis: University of Minnesota Press, 2015.

Ceaser, James W. "Foundational Concepts and American Political Development." In *Nature and History in American Political Development.* Edited by James Ceaser. Cambridge, MA: Harvard University Press, 2006.

Chang, David A. *The Color of the Land: Race, Nation, and the Politics of Landownership in Oklahoma, 1832–1929.* Chapel Hill: University of North Carolina Press, 2010.

Cheng, Eric P. *Hanging Together: Role-Based Constitutional Fellowship and the Problem with Difference and Disagreement.* Cambridge, UK: Cambridge University Press, 2022.

Cherokee Nation. *Laws of the Cherokee Nation.* New York: Legal Classics Library, 1995.

———. *Compiled Laws of the Cherokee Nation.* London: Forgotten Books, 2012.

Coates, Julia. "Forward." In Thomas Lee Ballenger and Chadwick Corntassel Smith, *The Development of Law and Legal Institutions among the Cherokees*, v–x. Norman: University of Oklahoma Press, 2010.

Cobb, Daniel M. "Devils in Disguise: The Carnegie Project, the Cherokee Nation, and the 1960s." *American Indian Quarterly* 31, no. 3 (Summer 2007): 465–90.

Cohen, Felix S. *Handbook of Federal Indian Law with Reference Tables*. Washington, DC: U.S. Government Printing Office, 1945.

Collins, Susan D. *Aristotle and the Rediscovery of Citizenship*. Cambridge, UK: Cambridge University Press, 2006.

Conley, Robert, Jr. *A Cherokee Encyclopedia*. Albuquerque: University of New Mexico Press, 2007.

———. *The Cherokee Nation: A History*. Albuquerque: University of New Mexico Press, 2005.

Corkran, David H. *The Cherokee Frontier: Conflict and Survival, 1740–1762*. Norman: University of Oklahoma Press, 1962.

Corn Tassel. "Let Us Examine the Facts." In *Native American Testimony*, 121–23. Edited Peter Nabokov. New York: Penguin Books, 1991.

Cox, Brent Alan. *Heart of the Eagle: Dragging Canoe and the Emergence of the Chickamauga Confederacy*. Milan, TN: Chenanee Publishers, 1999.

Cunniff, Michael G. "The New State of Oklahoma." *World's Work* 12, no. 2 (June 1906): 7618–19.

Curley, Andrew, Pallavi Gupta, Lara Lookabaugh, Christopher Neubert, and Sara Smith. "Decolonisation Is a Political Project: Overcoming Impasses between Indigenous Sovereignty and Abolition." *Antipode* 54, no. 4 (July 2022): 1043–62. https://doi.org/10.1111/anti.12830.

Cushman, Ellen. "'We're Taking the Genius of Sequoyah into This Century': The Cherokee Syllabary, Peoplehood, and Perseverance." *Wicazo Sa Review* 26 (2011): 67–83.

Dale, Edward Everett, and Morris L. Wardell. *History of Oklahoma*. New York: Prentice-Hall, 1948.

Dale, Edward Everett, and Gaston Litton. *Cherokee Cavaliers: Forty Years of Cherokee History as Told in the Correspondence of the Ridge-Watie-Boudinot Family*. Norman: University of Oklahoma Press, 1995.

Dean, Nadia. "A Demand of Blood: The Cherokee War of 1776." *National Museum of the American Indian* 14, no. 4 (Winter 2013): 36–40.

Debo, Angie. *A History of the Indians of the United States*. Norman: University of Oklahoma Press, 1970.

———. *And Still the Waters Run: The Betrayal of the Five Civilized Tribes*. Princeton, NJ: Princeton University Press, 1940.

Deloria, Philip J. *Playing Indian*. New Haven, CT: Yale University Press, 1998.

Deloria, Vine, Jr. *Custer Died for Your Sins: An Indian Manifesto*. Norman: University of Oklahoma Press, 1969.

———. "Forward." In *Native American Testimony*. Edited by Peter Nabokov. New York: Penguin Books, 1991.

———. "Self-Determination and the Concept of Sovereignty." In *Economic Development in American Indian Reservations*. Edited by Roxanne Dunbar Ortiz. Albuquerque: University of New Mexico Press, 1979.

Deloria, Vine, Jr., and David E. Wilkins. *Tribes, Treaties, and Constitutional Tribulations*. Austin: University of Texas Press, 1999.

Deneen, Patrick. *Why Liberalism Failed*. New Haven, CT: Yale University Press, 2018.

Denson, Andrew. *Demanding the Cherokee Nation: Indian Autonomy and American Culture, 1830–1900*. Lincoln: University of Nebraska Press, 2004.

Dow, Jay K. *Electing the House: The Adoption and Performance of the US Single-Member District Electoral System*. Lawrence: University Press of Kansas, 2017.

Du Bois, W. E. B. *The Souls of Black Folk*. Mineola, NY: Dover Publications, 1994.

Duncan, DeWitt Clinton. "The Outrage of Allotment." In *Native American Testimony*, 265–67. Edited by Peter Nabokov. New York: Penguin, 1991.

Duthu, N. Bruce. *American Indians and the Law*. New York: Penguin, 2008.

Edwards, Lydia M. "Protecting Black Tribal Members: Is the Thirteenth Amendment the Linchpin to Securing Equal Rights within Indian Country?" *Berkeley Journal of African-American Law & Policy* 8 (2006): 122–54.

Elliot, Jennifer. "Ga-ne-tli-yv-s-di (Change) in the Cherokee Nation: The Vann and Ridge Houses in Northwest Georgia.," *Buildings & Landscapes: Journal of the Vernacular Architecture Forum* 18, no. 1 (Spring 2011): 43–63. https://doi.org/10.5749/buildland.18.1.0043.

Evans, E. Raymond. "Notable Persons in Cherokee History: Dragging Canoe." *Journal of Cherokee Studies* 2, no. 2 (1977): 176–89.

Feeling, Durbin. ᎠᏕᎶᎭ ᏗᎧᏃᎮᏓ (*Cherokee-English Dictionary*). Tahlequah: Cherokee Nation of Oklahoma, 1975.

Feeling, Durbin, William Pulte, and Gregory Pulte. *Cherokee Narratives: A Linguistic Study*. Norman: University of Oklahoma Press, 2018.

Ferguson, Kennan. "Why Does Political Science Hate American Indians?" *Perspectives on Politics* 14, no. 4 (December 2016): 1029–38. https://doi.org/10.1017/S1537592716002905.

Finger, John. *The Eastern Band of the Cherokees, 1819–1900*. Knoxville: University of Tennessee Press, 1984.

Fixico, Donald L. *Termination and Relocation: Federal Indian Policy, 1945–1960*. Albuquerque: University of New Mexico Press, 1986.

Fogelson, Raymond. "On the 'Petticoat Government' of the Eighteenth-Century Cherokee." In *Personality and Cultural Construction of Society: Papers in Honor of Melford E. Spiro*. Edited by David K. Jordan and Marc J. Swartz. Tuscaloosa: University of Alabama Press, 1990.

Foote, Shelby. *The Civil War: A Narrative: Red River to Appomattox*. New York: Vintage, 1974.

Foreman, Grant. *Indian Removal*. Norman: University of Oklahoma Press, 1934.

Foster, George E. *Se-Quo-Yah: The American Cadmus and Modern Moses*. Tahlequah, OK: Office of the Indian Rights Association, 1885.

French, Laurence Armand. *Policing American Indians: A Unique Chapter in American Jurisprudence.* Boca Raton, FL: CRC Press, 2016.

Fritz, Henry E. *The Movement for Indian Assimilation, 1860–1890.* Philadelphia: University of Pennsylvania Press, 1963.

Frymer, Paul. *Building an American Empire: The Era of Territorial and Political Expansion.* Princeton, NJ: Princeton University Press, 2017.

———. "'A Rush and a Push and the Land Is Ours': Territorial Expansion, Land Policy, and U.S. State Formation." *Perspectives on Policy* 12, no. 1 (March 2014): 119–44.

———. "Why Aren't Political Scientists Interested in Native American Politics?" *Perspectives on Politics* 14, no. 4 (December 2016): 1042–43. https://doi.org /10.1017/S1537592716002929.

Garba, Tapji, and Sara-Maria Sorentino. "Slavery Is a Metaphor: A Critical Commentary on Eve Tuck and K. Wayne Yang's 'Decolonization Is not a Metaphor.'" *Antipode* 52, no. 1 (March 2020): 764–82. https://doi.org/10.1111/anti.12615.

Garroutte, Eva Marie. *Real Indians: Identity and the Survival of Native America.* Berkeley: University of California Press, 2003.

George, Henry. *Progress and Poverty.* London: Aziloth, 2016.

Goodwin, Doris Kearns. *Lyndon Johnson and the American Dream.* New York: St. Martin's Griffin, 1976.

Grann, David. *Killers of the Flower Moon: The Osage Murders and the Birth of the FBI.* New York: Vintage, 2017.

Grant, Ulysses S.. *Memoirs and Selected Letters.* Edited by Mary Drake McFeely and William S. McFeely. New York: Library of America, 1990.

Halliburton, R., Jr. *Red over Black: Black Slavery among the Cherokee Indians.* Westport, CT: Greenwood Press, 1977.

Hamilton, Alexander, James Madison, and John Jay. *The Federalist Papers.* New York: New American Library, 1961.

Haywood, John. *The Natural and Aboriginal History of Tennessee.* Nashville: George Wilson, 1823.

Hicks, Brian. *Toward Sun the Setting: John Ross, the Cherokees, and the Trail of Tears.* New York: Grove Press, 2011.

Hoig, Stanley. *Beyond the Frontier: Exploring the Indian Country.* Norman: University of Oklahoma Press, 1998.

———. *The Cherokees and Their Chiefs in the Wake of Empire.* Fayetteville: University of Arkansas Press, 1998.

Holm, Tom. "Indian Lobbyists: Cherokee Opposition to the Allotment of Tribal Lands." *American Indian Quarterly* 5, no. 2 (May 1979): 115–34. https://doi .org/10.2307/1183752.

———. "Untitled Review." In Crosslin Fields Smith, *Stand as One: Spiritual Teachings of Keetoowah; Awakening to the Original Truths,* 70–72. Ranchos de Taos, NM: Dog Soldier Press, 2018.

Hopkins, A. G. *American Empire: A Global History.* Princeton, NJ: Princeton University Press, 2018.

Hudson, Charles. *The Southeastern Indians*. Knoxville: University of Tennessee Press, 1976.

Jacobs, Wilbur R., ed. *Indians of the Southern Colonial Frontier: The Edmond Atkin Report and Plan of 1755*. Columbia: University of South Carolina Press, 1954.

Johnston, Carolyn Ross, ed. *Voices of Cherokee Women*. Winston-Salem, NC: John F. Blair, 2013.

Justice, Daniel Heath. *Our Fire Survives the Storm: A Cherokee Literary History*. Minneapolis: University of Minnesota Press, 2006.

———. *Why Indigenous Literatures Matter*. Waterloo, Ontario: Wilfred Laurier University Press, 2018.

Keith, Bill. *From One Fire: The Story of Cherokee Chief Bill John Baker*. Longview, TX: Stonegate Publishing, 2016.

Kettner, James H. *The Development of American Citizenship, 1608–1870*. Chapel Hill: University of North Carolina Press, 1978.

Kilpatrick, Jack F., and Anna G. Kilpatrick. *Friends of Thunder: Folktales of the Oklahoma Cherokees*. Norman: University of Oklahoma Press, 1964.

———, eds. *The Shadow of Sequoyah: Social Documents of the Cherokees, 1862–1964*. Norman: University of Oklahoma Press, 1964.

Kim, Yule, "The Cherokee Freedmen Dispute: Legal Background, Analysis, and Proposed Legislation," U.S. Congressional Research Service, order code RL34321, updated August 7, 2008, https://www.everycrsreport.com/files /20080807_RL34321_a3af70824a5ac2377f3625be371d61b58b32ff48.pdf.

Kushner, Aaron. "Cherokee Political Thought and the Development of Tribal Citizenship." *Studies in American Political Development* 35, no. 1 (2021): 1–15. https://doi.org/10.1017/S0898588X20000176.

———. "The Imposition of Freedom: Tribal Citizenship and the Case of the Cherokee Freedmen." In *American Citizenship and Constitutionalism in Principle and Practice*, 83–108. Edited by Steven Pittz and Joseph Postell. Norman: University of Oklahoma Press, 2022, 83–108.

Kushner, Aaron, and Stephen Clouse. "Citizenship and the Good Life: Cherokee and American Regimes in Conflict." *Political Science Reviewer* 47, no. 3 (2023): 1–34.

Lauber, Almon W. *Indian Slavery in Colonial Times within the Present Limits of the United States*. New York: Longmans, Green, 1913.

Leeds, Georgia Rae. *The United Keetoowah Band of Cherokee Indians in Oklahoma*. New York: Peter Lang, 2000.

Leeds, Stacy L. "Defeat or Mixed Blessing—Tribal Sovereignty and the State of Sequoyah." *Tulsa Law Review* 43, no. 1 (Fall 2007): 5–16.

Lemont, Eric D., ed. *American Indian Constitutional Reform and the Rebuilding of Native Nations*. Austin: University of Texas Press, 2006.

———. "Overcoming the Politics of Reform: The Story of the Cherokee Nation of Oklahoma Constitutional Convention.'" *American Indian Law Review* 28, no. 1 (January 2003): 1–34. https://doi.org/10.2307/20171713.

———. "Overcoming the Politics of Reform: The Story of the Cherokee Nation of Oklahoma Constitution Convention." In *American Indian Constitutional*

Reform and the Rebuilding of Native Nations, 287–322. Edited by Eric D. Lemont. Austin: University of Texas Press, 2006.

Limerick, Patricia Nelson. *The Legacy of Conquest: The Unbroken Past of the American West*. New York: W. W. Norton, 1987.

Lincoln, Abraham. *Lincoln: Selected Speeches and Writings*. Edited by Gore Vidal. New York: Vintage Books, 1992.

Littlefield, Daniel F., Jr. *The Cherokee Freedmen: From Emancipation to American Citizenship*. Westport, CT: Greenwood Press, 1978.

———. "Utopian Dreams of the Cherokee Fullbloods: 1890–1934." *Journal of the West* 10, no. 3 (Fall 1971): 404–27.

Litton, Gaston L. "The Principal Chiefs of the Cherokee Nation." *Chronicles of Oklahoma* 15, no. 3 (September 1937): 253–70.

Lumpkin, Wilson. *The Removal of the Cherokee Indians from Georgia*. New York: Dodd, Mead, 1907.

Lyons, Scott Richard. "Actually Existing Indian Nations: Modernity, Diversity, and the Future of Native American Studies." *American Indian Quarterly* 35, no. 3 (Summer 2011): 294–312. https://doi.org/10.5250/amerindiquar.35.3.0294.

———. *X-Marks: Native Signatures of Assent*. Minneapolis: University of Minnesota Press, 2010.

MacLean, Lauren M. "Marginalizing Politics: The Conceptual and Epistemological Barriers to American Indians." *Perspectives on Politics* 14, no. 4 (December 2016): 1044–45. https://doi.org/10.1017/S1537592716002930.

Mankiller, Wilma, and Michael Wallis. *Mankiller: A Chief and Her People*. New York: St. Martin's Press, 1993.

Martin, J. Matthew. *The Cherokee Supreme Court: 1823–1835*. Durham, NC: Carolina Academic Press, 2021.

Mayes, Joel B. "First Annual Message (Second Term) of Hon. Joel B. Mayes, Principal Chief of the Cherokee Nation Delivered at Tahlequah, I.T., November 4, 1891," 12. Indigenous Histories and Cultures of North America, https://www.indigenoushistoriesandcultures.amdigital.co.uk/Documents/Detail/first-annual-message-second-term-of-hon.-joel-b.-mayes-principal-chief-of-the-cherokee-nation-delivered-at-tahlequah-i.t.-november-4-1891/7019983?item=7019987 (accessed April 16, 2024).

McClary, Ben Harris. "Nancy Ward: The Last Beloved Woman of the Cherokees." *Tennessee Historical Quarterly* 21, no. 4 (December 1962): 352–64.

McLoughlin, William G. *Champions of the Cherokees: Evan and John B. Jones*. Princeton, NJ: Princeton University Press, 1990.

———. *Cherokee Renascence in the New Republic*. Princeton, NJ: Princeton University Press, 1986.

———. *Cherokees and Missionaries, 1789–1839*. New Haven, CT: Yale University Press, 1994.

Mellon, Knox, Jr. "Christian Priber's 'Kingdom of Paradise.'" *Georgia Historical Quarterly* 57, no. 3 (Fall 1973): 319–31.

Meserve, John Bartlett. "Chief Lewis Downing and Chief Charles Thompson (Oochalata)." *Chronicles of Oklahoma* 16, no. 3 (September 1938): 315–26.

Meserve, Charles F. *The Dawes Commission and the Five Civilized Tribes of Indian Territory.* Philadelphia: Office of the Indian Rights Association, 1896.

Mettler, Suzanne, and Richard M. Valelly. "Introduction: The Distinctiveness and Necessity of American Political Development." In *Oxford Handbook of American Political Development.* Edited by Suzanne Mettler and Richard M. Valelly. New York: Oxford University Press, 2016.

Miles, Tiya. "'Circular Reasoning': Recentering Cherokee Women in the Anti-removal Campaigns," *American Quarterly* 61, no. 2 (June 2009): 221–43.

———. *Ties That Bind: The Story of an Afro-Cherokee Family in Slavery and Freedom.* Oakland: University of California Press, 2015.

Minges, Patrick N., ed. *Black Indian Slave Narratives.* Winston-Salem, NC: John F. Blair, Publisher, 2004.

———. *Slavery in the Cherokee Nation: The Keetoowah Society and the Defining of a People, 1855–1867.* New York: Routledge, 2003.

Mooney, James. *Myths of the Cherokee.* Smithsonian Institution, part 1, paper no. 1. Washington, DC: Government Printing Office, 1900.

———. "The Sacred Formulas of the Cherokees." *Seventh Annual Report of the Bureau of Ethnology to the Secretary of the Smithsonian Institute, 1885–1886.* Washington, DC: Government Printing Office, 1891, 301–98.

Moulton, Gary E. "Editor's Introduction." In *The Papers of Chief John Ross,* Vol. 1, *1807–1839,* Edited by Gary E. Moulton. Norman: University of Oklahoma Press, 1985, 3–11.

———. *John Ross: Cherokee Chief.* Athens: University of Georgia Press, 1978.

Murray, Andrew. *Thinking About Political Things: An Aristotelian Approach to Pacific Life.* Hindmarsh, SA: ATF Theology Adelaide, 2016.

Nabokov, Peter, ed. *Native American Testimony: A Chronicle of Indian-White Relations from Prophecy to the Present, 1492–2000.* New York: Penguin Group, 1999.

Nelson, Joshua B. *Progressive Traditions: Identity in Cherokee Literature and Culture.* Norman: University of Oklahoma Press, 2014.

Obama, Barack. "A More Perfect Union." In *American Soul: The Contested Legacy of the Declaration of Independence.* Edited by Justin Buckley Dyer. New York: Roman & Littlefield, 2012.

Obermeyer, Brice. *Delaware Tribe in a Cherokee Nation.* Lincoln: University of Nebraska Press, 2009.

Orren, Karen, and Stephen Skowronek. "Have We Abandoned a 'Constitutional Perspective' on American Political Development?" *Review of Politics* 73, no. 2 (March 2011): 295–99. https://doi.org/10.1017/S0034670511000088.

———. *The Search for American Political Development.* Cambridge, UK: Cambridge University Press, 2004.

Oskison, John M. "The New Indian Leadership." *American Indian Magazine* 5 (Summer 1917): 93–100.

Otis, D. S. *The Dawes Act and the Allotment of Indian Lands.* Edited by Francis P. Prucha. Norman: University of Oklahoma Press, 1973.

Parker, Thomas Valentine. *The Cherokee Indians: With Special Reference to Their Relations with the United States Government.* New York: Grafton Press, 1907.

Parins, James W. *John Rollin Ridge: His Life and Works*. Lincoln: University of Nebraska Press, 1991.

Perdue, Theda, ed. *Cherokee Editor: The Writings of Elias Boudinot*. Knoxville: University of Tennessee Press, 1983.

———. *The Cherokee Removal: A Brief History with Documents*. 3rd edition. Boston: Bedford/St. Martin's Press, 2016.

———. *Cherokee Women*. Lincoln: University of Nebraska Press, 1998.

———. "Clan and Court: Another Look at the Early Cherokee Republic." *American Indian Quarterly* 24, no. 4 (Autumn 2000): 562–69.

———. "Rising from the Ashes: The Cherokee Phoenix as an Ethnohistorical Source." *Ethnohistory* 24, no. 3 (Summer 1977): 207–18. https://doi.org/10.2307/481695.

———. *Slavery and the Evolution of Cherokee Society, 1540–1866*. Knoxville: University of Tennessee Press, 1979.

———. "Traditionalism in the Cherokee Nation: Resistance to the Constitution of 1827." *Georgia Historical Quarterly* 66, no. 2 (Summer 1982): 159–70.

Perdue, Theda, and Michael D. Green. *The Cherokee Nation and the Trail of Tears*. New York: Penguin Books, 2007.

Philips, Joyce B., and Paul Gary Philips, eds. *The Brainerd Journal: A Mission to the Cherokees, 1817–1823*. Lincoln: University of Nebraska Press, 1998.

Piccolo, Samuel. "Indigenous Sovereignty, Common Law, and Natural Law." *American Journal of Political Science* (January 2023): 1–13. https://doi.org/10.1111/ajps.12762.

Pickett, Albert James. *The Annotated Pickett's History of Alabama and Incidentally of Georgia and Mississippi, from the Earliest Period*. Edited by James P. Pate. Montgomery, AL: New South Books, 2018.

Pierce, Earl Boyd, and Rennard Strickland. *The Cherokee People*. Phoenix: Indian Tribal Series, 1973.

Pinker, Steven. *The Better Angels of Our Nature: Why Violence Has Declined*. New York: Penguin Books, 2011.

Porter, Kenneth W. *The Negro on the American Frontier*. New York: Arno Press, 1971.

Prucha, Francis Paul, ed. *Documents of United States Indian Policy*. Lincoln: University of Nebraska Press, 1975.

———. *Indian Policy in the United States: Historical Essays*. Lincoln: University of Nebraska Press, 1981.

Reed, Julie. *Serving the Nation: Cherokee Sovereignty and Social Welfare, 1800–1907*. Norman: University of Oklahoma Press, 2016.

Reese, Linda W. "Cherokee Freedwomen in Indian Territory, 1863–1890." *Western Historical Quarterly* 33, no. 3 (Autumn 2002): 273–96. https://doi.org/10.2307/4144838.

Reid, John Phillip. *A Law of Blood: The Primitive Law of the Cherokee Nation*. DeKalb: Northern Illinois University Press, 2006.

Rickard, Jolene. "Diversifying Sovereignty and the Reception of Indigenous Art." *Art Journal* 76, no. 2 (Summer 2017): 81–84.

Rogin, Michael Paul. *Fathers & Children: Andrew Jackson and the Subjugation of the American Indian.* New Brunswick, NJ: Transaction Publishers, 1991.

Rosenblum, Nancy L. "Replacing Foundations with Staging: Second Story Concepts and American Political Development," in *Nature and History in American Political Development.* Edited by James W. Ceaser. Cambridge, MA: Harvard University Press, 2006.

Ross, John. *The Papers of Chief John Ross.* Vol. 1, *1807–1839.* Edited by Gary E. Moulton. Norman: University of Oklahoma Press, 1985.

———. *The Papers of Chief John Ross.* Vol. 2, *1840–1866.* Edited Gary E. Moulton. Norman: University of Oklahoma Press (1985).

Ross, Mollie. *The Life and Times of William P. Ross.* Fort Smith, AR: Weldon and Williams Printers, 1893.

Royce, Charles C. *The Cherokee Nation.* New York: Routledge, 2017.

Saltz, Ronald N. *American Indian Policy in the Jacksonian Era.* Lincoln: University of Nebraska Press, 1975.

Saunt, Claudio. "The Paradox of Freedom: Tribal Sovereignty and Emancipation during the Reconstruction of Indian Territory." *Journal of Southern History* 70, no. 1 (February 2004): 63–94. https://doi.org/10.2307/27648312.

———. *Unworthy Republic: The Dispossession of Native Americans and the Road to Indian Territory.* New York: W. W. Norton, 2020.

Schneider, Bethany. "Boudinot's Change: Boudinot, Emerson, and Ross on Cherokee Removal." *ELH* 75, no. 1 (Spring 2008): 151–77.

Sharkey, Marion L. *The Cherokee Nation.* New York: Alfred A. Knopf, 1946.

Shklar, Judith N. *American Citizenship: The Quest for Inclusion.* Cambridge, MA: Harvard University Press, 1991.

Simpson, Dorothy Audrey. *Quatie Ross: First Lady of the Cherokee Nation.* Berwyn Heights, MD: Heritage Books, 2018.

Smith, Benny. "ᎣᏍᏯ ᎠᏆᎬᎥᎠ Community Values." In *Cherokee Writers from the Flint Hills of Oklahoma: An Anthology,* 320–22. Edited by Roy Hamilton and Karen Coody Cooper. Stilwell, OK: INDIGITRONIC (distributed by the Cherokee Arts & Humanities Council, Inc.), 2011.

Smith, Chadwick Corntassel. Foreword to Mark Edwin Miller, *Claiming Tribal Identity: The Five Tribes and the Politics of Federal Acknowledgement.* Norman: University of Oklahoma Press, 2013, ix–xii.

———. *Leadership Lessons from the Cherokee Nation.* New York: McGraw-Hill, 2013.

Smith, Crosslin Fields. *Original Teachings Designed to Stand as One: Early Keetoowah Teachings and Traditions.* Ranchos de Taos, NM: Dog Soldier Press, 2021.

———. *Stand as One: Spiritual Teachings of Keetoowah.* Ranchos de Taos, NM: Dog Soldier Press, 2018.

Smith, Katy Simpson. "'I Look on You . . . as My Children': Persistence and Change in Cherokee Motherhood, 1750–1835." *North Carolina Historical Review* 87, no. 4 (October 2010): 403–30.

Smith, Linda Tuhiwai. *Decolonizing Methodologies: Research and Indigenous Peoples.* London: Zed Books, 1999.

Smith, Rogers M. *Civic Ideals: Conflicting Visions of Citizenship in U.S. History.* New Haven, CT: Yale University Press, 1997.

Smithers, Gregory D. *The Cherokee Diaspora: An Indigenous History of Migration, Resettlement, and Identity.* New Haven, CT: Yale University Press, 2015.

Squire, Peverill. *The Evolution of American Legislatures: Colonies, Territories, and States, 1619–2009.* Ann Arbor: University of Michigan Press, 2012.

Starkey, Marion L. *The Cherokee Nation.* New York: Alfred A. Knopf, 1946.

Starr, Emmet. *Early History of the Cherokees: Embracing Aboriginal Customs, Religion, Laws, Folk Lore, and Civilization.* Baltimore: Clearfield, 1917.

———. *History of the Cherokee Indians and Their Legends and Folklore.* Oklahoma City: Genealogical Publishing, 1921.

Stremlau, Rose. *Sustaining the Cherokee Family: Kinship and the Allotment of an Indigenous Nation.* Chapel Hill: University of North Carolina Press, 2011.

Strickland, Rennard. "Address: To Do the Right Thing: Reaffirming Cherokee Traditions of Justice under Law." *American Indian Law Review* 17, no. 1 (1992): 337–46. https://doi.org/10.2307/20068729.

———. *Fire and the Spirits: Cherokee Law from Clan to Court.* Norman: University of Oklahoma Press, 1975.

Sturm, Circe. *Becoming Indian: The Struggle over Cherokee Identity in the Twenty-First Century.* Santa Fe, NM: School for Advanced Research Press, 2011.

———. *Blood Politics: Race, Culture, and Identity in the Cherokee Nation of Oklahoma.* Berkeley: University of California Press, 2002.

———. "Blood Politics, Racial Classification, and Cherokee National Identity: The Trials and Tribulations of the Cherokee Freedmen." *American Indian Quarterly* 22, nos. 1–2 (Winter–Spring 1998): 230–58.

Sundquist, Matthew L. "*Worcester v. Georgia*: A Breakdown in the Separation of Powers." *American Indian Law Review* 35, no. 1 (2010): 239–55.

Swimmer, Ross O. "Firsthand Accounts." In *American Indian Constitutional Reform and the Rebuilding of Native Nations*, 80–181. Edited by Eric D. Lemont. Austin: University of Texas Press, 2006.

Tallbear, Kim. "Genomic Articulations of Indigeneity." *Social Studies of Science* 43, no. 4, Special Issue: Indigenous Body Parts and Postcolonial Technoscience (August 2013): 509–33.

Tamir, Yael. *Liberal Nationalism.* Princeton, NJ: Princeton University Press, 1995.

Taylor, Alan. *American Revolutions: A Continental History, 1750–1804.* New York: W. W. Norton, 2016.

Taylor, Graham D. *The New Deal and American Indian Tribalism: The Administration of the Indian Reorganization Act, 1934–45.* Lincoln: University of Nebraska Press, 1980.

Temin, David Myer. "Custer's Sins: Vine Deloria Jr. and the Settler-Colonial Politics of Civic Inclusion," *Political Theory* 46, no. 3 (June 2018): 357–79. https://doi.org/10.1177/0090591717712151.

———. *Remapping Sovereignty: Decolonization and Self-Determination in North American Indigenous Political Thought.* Chicago: University of Chicago Press, 2023.

Teuton, Christopher B. *Cherokee Stories of the Turtle Island Liars' Club*. Chapel Hill: University of North Carolina Press, 2012.

Teuton, Christopher B., and Hastings Shade. *Cherokee Earth Dwellers: Stories and Teachings of the Natural World*. Seattle: University of Washington Press, 2023.

Thomas, George. "What Is Political Development? A Constitutional Perspective." *Review of Politics* 73, no. 2 (Spring 2011): 275–94.

Timberlake, Henry. *The Memoirs of Lieut. Henry Timberlake: Who Accompanied the Three Cherokee Indians to England in the Year 1762*. London: J. Ridley, 1765.

Tocqueville, Alexis de. *Democracy in America*. Edited and translated by Harvey C. Mansfield and Delba Winthrop. Chicago: University of Chicago Press, 2000.

Tuck, Eve, and K. Wayne Yang. "Decolonization Is Not a Metaphor." *Decolonization: Indigeneity, Education & Society* 1, no. 1 (2012): 1–40.

Tucker, Norma. "Nancy Ward, Ghighau of the Cherokees." *Georgia Historical Quarterly* 53, no. 2 (June 1969): 192–200.

Tulis, Jeffrey K., and Nicole Mellow. *Legacies of Losing in American Politics*. Chicago: University of Chicago Press, 2018.

Valdivia, Katherine Becerra. *Indigenous Collective Rights in Latin America: The Role of Coalitions, Constitutions, and Party Systems*. Lanham, MD: Lexington Books, 2022.

Vermeule, Adrian. *Common Good Constitutionalism*. Medford, MA: Polity Press, 2022.

Vigil, Kiara M. *Indigenous Intellectuals: Sovereignty, Citizenship, and the American Imagination, 1880–1930*. New York: Cambridge University Press, 2015.

Wahrhaftig, Albert L. "In the Aftermath of Civilization: The Persistence of the Cherokee Indians in Oklahoma." PhD diss., Department of Anthropology, University of Chicago, 1975.

———. "Making Do with the Dark Meat: A Report on the Cherokee Indians in Oklahoma." In *American Indian Economic Development*. Edited by Sam Stanley. Berlin, NY: De Gruyter Mouton, 2011.

Wahrhaftig, Albert L., and Jane Lukens-Wahrhaftig. "New Militants or Resurrected State? The Five County Northeastern Oklahoma Cherokee Organization." In *The Cherokee Indian Nation: A Troubled History*, 223–46. Knoxville: University of Tennessee Press, 1979.

Wardell, Morris L. *A Political History of the Cherokee Nation, 1838–1907*. Norman, OK: University of Oklahoma Press, 1938.

Ware, Amy M. *The Cherokee Kid: Will Rogers, Tribal Identity, and the Making of an American Icon*. Lawrence: University Press of Kansas, 2015.

Washington, George. *George Washington: Writings*. Edited by John Rhodehamel. New York: Library of America, 1997.

Watts, William Jefferson, and Henry Edwards Huntington. *Cherokee Citizenship and a Brief History of Internal Affairs in the Cherokee Nation*. Muldrow, Indian Territory: Register Print, 1895.

Wax, Murray L., and Rosalie H. Wax. "Religion among the American Indians." *Annals of the American Academy of Political and Social Science* 436 (1978): 27–39.

Weaver, Jace. *That the People Might Live: Native American Literatures and Native American Community*. New York: Oxford University Press, 1997.

West, Thomas G. *The Political Theory of the American Founding.* Cambridge, UK: Cambridge University Press, 2017.

Williams, Samuel. "An Account of the Presbyterian Mission to the Cherokees, 1757–1759." *Tennessee Historical Society,* series 2, vol. 1, no. 2 (January 1931): 125–38.

———. *Early Travels in the Tennessee Country.* Johnson City, TN: Watauga Press, 1928.

Wilkins, David E. "Absence Does Not Make the Indigenous Heart Grow Fonder." *Perspectives on Politics* 14, no. 4 (December 2016): 1048–49. https://doi.org /10.1017/S1537592716002954.

———. *Documents of Native American Political Development: 1500s to 1933.* New York: Oxford University Press, 2009.

———. "A Most Grievous Display of Behavior: Self-Decimation in Indian Country." *Michigan State Law Review* 2 (June 2013): 325–38.

Wilkins, David E., and K. Tsianina Lomawaima. *Uneven Ground: American Indian Sovereignty and Federal Law.* Norman: University of Oklahoma Press, 2001.

Wilkins, David E., and Shelly Hulse Wilkins. *Dismembered: Native Disenrollment and the Battle for Human Rights.* Seattle: University of Washington Press, 2017.

Wilkins, Thurman. *Cherokee Tragedy: The Ridge Family and the Decimation of a People.* Norman, OK: University of Oklahoma Press, 1986.

Wilmer, Franke. "Indigenizing Political Science or Decolonizing Political Scientists?" *Perspectives on Politics* 14, no. 4 (December 2016): 1050–51. https://doi .org/10.1017/S1537592716002966.

Wimberly, Dan B. *Cherokee in Controversy: The Life of Jesse Bushyhead.* Macon, GA: Mercer University Press, 2017.

Wisecup, Kelly. "Practicing Sovereignty: Colonial Temporalities, Cherokee Justice, and the 'Socrates' Writings of John Ridge." *Native American and Indigenous Studies* 4, no. 1 (Spring 2017): 30–60. https://doi.org/10.1353/nai.2017 .a661471.

Woodward, Grace Steele. *The Cherokees.* Norman: University of Oklahoma Press, 1963.

INDEX

Cherokee Nation: alliances and war, 34, 81–83; bureaucracy and nationalism in, 189–90n7; Curtis Act and, 115; Dawes Commission and, 112, 115–16; Dawes on, 107; DNA tests and, 2–3; dormancy of, 142–43; early settlers of, 204–5n186; emancipation and, 214n48; English language and, 128; enrollment numbers, 154, 175–76; incestuous relationships and, 197n14, 200n85; internal conflict over removal, 72–76; Jewish descent, 201n101; Mexico and, 128–29, 220n60; misconceptions of, 1–2; nationhood and, 120; off-reservation residents of, 100, 159; "Origin of Corn and Game" and, 27–29; Priber and, 35–37; procreation and, 197–98n16; racial awakening in, 114; reduced role of, 117; restructuring of, 138–39; revival of, 178; scholarship on, 6–7; towns of, 29–30, 200n75; traditionalist commonwealth and, 129–30; uniqueness of, 44–45; unity and, 75–77, 142; values and cultural resilience of, 183–84, 187; Washington treaty delegation of, 88–89. See also blood quantum; clan membership; Eastern Band of the Cherokee; foundational ideas; freedmen; Indian-white relations; southern Cherokees; tribal citizenship; tribal governance; tribal sovereignty; United Keetoowah Band (UKB)
Cherokee National Historical Society (CNHS), 138
Cherokee Nation Membership Act, 155
Cherokee Nation v. Georgia, 71
Cherokee Phoenix, 58–59, 162
Cherokee Register, 163

Cherokee Rolls, 146, 149. *See also* Dawes Rolls
Cherokee towns, 29–30, 200n75
Chewie, John, 139
Chickawa, 20, 53, 56, 84, 179
Christianity, 37–39, 63–64, 160–61, 227n80. *See also* religion and spirituality
citizenship in the Cherokee Nation. *See* tribal citizenship
citizenship in the US, 15–16, 33, 129, 182, 184–87; consent and, 4. *See also* tribal citizenship
civilization policies: acculturation and, 47–49, 51; Cherokee Constitution and, 53–54; development of, 46–47; land cessions and, 50–51; missions and, 50; problems with, 47; property ownership and inheritance in, 48; unintended consequences of, 66–67
"civil religion," 186–87
Civil War, 81–83
clan membership: 1975 constitution and, 148; belonging and, 13, 20–21, 32–33, 53, 56, 179; blood and, 21; changes in, 11, 53; Cherokee Constitution and, 60; foundational and policy ideas about, 33; intermarriage and, 55–56; kinship structure and, 11; as matrilineal, 21–22; "membership" and, 4; "Origin of Corn and Game" and, 27; ownership and inheritance implications for, 48; purpose of, 22–23; responsibilities and, 32; threats to, 41. *See also* Blood Law
Clinkenbeard, J. L., 119
Coates, Julia, 159, 182
Cobb, Daniel M., 138
Cohen, Felix S., 11, 135
Collier, John, 135, 137
Community Action Program, 140

Idea Pyramids about Cherokee
citizenship, 9–10, *33*, *65*, *95*, *124*,
150. *See also* foundational ideas;
policy ideas; tribal citizenship
identity: blood quantum and,
135–36, 140; Indigenous heritage
and, 15; Indigenous status and,
123; "nationhood" and, 189–90n7;
United States and, 16–17,
19. *See also* belonging; clan
membership; tribal citizenship
Indian Child Welfare Act (ICWA),
151–52, 176–77, 225n22
Indian Citizenship Act, 133
Indian Civilization Act, 50
Indian Civil Rights Act, 140, 148
Indian Claims Commission Act, 136
Indian removal, 13, 47, 70–75.
See also land cessions
Indian Removal Act, 70–71
Indian Reorganization Act, 135–36
Indian Self-Determination and
Education Assistance Act, 141
Indian Territory, 102–3, 110, 125–26,
127. *See also* Oklahoma; Sequoyah
Convention
Indian-white relations: civilization
policies and, 46–48; Dawes on
land and trust in, 107–8; dignity
and respect in, 185; freedmen
and, 118, 168; ICWA and, 151–52;
Indian Reorganization Act and,
135; integration and removal
in, 72; noncitizen jurisdiction
and, 104–5; political science
scholarship and, 6–7; post-
allotment tribal leadership and,
132–33; postwar, 137; Potter's
Field and, 102–3; traditionalist
and, 127–28; tribal citizenship
and, 123, 177; tribal sovereignty
in, 66–70; *United States v. Rogers*
and, 81; US involvement in
Cherokee policies in, 94–95; war
and alliances in, 41–46. *See also*

allotment; Curtis Act; Dawes
Commission; Indian removal;
individual acts and policies
Indigenous heritage claims, 2, 5,
15–16, 18
individualism, 17–18, *63*, 78
intermarriage, 55–56, 79, *99*, 126.
See also marriage and partnerships
intertribal compact, 80, *94*
intruders, 69, 86, 100, 103–5. *See also*
white settlers

Jackson, Andrew, 70
Jefferson, Thomas, 47–48, 51
Johnson, Andrew, 89
Johnson, Willadine, 170–71
Johnston, Carolyn Ross, 27
John Three Sixteen, 113
Jones, Evan, 82
Jones, John B., *94*, 100–101
Judicial Appeals Tribunal, 148, 163
Justice, Daniel Heath: on allotment,
120; on "Beloved Path," 44; on
"by blood" amendment, 167;
on disconnection, 17; on good
life, 29; on "Origin of Corn and
Game," 27; on peoplehood,
189–90n7; on resistance to US
imperialism, 46; on stereotypes, 2

Keeler, William Wayne, 136–37,
138–39, 140–41
Keen, John, 159
Keen, Ralph, II, 174
Keetoowah Society, 82, 113–15,
128, 222n104. *See also* Nighthawk
Keetoowah Society; United
Keetoowah Band of Oklahoma
(UKB)
Keetoowah way, 17, 185
Kilpatrick, Anna, 26
Kilpatrick, Jack, 26
Kingdom of Paradise (Priber),
35–36
Knights of the Golden Circle, 82

Nixon, Richard, 140–41
Nofire, Wes, 173–74
Norman, James A., 125

Obama, Barack, 184
Office of Economic Opportunity
(OEO), 140
Oklahoma, 124–25, 127–28, 139.
See also Indian Territory
Oklahoma Constitution, 125
Oklahoma Indian Welfare Act, 136
Old Settler Cherokees, 72, 75. *See also*
Keetoowah Society
Old Tassel (Corn Tassel), 44–45
Original Cherokee Community
Organization (OCCO), 139
Origin of Corn and Game (Cherokee
story), 25–29
Osage Nation, 80
Oskison, John M., 128

Parker, Isaac C., 104
Pathkiller, 48, 50
peoplehood, 189–90n7
Perdue, Theda, 28, 70, 82
Perryman, Patsy, 98
Petite, Phyllis, 98
Pike, Albert, 83
policy ideas: 1827 constitution,
62–63; 1839 constitution, 78;
1970s, 151; concept of, 9–10, 15,
56; membership and, 33; Treaty
of 1866 and, 95–96. *See also*
foundational ideas; Idea Pyramids
about Cherokee citizenship; tribal
citizenship
political development, 9–10
political science, 6–8
Porter, Kenneth W., 41
Porter, Pleasant, 125
Poteete, Troy Wayne, 160
Potter's Field, 102–3
poverty: allotment and, 129–34;
communal tenure and, 106, 108–
9; "culture" of, 164; missionaries

and, 39; 1970 census and, 141;
War on Poverty and, 139–40
Priber, Christian Gottlieb, 35–37,
53, 179
Principal Chiefs Act, 141
procreation, Cherokee theory of,
197–98n16
property ownership, 48, 108–9.
See also allotment; confiscation
laws; land in common

Qualla Boundary, 210–11n108
quasi-slavery, 39–40

race: *blood as ancestry* and, 77–78, 84;
Cherokee identity and, 12–13,
52; marriage regulations and,
79; tribal citizenship and, 60–61.
See also freedmen
racial awakening, 114
Ragsdale, Pat, 164
railroads, 88–89, 90, 92, 105, 107–8
Rector, Henry Massie, 82
red (war chief) government, 30
Reed, Julie L., 15
Reid, John Phillips, 51
religion and spirituality: 1999
constitution and, 160; Cherokee
Constitution and, 59; Christianity and, 37–39; clan membership
and, 32; as policy idea, 63–64,
78; practices of, 227n80.
See also Cherokee cosmovision;
missionaries
relocation program, 137–38
Richardson, Chaney, 97
Ridge, John, 52, 55, 59, 73, 75–76,
82–83
Ridge, Major, 45, 49, 73, 75
right living *(osda iyunvnehi)*, 23, 33
Rogers, William C., 125, 130
Rogers, William. S., 81
Rogin, Michael, 18
Ross, John: 1827 constitution and,
57, 58; Cherokee unity and,

64–65, 72; citizenship bills and, 68–69, 79; Civil War and, 81, 83; freedmen and, 87; internal conflict and, 76–77; Mexico and, 128; removal and, 73–75; slavery and, 61; Treaty of 1866 and, 88–89, 90
Ross, Louis, 72, 98–99
Ross, William Potter: on Cherokee values, 108, 184; chiefship of, 101–2; goals for Cherokee Nation, 100; on land in common, 102–3; railroad and, 105; six-month provision and, 96; Treaty of 1866 and, 91–92
Ross v. Neff, 154
Runningwolf, Jim (fictional character), 134

Sanders, Jack, 160
Santa Clara Pueblo v. Martinez, 11, 152
Scott, Winfield, 74–75
self-determination, 140–41, 144, 167–68, 177. *See also* tribal sovereignty
selfishness and civilization, 107–8, 110, 112–13. *See also* individualism
Sequoyah, 51–52, 76
Sequoyah Convention, 125–27
settler colonialism, 6. *See also* Indian-white relations
Seven Years' War, 41–42
Shade, Hastings, 24, 63
Shawnee Nation, 14, 94, 112, 163, 167, 180
Sheppard, Morris, 97
Shoe Boots, 61
sin, 38–39. *See also* Christianity
six-month provision, 93, 96
slavery: acculturation and, 13; Cherokee adoption of institutionalized, 40; Cherokee Nation end of, 92, 96; Cherokee views on, 81–83; quasi-, 39–40; racial hierarchy and, 61

Smith, Benny, 29
Smith, Chad: administrative legacy of, 163; on citizenship, 168; "Economic Trail of Tears" and, 138; elections and, 156–57, 164, 170; *gadugi* and, 15, 18, 183; marshal service and, 154
Smith, Crosslin Fields, 22, 24, 26, 143
Smith, Linda Tuhuwai, 8
Smith, Pig Redbird, 113
Smith, Redbird, 18, 113–14, 121–22, 130–31, 181
Smith, Sam, 130, 131
Smithers, Gregory D., 113
Soto, Hernando de, 34
southern Cherokees, 88–92. *See also* Cherokee Nation
Starr, Emmet, 37, 52, 131, 203n164
statehood debate, 125–26
State of Sequoyah, 125–27
Stitt, Kevin, 175
storytelling, 24–29
Stremlau, Rose, 29, 123–24
Strickland, Rennard, 31, 34, 48, 49, 123, 205n203
Stuart, John, 42, 203n164
Sturm, Circe, 100
Sweepstake Act, 86
Swimmer, Ross, 141–42, 147, 149, 151, 153, 155
syllabary, Cherokee, 51–52, 206n227

Taney, Roger, 81
Taylor, Alan, 203n164
Teehee, Kimberly, 2, 5
Temin, David Myer, 6, 225n22
termination period, 14, 130, 133, 137, 145
territorial bills, 89, 101–2
Teuton, Christopher B., 6, 15, 24, 26, 63
Texas Cherokees, 128, 210n90.
Timberlake, Henry, 23

INDEX

and, 135; Keeler and, 136–37; land in common and, 108–9; Milam and, 136; OCCO and, 139; OEO and, 140; as policy idea, 63, 78; "political dormancy" and, 120, 218n161; political science and, 6–8; political transition and, 34–35; preservation of cultural traditions in, 123; reduced role of, 117; restructuring of, 151–52; role of councils in, 30; self-determination and, 141; Smith administration and, 164–66; sovereignty and, 68–69; Swimmer and, 141–42; trial by jury and, 207n18; unicameralism and, 147. *See also* Sequoyah Convention; tribal sovereignty; *individual constitutions*

tribal sovereignty: 1999 constitution and, 163–65; Act of Union and, 76; allotment and, 120–21; Cherokee Constitution and, 67–69; citizenship and, 93; court cases and, 71; cultural integrity and, 18; decolonization efforts and, 140; freedmen citizenship and, 99–100; Georgia and Cherokee Nation, 70; ICWA and, 176–77; Nero lawsuit and, 146; noncitizen jurisdiction and, 104–5; *Ross v. Neff* and, 154; Smith administration and, 165; territorial bills and, 101–2; Treaty of 1866 and, 123; tribal citizenship and, 168–69; US intervention and, 117–18; US policy and, 111. *See also* Indian-white relations; self-determination; Sequoyah Convention

Trump, Donald, 2

Unassigned Lands, 87
unicameralism, 147, 159

Union soldiers, 97
United Keetoowah Band (UKB), 136, 143, 154–55, 222n109
Unites States v. Rogers, 81
Upshaw, A. B., 104–5

Vann, Joseph, 72
Vann, Marilyn, 12, 165–66, 172–73
voting, 145–46, 152, 153–54, 170

Walkingstick, David, 171–72
war and alliances, 41–46, 49–50, 81–83
Ward, Nancy, 43–44, 50–51, 204n169
Wardell, Morris L., 117
War on Poverty, 139–40
Warren, Elizabeth, 2, 5
Washbourne, J. W., 88–89
Washington, George, 46–47, 205n194
Watie, Stand, 73, 76, 77, 83, 88
Watson, Diane, 168
Watts, William Jefferson, 86–87, 94, 103–4
Wheeler, Perry, 153
Wheeler-Howard Act. *See* Indian Reorganization Act
White, Randy, 231n15
white civilization, 39, 62, 81–82. *See also* civilization policies
white (peace chief) government, 30
white settlers, 87, 107, 110. *See also* intruders
Whitmire, Eliza, 74, 97
Wilkins, David E., 4, 7, 144
Wilkins, Shelly Hulse, 4, 144
Wilkins, Thurman, 45
Wilmer, Franke, 8
Worcester, Samuel Austin, 71
Worcester v. Georgia, 71

Young, Charles Sumner, 130
Young Tassel (John Watts), 44

259

www.ingramcontent.com/pod-product-compliance
Lightning Source LLC
Chambersburg PA
CBHW020348100426

42812CB00035B/3392/J